A FIRST BOOK IN POLITICS AND GOVERNMENT

to prevent its application in other introductions. General courses in political science, courses concentrating on public policy, courses focusing on such themes as problems of democracy all seem to be well suited for the points made in this book and for its methods of pursuit. Such decisions are, of course, basically pedagogic and belong properly to teachers. I hope they will see many possibilities.

What is true for the problem of varied content may also be the case for courses of varying length and for work at different levels of study. In a short course, the book might serve as the core of the discussion, around which a number of well-chosen supplementary books with ancient or current content might be organized. In a semester's work it would serve only as an introduction to the remainder of the work, which might consist of anything related to presenting the material. In the latter case, no more than two or three weeks need be given to it.

Aside from the question of level, teachers understandably may disagree on matters of stress in the treatment of this subject. Neither the logic of the book nor the substance of the discussions preclude variation of theme, content, or method. Teaching situations vary widely and it is hoped the book will prove adaptable for a variety of these situations. As long as the teacher keeps firmly in mind the central purpose of the book, such adaptability seems built into it. The choice of topics not only reflects the daily sequence of life, but also demonstrates the inescapable character of the activities and the surprisingly wide range of connections each of these has in political time and space.

I trust that your students, confronted with these wide-ranging political implications of their own daily lives, will, with the guidance of competent teaching, be led to examine and reflect about politics out of necessity and with interest and imagination.

Acknowledgments

The people who animate these pages are real, even though the protection of their identities required changing their names, and many of the things said in this book have really been said by them in my classes over the years. However, neither the students nor the teacher always had the presence of mind that they display on occasion in the dialogues as they were written. Nor did they have the chance to "revise and extend" their remarks to make them as coherent as it is hoped they are in these pages.

The dialogues owe much to many persons, only some of whom can be mentioned: my sons Edward and Daniel, who liked them as they were unveiled during the dinner hour and who found on occasion that the heavy hand of the teacher needed lifting; my patient wife, Nahoma, who has been hearing bits and pieces of them for some time and who likes this version; my colleagues in the Political Science Department at Hofstra University, who were helpful as monitors of substance and kept me from straying into gross error—especially Paul Harper and Tom Lauth whose combined sardonic smiles and raised eyebrows were formidable barriers. My critical friend Linton Thorn was present at the creation almost from day to day and helped in the severance of the umbilicus; a more helpful "significant other" could not be imagined. Alfred Cohn saw through some of the intellectual and verbal fat and noted the need for fun; while Rhoda Nathan's sharp eye for the permissible limits of linguistic convention restrained me, even when she wasn't watching.

This is also the proper place for thanking Ted Lowi, whose early encouragement and subsequent critical reading and advice were immensely helpful and valuable.

The largest debt is owed to my students, past and present, whose lively responses and challenging questions have taught me about teaching and who helped in keeping alive hope for the utility of learning. I hope that they, and others like them, will enjoy reading what they said and what they would have said had they had another chance.

The conventions of the tribe, of which I approve, require me to say also that my friends and my students stand absolved of whatever remains of error, cant, fault, and other shortcomings. These are all mine.

Hampstead, New York   H. D. R.
January 1972

Contents

Preface   v

1.
My Home Is My Castle

    The terms of the dialogues are set down, the spirit of inquiry is established, and the first question is posed: What have you had to do with politics and government today? The responses show the political connections between a peaceful night's sleep and the problems of public safety. Government is shown in its primary function as protector against disorder and crime and promoter of safety and peace.   1

2.
The Pillow

    Protecting people against pillows of diseased content and misrepresentation is a governmental matter. The sources of public commercial regulation are examined and the conflict between public and private regulation is considered. The discussion turns to the mechanisms of representing the people in lawmaking. Nominations and elections of legislators in the party system are looked at and the partisanship and political activity of the electorate is described. Differences and similarities of parties and their control of government are evaluated. The multiple and sometimes conflicting character of self-interest is demonstrated.   9

3.
Power for the People

The reliable and plentiful supply of inexpensive electricity is examined as a political product. The economics of private and public enterprises are compared as part of the controversy over public and private power. Government is shown as a producer of power for unique purposes, such as war; and the peculiar problems of public enterprises, such as political influence, efficiency of operation, and costliness, are referred to. Theories and controversies over public enterprises are viewed against the backdrop of ideas of capitalism and socialism, and private versus public interest. 28

4.
The Alarm Clock

The price of an alarm clock is the point of departure for a dissection of international trade policy and tariffs. Economic competition and cooperation among nations in the interchange of goods, including pressures for protection and for free trade, is the focus. The linkages between private interests and public policy are laid bare in the form of interest groups and politically interested legislators, acting in defense of their supporters. Maintaining friendly relations with political and military allies is examined as a complication of commercial relations. 44

5.
The Bathroom and Beyond

Unsurprisingly, the political connections between the elimination of human body waste and the technical-social problems they create leave much to be discovered despite the familiarity of the separate functions. Varieties of disposal, especially public ones requiring decisions about taxes, location, pollution, and other subjects centered on political life are considered. These problems are related to population density and public health. The intimacy of the functions, when connected to the extremely serious public nature of their consequences, makes a particularly important lesson in politics. 53

6.
Water, Water Everywhere

> The major point of this discourse is that governments are usually obliged to secure water as a condition of their own ability to endure, as well as for the life of their people. Controversies over water, such as that concerning fluoridation, are adverted to. A student makes a foray into theorizing about the relation between government and the need for water and is led into byways of speculation. Another student learns about the parameters of private ownership and public authority. 59

7.
A Healthy Body

> The focus of this discussion is the contents of the medicine cabinet and their politics. Typical ailments and remedies are described, leading to talked-about public laws on medications, proprietary, private, and public interests, patents and prices of drugs. Public health and the controversy over the systems of delivering medicine are debated via definitions of private and socialized methods. Attempts are made at establishing functional definitions of politics as a help in distinguishing between public and private medical practices. 68

8.
The Clothes We Wear

> The politics of plant and animal fiber, especially wool and cotton, in securing supply and in mediating over prices and over land and labor, both within nations and between them, is discussed. Chattel slavery and territorial expansionism as political benefits for the fiber economy are considered. The presence, character, and significance of interest groups is examined and their social bases and comparative power is evaluated. Distinction is made between electoral politics and interest politics; and techniques of public intervention, such as subsidies and production control, are described and their political meaning is assayed. 78

9.
Give Us This Day Our Daily Bread

The political implications of food are many: the management of surpluses, the control of quality, the adequacy of the supply. Food and war are politically related as are the incongruities of the boundaries of political systems and food supply areas. Imperialism and autarchy are discussed as alternate policies in the relation between large and small nations. A lively debate in political analysis ensues: Is it more important to know "who gets what" than "how" they get it? Institutions and processes are considered as outputs of political conflict. 92

10.
The House I Live in

We discover that our homes are rich sources of political comprehension. Zoning and its controversies point to majority and minority conflicts and theories; political combat takes place in differentiated arenas, where winners and losers confront and reconfront each other. The deep social cleavages of class and race in housing policies are central to the dialogue as well as the differential capacity for political influence of rich and poor. The administrative and managerial problems of public housing—the supposed solution for slums—are displayed with their sometimes heartrending personal consequences. Class and race conflict as agents of politicization are considered. There is some byplay about the virtues of professorial detachment in the dissection of serious political problems. 115

11.
The Joys of Transport

Transporting people means political conflict, we find. The demands of the automobile users and the advocates of mass-transportation conflict in the economy and in the polity, and the results of that friction are discussed. The linkages between public policy, the structure of social power complexes, and favored political "solutions" are shown. An improbable form of government is invented to protect the private convenience from the public demand. But the problem-ridden enterprises of public transportation show that some political solutions are as full of troubles as are nonpolitical ones. 138

12.
Schooldays, Schooldays

The political nature of education—process, content, and structure—is discussed. Fundamental issues of politics, such as loyalty and the fitness to rule, are opened and schools are seen as ancillary as well as contrary to political systems. The political function of managing schools to match the aims of public life is debated. The deep conflicts over race in schools is seen in a new light: defenders and attackers of segregation make use of the same political means to protect their interests. 149

13.
". . . By the Sweat of Thy Brow . . ."

The universal need to work is examined for its political content. Professional and vocational competence as an object of public laws and government's interest in able and politically reliable public servants are discussed and described. School is shown to be publicly prescribed work. Modern welfare law is seen as an outcome of the nineteenth- and twentieth-century class struggles. Socialist ideals, movements, and leaders, struggling over redefinitions of property, class, and power, are seen as social-ideological results of the age of industrial mobilization. Competing political doctrines of authority, work, and power are examined; and the economic relationship, when linked to social class, is seen as a major source of understanding the problems of power in society. 166

14.
Arrivals

Is there a politics of being born? The affirmative reply to this interesting question ranges far and wide, covering public control of health services, sexual practices and their regulation, censorship, and marriage and the family. Public interest in the linked preservation and protection of marriage as a legal relation and of property as a social and private asset is discussed, as is the interest in the protection of children as society's weaklings and in their nurture as future citizens. The complex problems of birth control and population growth are calmly dissected, while students weigh moral values in the process of recognizing political necessities. 189

15.
Departures

As with life, so with death: politics presides at many points, it is discovered. Public interest in death's pathology, from crime to disease, is great, as it also is in burial places and practices. The political power of the mortuary professions in defining the legal requirements of their work is disclosed. There is a discussion about the political meaning of war as contrived mass death. The willingness of civilization to make political use of the readiness to die and of the fear of death for great causes is quietly examined, as is the building of nations by means of war and the conduct of controversies between them through war. Loyalty, self-sacrifice, patriotism, and peace are major themes. 200

16.
From Here to Eternity?

The teacher challenges his students to speculate deeply and openly about the meaning of politics. Students in turn are interested in solving new social problems, while they fear the consequences of increasing political power. The many-faced character of politics is reviewed: public good and public danger go hand in hand; irresistible power seems matched with great impermanence. The summary attempts to discover the nature of politics itself and lists some major characteristics; it ends by concentrating on speculation about happiness, justice, oppression, and freedom. The dialogues conclude by asserting that a good beginning has been made. 212

Contents by Topic

Topic	Dialogues
Authority	1, 6, 12, 13, 14, 16
Capitalism	3, 8, 13
Community	1, 5, 6, 7, 8, 10, 14, 15, 16
Democracy	8, 10, 12, 13
Economics	2, 3, 4, 6, 7, 8, 9, 10, 11, 13
Elections and Voting	2, 10, 12, 13
Ideology	2, 3, 6, 13, 15
Interest Groups	2, 4, 8, 9, 10, 11, 13
Justice	6, 10, 12, 13, 16
Loyalty	6, 12, 15, 16
Nationalism	4, 8, 9, 12, 15, 16
Political Parties	2, 6, 9
Political Socialization	2, 12, 14, 15, 16
Politics Explained and Defined	3, 6, 7, 8, 9, 10, 12, 13, 14, 15, 16
Power	2, 3, 6, 12, 14, 16
Prejudice, Racial Segregation	1, 8, 10, 12
Representation, Legislation	2, 4, 8, 9, 10
Revolution	6, 9, 12, 16
Social Classes	10, 11, 13
Socialism	3, 7, 13
Taxation	2, 3, 4, 6, 7, 10, 11, 13, 16
Technology	5, 6, 7, 8, 9, 10, 11, 13
Violence	1, 2, 6, 13, 14, 15, 16
War	8, 9, 15, 16

xvii

Contents
by Public Policy

Dialogue   **Public Policy**

1. Personal and Public Safety: Public Order and Police
2. Public Health Regulation: Maintenance of Competition for Power
3. Public Utilities: Regulation and Ownership, Public Enterprises
4. International Trade Management: Tariffs
5. Private and Public Sanitation
6. Water Supply: Sufficiency and Purity
7. Personal and Public Medical Health: Choices of Modes of Delivery and Justifications
8. Fiber of Plant and Animal for Clothing: Economic and Social Imperatives for Domestic and International Life
9. Foodstuffs: Milk, Sugar, and Bread; Rationing, Inspections, Processing, and Supply
10. Housing: Zones, Slums, and Justice
11. Transportation: Mass versus Private
12. Education: Loyalty, Learning, and Racism
13. Employment: Licenses, Wages, Unions, Social Classes, and Political Movements
14. Births: Health, Legitimacy, Property, Marriage, Sex and Morals, Population Control
15. Deaths: Burial, Pathology, War, Loyalty, and Nationalism
16. Politics as the Generic Solution for Problems Management: Power, Freedom, Justice, Law, and Authority

A FIRST BOOK IN POLITICS AND GOVERNMENT

1

My Home Is My Castle

It is the first day of the new semester. The college classroom is filled to near capacity and the class in political science is about to begin. It is an introductory course, and some students have acquired the texts and other reading materials, others have syllabi in their possession, foresightedly acquired while visiting the departmental offices.

The door opens and the professor enters. He bids the students a brief welcome and then casts a deliberate, slow look over the new assembly, making sure to get a physical impression of each student.

"Well," he says after a while, "from what I can tell by looking at you, we may well have a good semester together."

Puzzled glances are exchanged among the newlings. The teacher rearranges the window blinds and the openings of the windows to suit himself and begins the work of the semester, saying "Which one of you has had any kind of direct, firsthand contact with government or politics before you came to class this morning?"

Thoughtful silence follows the question. Does he mean it? Could he be serious?

Slowly at first, then more quickly, a few hands go up.

"Yes, sir, back row, name please?"

"Miller, sir."

"Yes, Mr. Miller."

"Well, I listened to the radio coming to class in my car just now and there was a report about yesterday's Supreme Court ruling on school integration."

"Strike one!"

"But . . . you said politics."

"Yes, but I also said 'direct, firsthand contact!'"

"But, I heard it with my own ears, coming directly over the car radio."

"Yes, but were you a litigant in the case?"

"A what?"

"Litigant—did you appeal the case to the court yourself? Were you the lawyer, or one of your immediate family? That would be direct. Otherwise, we're dealing with secondhand reports about people other than yourself."

"Yes, that's so, but we're all in the same country and the decisions affect all of us, so that's pretty direct, wouldn't you say?"

"A good point, and I hope that you'll remember it in the weeks ahead but, not close enough to meet my condition. Many political events are, in fact, limited to a very few people, even though they are significant to many others far less directly involved, as in the case of Supreme Court opinions. No, Mr. Miller, I'd deny you directness, but grant that listening in about political events does involve you in some special way. Among political scientists that kind of involvement, if carried no farther, has been called 'spectator participation.' You were being an onlooker at that moment, but in such a way as to give you the sense of more direct participation without actually doing anything."

"No," the teacher continued, "what I'm after here is direct, *personal, firsthand, nonmediated* experience which you have had *today*."

The remaining hands disappeared slowly. The teacher waited for a few moments, searching in the puzzled faces of his newly acquired charges for a glimmer of recognition.

Hesitatingly, a young freshman in the first row cocked her head, raised her hand slightly and, without waiting for the professorial nod said, "I'm Carole Barrington. On the way to school today I traveled on a public road. I would have had difficulty in getting here without it, but before I set foot on *it* I certainly had no contact with anything that government does or with politics either."

"Nice, Miss Barrington, but not nice enough. Are you willing to serve as my witness for a few minutes so that I can show you, and the class, what I mean?"

Miss Barrington, sensing some kind of entrapment, shrank back a little, saying, "Well, I don't know, it depends on what kind of questions you're going to ask me in front of all these people."

"Actually," said the professor, "I should warn not only you, Miss Barrington, but the other students as well, that some of the questions might be embarrassing. Others will sound strange. From experience with this kind of interrogation with other students I know that some things embarrass people. Frankly, I *will* be tempted to get very close to your intimate lives just to help you see the character of what we talk about when politics and government are used as terms describing certain kinds of social relationships. So, in answer to your question, I'll admit that I may ask you some questions which, under ordinary circumstances, professors simply don't ask. If it gives you any comfort I'll promise here and now that you'll be no exception. Everybody in this class should be prepared to get picked on. Moreover, I'll indicate the line of questioning ahead of time so as to enable you to keep out of it for a while, at least. So long as you don't expect to get away scot-free. I'm going to make sure that by the end of this discussion everybody here will have had a chance to participate. Getting right down to cases, Miss Barrington, I will start asking questions about bedrooms. Now, if that lets you out until we get to another part of the house, OK."

The student reddened somewhat and hesitated. The professor turned away from her and said, "All right, then, where's the volunteer who is willing to talk in some detail about sleeping habits?"

When the low laughter had subsided a few hands were up again. Before turning to one of the eager volunteers, the professor said to Miss Barrington, "Thank you for the present, miss. We'll get back to you later, right?" She nodded and prepared to listen.

"Now, then—your name, please."

"I'm David Murray, and I'm ready for you. While you were talking to that girl over there I've been thinking about what you might be driving at. I don't think that how I sleep, where I sleep, and all that stuff, has anything to do with politics. I think you're just trying to get our attention here by some sort of trick because everybody's always talking about sex, and reading about it and it's a cinch to get attention in a class full of students."

"Mr. Murray," said the professor, "I'm disappointed in you. Now I didn't say anything about sex. I just talked about sleeping habits or bedrooms. Let's stay close to the subject. But I promise you that we'll get to sex, too, and how it relates to politics, but not for a while yet. Do you want to stay with me even though I won't talk sex with you or do you want to get off, too?"

"No, no, I'll stick with it, but I'm suspicious."

"No need for that, Mr. Murray."

"All right," Mr. Murray nodded pleasantly.

"How did you sleep last night?"

"Pretty good, I'd say."

"No eager sleeplessness about getting to class on time, or worries about what kind of courses or teachers you'd wind up with?"

"No, I'm a junior and I'm over that. What could they possibly throw at me that I haven't been through already?"

"Good. Was your front door locked during the night?"

"I guess so, I don't know. One of my parents usually takes care of that."

"Would you have slept less well had you known that it was open?"

"I don't really know that, either. I suppose I've slept many a night without the door being locked but I didn't know about it. Somebody is sure to forget a thing like that once in awhile."

"Do you suppose, Mr. Murray, that a lot of doors remain unlocked in this country at night?"

"I suppose a lot of them must."

"And, what do you think happens to the houses or their inhabitants when that occurs?"

"Well, I don't really know. I suppose here and there people get robbed or something of that sort. But I guess that people who are fearful really watch out for that. If I lived in the slums of a big city or maybe any place in a big city, I'd be careful enough to lock up at night. Sometimes you read stories in the papers about people who have three or four locks on their doors and a sort of bar. They feel a lot safer that way."

"Do we know very much about the relationship between burglaries and locked or barred doors and windows?"

"I suppose somebody must know it, but I don't."

"Would you think that burglaries and other offenses requiring the invasion of the home are seriously retarded that way?"

"I don't know. I suppose it must have something to do with it. After all, burglars have tools. How would they know ahead of time if doors are locked? They aren't going to go around trying out if doors are open. They might never find any."

"Good point. In other words, you don't think it's really that much trouble to get into a place that you really want to invade."

"Right. Those guys know a lot about the kinds of locks there are and about alarms and things. Besides, a lot of them are probably skilled at telling whether a place can be knocked over, or whether it's too risky, or even whether it's worthwhile. There's not a hell of a lot to find in my house. Maybe that's why I never worried much about it. But tonight I'm going to."

"Do you suppose that burglaries in unlocked homes exceed those in locked ones, anyway?"

"I don't know. I'd be willing to guess that they don't, because if people in unlocked houses were burglarized even once, they'd probably get locks and so there would be less and less unlocked places in time, as the news about burglaries got around."

"Right. Now we are at least moderately sure that locks don't prevent more than a certain percentage of intrusions, and open houses don't attract more than a certain proportion of burglaries, right? Now then, let's take it a step further. Why is it that burglars can't do a lot of shopping around for unlocked places?"

"Well, it takes time, I guess and it's risky. There are, after all, people around at all hours of the night, even in the country, I suppose, and there are also, of course, policemen whom you don't want to make too suspicious."

"Policemen?"

"Yes, and in some places there are regular patrols or beats. Here in the suburbs they cruise around in cars, and in the cities they're on foot patrols, too. The crime rate in the cities is very high and you need a lot of cops."

"So, taking it all together, you think you were safe last night because of the chancy business of burglaries and because of the fact that there are cops around to watch while you're sleeping."

"I've never thought of it like that, but I suppose that's about right."

"A little while ago you said that after this conversation you'd start worrying about the locked door, and we also established that there's probably not too much to worry about. Are the police engaged in private enterprise? Is the police business a very profitable one? Do private companies hire them and in turn contract with villages and towns and so on for their services?"

"You're putting me on, doctor."

"Yes, I am. Who are the police working for?"

"The government, of course. There are all kinds of cops. Village, city, state. I've never seen a federal policeman, though. Oh, yes, there are private police, too.

"So finally, we're in a position to say that the government saw to it that you slept well last night?"

"I'm not completely sure I'd go along with that, and there are a couple of reasons. You talk as if the government is the only protection there is against this kind of trouble."

"Well, isn't it?"

"No, now that I think of it, I don't believe it is. After all, the country isn't completely made up of dangerous criminals who have to be watched all the time. The great majority of people are law abiding citizens who wouldn't hurt a fly. You don't have to be afraid of them."

"Would you be willing to support a bill which would reduce the police force in your community or maybe even send them home altogether for that reason?"

"No, I wouldn't, because they're pretty important, after all. But they are only after a few people and, actually, they couldn't protect more than a few, either, if it came to that. I mean, if for some reason there should be a sudden rise in the rate of crime, the police couldn't cope with it. You'd have to call out the National Guard or even Federal troops."

"Of course, Mr. Murray, in this country that never happens, right?"

"Everybody knows it happens all too often. At least, too often to suit me. A lot of people seem worried about it, anyway."

"What are they proposing to do?"

"Well, they're in favor of more police, of course, and they're also against the people who cause the trouble."

"Can somebody else get into this conversation?" The question came from another student. He identified himself as Joe Nathan.

"Yes, Mr. Nathan, what's your pleasure?"

"That was pretty interesting, but kind of simple. I'd like to say that not everybody feels himself equally protected by the police. There are a lot of complaints about police brutality, about corruption, and even that some policemen use their authority to go on vendettas against some organizations, and certain groups."

"No doubt," replied the teacher, "the points you raise are critical, especially now, but we were mainly talking about being able to sleep well at night and what it might have to do with government and politics."

"All right, and so was I, and I was saying the government is not even all that effective in protecting us. I think it's really overdoing it to say that the police stand between us and disaster. Most of the time the disaster doesn't threaten and some of the time the government seems almost helpless against it. A lot of crime goes undetected and some of the detected crime goes unpunished, and some of the punished criminals go right back to the old stand after they've served their time. I also think that the secret of being able to live in a safe society is really that people in general trust each other about most things and that they are not motivated to rob and steal, and that they are raised by their families and schools to respect each others rights and property."

"That was very well thought out, Mr. Nathan, and particularly well stated. But don't you think that government and politics have anything to do with the things you have listed?"

"I knew you would say that, I just knew it," Mr. Nathan said, somewhat agitatedly.

"How come you knew it?"

"I'm beginning to get the drift of this whole thing, I think. You're trying to say that everything we are we owe to the government."

"Well now, Mr. Nathan, I must tell you that if I did believe that, I would not say so, not now anyway. My job here is quite different, but I hope this will become clear later during the semester. We can't learn everything at once. No sir, that's not the drift of my intention here, I assure you."

The professor, who had himself become somewhat agitated during this denial, paused for a moment, while considering the possible consequences of his own vehemence on the spirit of the class. He sensed that the tension in the room had risen somewhat, and from experience considered that a gain. It increased the circle of attentive students, but he also knew that more than a certain amount of antagonism was damaging. He decided to go ahead and turned to the class in general:

"So far, the discussion leaves very little doubt that the safety of your bedrooms, actually of your whole house, is in large part a societal product in which the government is in some way powerfully involved. We have some doubts about the precise nature of that involvement, and that is proper. It is a matter over which reasonable and well-informed people may differ. Now the next question on this subject is this: Is there anyone in the class who would like to voice a particularly strong disagreement with what has been said so far on the subject of your safety last night, by myself or by anyone else during the last few minutes?"

"Yeah, I have something to say," said a student in the first row.

"Your name is . . .?"

"Emily Andrews, and what I want to add is this. I think that feeling safe, since it is a matter of feeling, is purely psychological, and has little to do with reality, as we ordinarily think of it. Insecurity is a psychological condition more than it is a social fact, I believe. There's nothing the government can do to make people feel safer."

"One hears such arguments often these days," replied the teacher. "I must say that I'm not convinced by them. Even if we conceded the essential point, we would have to be able to explain how it happens that when governments fall, or when political crises occur, they produce large-scale psychological insecurities among the governed, who, before the crisis struck, seemed to be going about their daily lives without signs of distress. They congregate in large numbers in the streets, or in front of the buildings where powerful men or institutions are housed, they threaten each other or they set upon their former leaders and kill them. They rampage through the streets, burning and looting, and they cry out for leadership, stability, and security."

Miss Andrews replied, "But I always thought that crises were produced by psychological causes."

"And I," said the teacher, "am aware that crises have many different kinds of so-called causes, even though I agree that they have what are called psychological ingredients. I simply don't agree that security is purely an internal human condition. There is probably some limit beyond which no government can make people feel more secure, but I wonder what the possibilities are of producing insecure feelings among people by threatening them or by failing to protect them?"

Miss Andrews nodded silently, even though her agreement was not entire.

"Now are there any other points to be made?"

A hand in the middle of the class.

"I'm Sheilah Lowe," the auburn-haired girl said, "and I would like to agree a little with Miss Andrews. You are partly right, but so is she. For example, there are a lot of people who keep weapons in their homes for what they call self-protection when there is no need for them. Some people have dozens of guns of all kinds, and knives and clubs. I read a story recently about a community in which there was a riot, actually a kind of fight between teen-agers. A dozen or so kids were involved. The news spread like wildfire and within a few hours all the guns in the local sporting-goods stores had been sold out and all the ammunition was gone, too. Many people don't believe the government is strong enough to protect them when something like that happens. A lot of these people are just sick with paranoia, or with race prejudice, and that's psychological. I think you overlooked that just now."

"Miss Lowe, I'm grateful to you for making the case. Do you know that the gun buyers are paranoids or racists just from their response to exaggerated news of a race riot? Are you quite right in suggesting that they are wrong in believing that the government is unable to protect them against such dangers? Isn't it true that when the spirit of mob action takes hold, local and state governments intervene only after things have gotten very dangerous, even after people have gotten killed, and houses have been burned down? Are these fearful people so terribly mistaken in their beliefs that you would be entitled to label them sick or prejudiced?"

"Well, maybe that's strong language, but I'm just afraid of people who keep guns. They must be preparing to use them against somebody. I feel if less people had them, fewer people would feel insecure. I'm sure I don't know how to make them feel that they are safe, of course."

"Can this be accomplished to some degree by putting arms into the hands of the government only?"

"Yes, I'm in favor of outlawing guns, but I'm just as scared of people in government having guns. They can be dangerous, too."

"Would you be less feaful if only those who are legally entitled to restrain others from doing harm could carry weapons?"

"I don't really know. The whole subject scares me to death. I really can't even think straight about it. I'm one of those fearful people, I guess."

"All right," said the professor, with an air of wanting to put an end to the discussion. "I think we have done some small justice to the subject for the present. Why don't we let go of it for now by saying, somewhat repetitiously, that our collective and individual safety at night is a very important subject of public policy in which government figures prominently and, sometimes critically, but not exclusively."

2

The Pillow

The class seemed satisfied, with the exception of one student, whose hand was raised, but the teacher was not intending to stay with the problem for now and asked him:

"Would you be willing to begin the discussion of another, somewhat connected, subject with me?"

The student, who identified himself as John Mason, said, "Well, all right, I'll go along, but I'd sure like to get back to that subject some time soon. I think it's so important that it puts all other problems in the shade, by comparison. If you don't have a stable order with people feeling safe, and actually being safe, the whole society becomes an armed camp and everybody has to live behind high walls. All of the weak and the poor and the disadvantaged are in trouble from the strong, the powerful, and the aggressive. I always thought that was the first principle of government, to keep order for the purpose of safety."

"We must move on, Mr. Mason. Before we do, may I say something to the whole class? So far, I'm favorably impressed by this discussion. It's very good. Let's make sure we continue at this level for the rest of the semester. Now, Mr. Mason, on the assumption that you did spend a peaceful night, let me ask you whether your head was elevated by a pillow while you were sleeping?"

"As a matter of fact, it was. I thought we were going to talk politics."

"We were, and we are."

"How so?"

"The pillow."

"The pillow?"

"Yes, the pillow."
"I don't get it."
"You will, shortly."
"That I'd like to see."
"I value nothing so much as eager students."
"Oh, this is killing me."
"It could, possibly."
"What?"
"The pillow."
"The pillow?"
"Yes."
"How could a pillow kill me?"
"Give it some thought."

Mason, thinking, a study in concentrated, brow-furrowing labor. The teacher waits. The class smiles, mostly. A whisper is heard, "What is this, political science?"

"All right. I guess it could kill me if it had something in it that was unhealthy for me to breathe."

"You're making it easy for me, Mr. Mason. How do you know there's nothing like that in the pillow?"

"I don't actually know it firsthand, but I guess I trust the merchants who sold it to me, or whoever bought it does."

From the middle of the classroom an interruption. A student more mature in years than the rest.

"You don't have to worry about trusting merchants on a thing like that. They can only sell pillows that have an inspection label on them, anyway."

Mason turns towards the lady.

"I never knew that. Who inspects the pillows, the government?"

The teacher, having set it up so that one of the students would say the magic word, regarded the conversation with satisfaction.

"Well, who does inspect it?"

The housewife: "I don't exactly know that, but when I buy pillows I always read the label that's sewn into one of the seams. It gives you the content, it has the manufacturer's name on it, I think, and it says "DO NOT REMOVE" in great big letters. I don't even know if I'm not allowed to remove it or if that's just for the retailer."

"Is there any evidence that the government is involved at all?"

"Yes, I think it says something about some agency or some law that requires the inspection and the label. I don't remember."

"Would you think that the makers and sellers of the pillows would likely provide all that information voluntarily?"

"Well, they might in order to compete with other pillow makers, but

I sort of doubt it. They would probably just label it by saying kapok, or horsehair, or down, or something else. But it might not be very reliable. People might be tempted to fill pillows with cheap stuffing, and sell it at a higher price."

Mason interrupts, "But I thought we were talking about health here, and not just price or quality."

The teacher: "Yes, we were. Are they related? Is it possible that the health regulation and the quality control are, in fact, the same thing?"

Mason, responding, says, "I think to some extent, yes. There must be a lot of dangerous materials. I suppose if you require. . . ."

Interrupting with pointed finger, the teacher says, "If you what?"

Mason, responding, "Require . . . ah . . . compel."

Interrupting himself, "I got it, yes, of course. I was able not to worry about that pillow because somebody else was being required to do something or forbidden from making a false statement about what he was selling."

"That is the heart of it," says the teacher, with satisfaction, and continued, "Our problem is to identify *who* made the requirements, for what reasons they were made, and how they are enforced. How do you suppose the regulation of the content of pillows got started, anyway?"

"Somebody must have complained," said Mason, leisurely.

"Complained?" asked the teacher. "To whom, and about what?"

The amused student responded, "Well, maybe dirty feathers made him mad and he ran back to the feather merchant, complaining."

"And then what?" prodded the teacher.

"Maybe he said that it was tough luck and that he wasn't going to do anything about it."

"And then what do you imagine might have happened?"

"Maybe the buyer sued the seller in a court."

"What would he accuse him of?"

"Oh, I don't know. Maybe fraud or something like that."

"What do you suppose was fraudulent in the sale of the pillow."

"Well, the feathers were dirty."

"Is that fraud?"

"Aren't they supposed to be clean?"

"Supposed to be? Who says so?"

"Well, I'm not sure. Isn't it common sense?"

"Common sense?" asked the teacher, puzzled.

"I mean, doesn't everybody know that?"

"I have no way of knowing if everybody knows it. We are trying to understand where the government got into the act of regulating the content of pillows, and your train of reasoning obviously leads to the conclusion that the government regulates this because it's common sense.

What we are trying to find out is how that regulation, which you say is common sense, got started in the first instance, and not that it can result in legal action. I thought you were leading us down the plausible road when you started to talk about somebody complaining about dirty feathers to the merchant and finding that the seller owed no obligation to the buyer, under the law then prevailing. Likely as not, this possible reason was as important as another one: The content of pillows is, as you suggested, at the source of certain illnesses that can be generated in the respiratory tract of humans—psittacosis, for example, or tuberculosis, or any number of allergic reactions as well. So, let's say that some doctor or laboratory scientist detected diseases transmitted by pillows and urged the sick and angry buyers to complain."

"But," protested the student, "what good would that do? If the law said that the sellers have no obligation to sell clean feathers could anybody force them to make good?"

"Under certain circumstances, and in very limited ways, yes, a court could, but that's not our problem. Let's confine ourselves to the law as it is then written, and which assumes that no such obligation exists. What can the sick and angry pillow buyers do about that?"

"They can get the law changed."

"How do they do that?"

"Don't they have elected representatives in the government?"

"Elected representatives?" the teacher asked. "Why bring that up?"

"Well, but they make the laws, don't they?" the student replied.

"Yes, but I thought that you were trying to say something else. It seemed to me that you had put a stress on the words elected and representative. You might have chosen to say legislature, for example. Why didn't you say it that way?"

"Well, I'm not sure. Maybe I'm just used to talking about it the other way."

"I see. But can you see the difference between the two ways of talking?"

"Actually, I don't know what you mean. Isn't it really the same thing? I mean the legislature consists of elected representatives, doesn't it? That's the idea in a democracy, I thought."

"Yes, I agree, but there have been, and are, ways of composing a legislature other than by election."

"But that wouldn't be democratic, would it?"

"And so you were trying to stress something about the legislature's democratic character, weren't you, when you spoke of it as being composed of elected representatives, right?"

"Yes. Doesn't the United States Constitution see to it that that's how the legislatures are made up?"

"Yes, it does. And it also guarantees to each state a republican form of government. That's usually taken to mean that the members of the lawmaking body have to be popularly elected."

"So what's our problem?" the student said. "Couldn't we just assume that and go on with the discussion?"

"Yes, we could, but there are some very important lessons about politics concealed in that phrase, 'elected representatives'. It's not so simple a matter, after all, to elect representatives."

"But why? We go to the polls on election day and vote for the candidates of our choice, and whoever gets the most votes wins. That doesn't sound complicated to me."

"With your permission, Mr. Mason, I'll take that sentence and raise some questions about it. Perhaps the complexity will then become apparent. You say first that 'we go to the polls'. Now who is this 'we'? Is it everybody, or everybody over twenty-one years of age, or over eighteen, or everybody who is a citizen, or who is literate, or who is properly registered, or who is not in prison or in a mental institution, or who has a certain amount of property, or money to pay a poll tax, or who's been in the state a year, the county ninety days, or who's not traveling that day, or everybody except women? And, lastly, who is to say who this 'everybody' is composed of? Are you beginning to get the drift of the complexity of the very first phrase in your answer?"

Mason did. "I knew all that, of course, or at least some of it. I'm really surprised what lies behind some of the simple words we use."

"All right, now. Can we deal with the substance of the issue raised by my questions about who this supposedly clear 'we' is that does the voting? Perhaps, if Mr. Mason wouldn't mind, we can go to someone else. Who'd like to have a go at it?"

A girl near the window responded with a wave of her hand, calling out, "May I? My parents are very active politically, and I sort of grew up in it."

"What did you grow up in?" the professor teased.

"Politics, I meant. You know, getting out the vote, registering people, organizing rallies, and all that."

"Your name?"

"I'm Angela Peretti."

"Now, Miss Peretti, what do you think was the point of taking that sentence apart at the point I did?"

"I guess you wanted to show that there's a difference between what the word 'we' really meant the way he used it, when he said 'we' vote."

"Yes, we established that, but what do you think I did show?"

"That only a certain portion of the population is really entitled to vote in the first place. A lot of people are excluded."

"Good, so far. Some of the qualifications for voters I mentioned are, of course, no longer in effect, are they?"

"Well, I guess you meant to show that the qualifications keep changing, right? That's true, I know. Now almost everybody in this room is entitled to vote, but until 1971 they were not. The same with women. They got the vote in 1920."

"Fine, Miss Peretti. And that brings us to the other matter. Who decides who is to get the vote?"

"Oh, I guess the legislatures do."

"The legislatures? Do you mean the elected representatives?"

"Well, anyway, the people who got elected by the people who were entitled to vote, that's right. . . . Oh, I see what you mean. The people who decide whether to extend the vote to other people in society are those who were elected by the ones already entitled to vote. We talked a lot about that when we agitated for the eighteen-year-old vote."

"Yes, that's certainly one good point. If the incumbents owe their authority to voters who don't want to share their voting power, the going can be pretty rough for those trying to get admitted to the electorate. And there's also another problem here, as you probably know. When you asked to participate in the discussion, Miss Peretti, you spoke about having helped your parents to get out the vote. What did you mean by that? Why does the vote have to be gotten out?"

"Well, I don't know, but I found out that there are a lot of people who just don't vote. Some of them have the kookiest reasons, and some of them won't even talk about it. It's very hard work, I found out, to get people to vote, especially in party primaries and off-year elections, when there's no voting for the United States President."

"In other words, the people who get elected are voted in by something less than all of those who are entitled to vote. What explains the fight for the vote, in that case, Miss Peretti? After all, each addition to the electorate has had to be fought over very bitterly and some of them for a long period of time."

"My father says that it's just a battle between the activists in every group, and that the bulk of the population just sort of goes along. They're more or less onlookers, he thinks. A lot of them aren't good citizens at all, because they don't seem to care about voting. I got involved with people who vote and when I talked to them I found out that they don't even know who they're voting for, or what. It sometimes looks like the voters have reasons for voting that are no better than those of the nonvoters. All that apathy is very disillusioning."

"It seems," the teacher said, "that we've found out quite a bit about the first phrase in Mr. Mason's sentence. There is a difference between the legal definition of voters and the actual participants: the legal definition is subject to change; and the level of participation in elections varies. Now we have to go to a more serious matter, perhaps, if that's possible. You will note that Mr. Mason asserted that we go to the polls and on election day vote for the candidates of our choice. Miss Peretti, you seem to be an experienced politician; could you tell us where these candidates appear from to be voted on, and how it happens that in the United States there are, in most cases, just two people running for every public office?"

"Well, first off, the candidates get nominated by the political parties."

"All candidates, Miss Peretti?"

"Yes, I guess so. Sure. Anyway I've never heard of anybody else nominating any. Does it ever happen?"

"Yes, there are certain kinds of non-partisan elections in the United States, but the vast majority of them are partisan and seem to have been that way for almost two hundred years. But isn't it interesting that the nominations are a party business? How do you suppose parties can keep other people from getting nominations?"

"I thought there was a law. It says that you have to go through certain steps, like getting signatures on a petition and having yourself voted on in party primaries, and so on."

"Are those laws also made by legislators, or, as we have called them here, the elected representatives?"

"Yes, I think in the United States the state legislatures have almost complete control of the elections law, don't they?"

"Yes, they do, except for the limitations imposed by the federal Constitution and by federal law relating to certain kinds of discrimination. But the point is still good. The nominations process is a party process, but regulated by the law, which is made by the parties' representatives in the legislatures. One of the purposes they have there is to keep other parties from forming, within the bounds of fair procedure. But that's not enough, is it, Miss Peretti? There's quite a struggle over nominations in political parties, isn't there? How do these conflicts get settled?"

"Well, I don't know how it works in other places, but in our county there are a lot of different committees in each jurisdiction, and you have to be a county committeeman to participate in them, and they decide. Then the people who get picked have to get a certain number of party signatures on a petition and their names appear on a primary ballot. If you're a party member you can vote in that election."

"But what would there be to vote on, Miss Peretti?"

"Well, sometimes some people aren't satisfied with the party choice of candidates and they run against them. They have to get a certain number of signatures on a designating petition, too, and then they can appear on the primary ballot and then there's a choice."

"But still isn't it true that only party members are allowed to participate in the voting?"

"Yes, we have a closed primary in this state. You have to be an enrolled party member to be permitted a vote in the primary."

"Where do you enroll?"

"When you register to vote you can choose a party and then you are entitled to vote. If you don't enroll you cannot vote in party elections."

"In other words, Miss Peretti, parties have a monopoly of the nominations process, which is protected by the law."

"That's right. I think the only way to get away from them is to start your own party, and even then you have to have petitions and nominations just like the other parties. And then the new party has to follow the law of nominations just like the old ones."

"You have your elections law pretty straight, Miss Peretti."

"Well, you have to. It's very complicated and if you want to be influential in politics you have to know it."

"You might add that there are other processes of nominations aside from the primary. There's the national convention system and there are some states which employ conventions at the local level. And now we have to push our question a few steps further still. A couple of times during Miss Peretti's narrative, the word 'party' was used in three different ways. First, in describing the nominating process, she spoke of the party organization. Then she spoke of the voters who, after all, are part of the party as well—imagine a party without supporters. Thirdly, both Mr. Mason and Miss Peretti described the party as an activity in government—the making of laws about clean pillows, and the regulation of such things as the vote, including even the activities of political parties. We now have to turn to that segment of the party which makes the other two parts possible. Without supporters there are no parties, if we are thinking of democratic government and of voting—which is the official way of constituting the government or electing its officials. Otherwise we wouldn't really understand what was meant by the term 'elected representatives' and we might have difficulties seeing why they react the way they do when asked to make laws about such things as dangerous fillings in pillows. Let's go about that in the simplest way I know: How many of you in this room are aware of the general political leanings of your parents? Will you please raise your hand?"

Students all over the room raised their hands and, while they did, looked around to see who had similar knowledge. Soon almost all of the hands were up. Before the teacher could ask his own questions, a student asked, "Do I raise my hand if I know my parents to be independent politically?"

"Independent?" the teacher asked.

"Well, they don't generally vote the party line."

"Yes, independence is a political inclination, isn't it?"

The count revealed that 90 percent of the students had raised their hands. The teacher asked, "Now then, what have we found out from this elementary-school workout?"

A young man in the front row called out, "Well, it means that a lot of parents have political loyalties, doesn't it? I mean that's obvious. Look at all the hands."

"Right. It does mean that. Who are you?"

"I'm Mark Ronald. Isn't that right, what I said?"

"Yes it is. What else did we learn, Mr. Ronald?"

"I guess we learned that some people *don't* know their parents' political leanings, right?"

"Do you find that unusual?"

"Yes, sure. How could you not know that? I mean you live with your parents all your life and you're all the time having political arguments, how could you not know that?"

"Well, Mr. Ronald, that's an interesting problem. Perhaps we can get to that later. Now, of those who raised their hands, which of you think your parents support one or the other major party, or a minor political party more or less regularly?"

The number of hands was down somewhat.

"Now what have we learned, Mr. Ronald?"

Ronald looked around to see the hands and said, "Most people here seem to identify with some party or other."

"Right. Now let's get to the next question. How many of you in this classroom do not share the general political orientation of your parents?"

About seven or eight hands went up.

"Now, Mr. Ronald, what have we learned?"

"Well, you could put it two ways. You could say that the great majority of this class share their parents' general political orientation, or you could say that they are less partisan than their parents."

"Good. I thank you. Now suppose we had your parents here so that we could ask them whether they knew what the partisanship of *their* parents had been. What answer would they give us, do you suppose?"

Ronald was on the spot again. "I think it might be the same. Maybe their parents were like them, just like our parents are like us. It's amazing. I'm very surprised. But I read someplace that young people don't identify with political parties the way the older generation does. Is that true?"

"Yes, it appears to be, but what will happen when you become the older generation? Will your partisanship increase between now and then?"

"Well, I don't know, but why should it?"

"That, sir, is a very complex matter which I can't get into right now, but you should keep it in the back of your mind anyway. The problem for us, Mr. Ronald, is this: even though attachment to parties or identification with them may vary from time to time, or among certain people, the overall proportion of the population committed to some degree of partisanship is quite high, high enough for us to be justified in speaking realistically of an electoral party."

"But if the voters should get disgusted with parties, what would happen?" Ronald wanted to know.

"What happens now, do you suppose?" the teacher asked.

"I don't know."

"The usual pattern seems to be that people unhappy with one party start another one, or try to, or switch from one to the other temporarily. There seems precious little alternative to that in modern democratic systems of government."

"I don't see why that should be, though. If a party doesn't represent one's wishes, or if none of them do, you could just leave the whole thing and retire from politics, couldn't you?"

"Yes, one could, but how much sense would that make? Consider the reasons for the discontent. Usually it is based on some major issue which the discontents feel the parties have failed them on, or the nomination of some candidate which displeases them. Those reasons tend to propel people toward parties of dissent or of the opposition. But when people retire from partisanship they are, in a sense, picking up their marbles and leaving the game. The game itself goes on, and when you leave it you surrender your chance of winning something to other people who are keeping their marbles in the game. If you care enough about the outcome of that game to leave it because of the conduct of your own party, you probably care enough to look for a likeminded set of players. But leaving it to others ignores the fact that the game I'm talking about is really the only game in town. If you want to play, that's where you have to go."

"But why should it be the only game in town? You could have other games, couldn't you?" Ronald responded.

"Could you? What other games could you have?"

"Well, maybe I didn't quite understand what the game is you're talking about. You don't seem to think one could."

"What do you think the game is?"

"Well, I thought it had to do with electing representatives and all that. Isn't that right?"

"Yes, that's right," the teacher encouraged. "What is the fundamental rule of that game, though?"

"The high man wins, I guess."

"You guess?

"All right, then . . . majority rule. But it doesn't sound fair. You should be able to pick up your marbles if you want to, shouldn't you?"

"No one denies that, Mr. Ronald. Anyone can leave the game. But it *is* the only game in town. There is only one legitimate legislature to which representatives get elected, one United States Congress, one president, governor, mayor, etcetera, etcetera. Not playing the game means not being able to win, and it maximizes chances that the others, who are playing without you will divide up the proceeds of the game without dealing you in. In effect, the impact of 'high man wins' or in other words, majority rule, gives everybody who can vote a marble with which he can help decide winners and losers. Even if that's not as it should be for various reasons, it is more satsifactory than not being in the game at all."

"But a lot of people aren't in it, just the same, isn't that right?"

The challenge had come from another student who had sat quietly, but with increasing irritation at the teacher's insistence about the only game in town.

"Yes, that right. A lot of people aren't in it."

"They don't seem to mind so much," the student argued.

"And what's your evidence for that assertion?" asked the teacher.

"Well, they could participate if they wanted to, but they don't. A lot of people don't vote at all, and a lot of people don't care about political party activity, but they don't seem all that unhappy about it."

"You have hold of some major facts here, but, all the same, I'm not sure you're close to the truth of it," the teacher replied. "Will you introduce yourself?"

"I'm Bea Robbins. But how can that be? People could participate if they wanted to, couldn't they?"

"Are you sure, Miss Robbins? How about eighteen-year-olds before 1971, or Negroes, or Indians, or women before 1920?"

"I don't mean that. I know about that, but even in the groups you mentioned there are a lot of people who won't take part in any of the things you mentioned, but they could. That's what I mean."

"I see," replied the teacher. "Well, we'll concede that some among the nonparticipants may indeed be satisfied with the way the actual players of the game decide things. But have you noticed that there is a real difference in the social characteristics of the participants and the nonplayers, Miss Robbins?"

"A difference?"

"Yes, a real difference. The political, and partisan, participants are, on the whole, better off financially, of higher status socially, better educated, of higher occupational ranks, and are more active participants in many things besides politics than the nonparticipants. Even where there are no legal barriers, Negroes and working people vote less and participate less than do whites and middle class people and professionals. Some have suggested that by the rules of logic the very people who aren't playing have the most to gain from the only game in town. After all, statistically, they look like losers."

"Maybe they don't participate just because they have no marbles to get into the game with," a voice was heard to say.

When the teacher turned to look for its owner, he found it to be Mark Ronald.

"That was pretty good, Mr. Ronald. Do you mean to say that you need more than just the right to vote in order to exercise it? What do you suppose you need?"

"Well, I guess you have to know what's going on in the first place, right? And, let's see, you have to care somehow; it has to be important to you. I don't know what else it could be."

"How about being able to believe that it makes a difference whether you participate on the game?" the teacher prompted.

"That's hard, isn't it? I mean, so many other people take part too. People don't think their own vote makes a difference when millions of others also vote. How can they? It seems absurd."

"Well, perhaps it does, to you, but those who participate don't think it absurd, and there is at least one inferential way of proving that it is not."

"I'd sure like to hear that," Ronald exclaimed eagerly.

"You're about to," the teacher promised. "Think about the possibility that the so-called losers in society who are also the political nonparticipants owe their position partly to their nonparticipation, while the winners owe theirs in part to their activity."

Mr. Ronald thought hard, and having done so, whistled softly through his teeth. He was, for the moment, without words. The teacher continued.

"In other words, when the thing is looked at from the point of view of how the elected representatives decide who is to be benefited in society, they favor their own supporters who are easy to identify. In addition, the game players get very resentful when some of the nonplayers want in. They suspect ever so dimly, and some perhaps not, that players stand a chance of getting something for their trouble, but that nonparticipants can be ignored."

Ronald continued to seem surprised at the new interpretation. Angela Peretti, the partisan activist, came to his help.

"It's very hard to explain to people why they should vote, though, professor. I think we've tried all of the ways there are and still many of them don't go. One man in our district won't vote because the voter registration is used to make up the list of jurors in the county courts and he doesn't want to serve on juries. So he doesn't vote."

"Miss Peretti, did you hear me say that I advocated that everybody should vote? I thought I had merely described the difference between the voters and the nonvoters and given some explanation of their possible reasons and their consequences."

"But don't you think that everybody should vote who has the right to?"

"My own preference is to vote, of course, but it is understandable, and may be politically quite smart for someone who has been a faithful participant not to vote, may it not?"

"But why? You said that the nonparticipants get cheated because they're out of the game. Why let yourself be cheated?"

"Well, Miss Peretti, if political leaders who have been operating with your support are deprived of it, they may want to get busy to get you reinterested and look at problems your way, isn't that right? That would make nonparticipation a sensible act, wouldn't it?"

"Maybe, but not every politician is as easily scared as that. If he has a lot of support, he can afford to lose a few, can't he? He'd have that much less to worry about."

"That's good reasoning, and very promising for your future, but politicians are gregarious people who worry when people threaten not to love them any more. But, I agree, it depends quite a bit on the particular situation. In general, participating seems to have much higher payoffs. But, remember, one of the criteria of democratic political life is that people make their own choices and abide by the consequences. That includes political participation."

Mr. Ronald's hand was up again. "Now let's say I accepted your argument about the only game in town and about the difference between winners and losers; there's still a lot about party politics I don't get. For example, it's very hard to see the difference between some of the candidates for public office. They seem all to be saying the same things, and a lot of things they say are very ambiguous. That makes it hard to see why so many people keep on voting and supporting one or the other party so consistently. And another thing, a lot of people I know who belong to the same party disagree with each other more than some people who belong to different parties. Is there any sense to that?"

"Are you asking for an explanation or for approval, Mr. Ronald?"

"Doesn't that seem hard to explain, to you?"

"You've trapped me, sir. If I say no, I'll sound arrogant and if I say yes it might be construed as if I agreed with your judgment. What shall I do?"

"Tell the truth," the student replied.

"You don't seem to like some of the truth I have to tell here, Mr. Ronald."

"I'm still listening, aren't I?" he replied.

"Good. Then we can proceed. There are many ways of analyzing what you obviously identified as a problem in electoral choice. If you look at the partisans, that is the party supporters, you will see that they are variously composed. People belong to parties or identify with them for many different reasons, in the United States a little more various than in some other places. Some people of each of the categories of the population may be found in each party, from rich to poor, black to white, and also by religion, region, social status, and so forth. At the same time, the composition of the parties differ, and the most important differences seem to have to do with social class, with race, religion, status, and economic interest. In modern societies, political parties often represent the major differences between the rich and the poor, the well located and the dispossessed. But each party is a historical fixture too, and therefore represents past political loyalties as well, and so a mixture of supporters is always present.

"Another way of seeing it, is that parties represent one of the ways in which certain groups in the society have to cooperate in order to get at least a part of what they need. That their cooperation is a result of the need to produce a numerical majority at the polls. That, at least, makes it clear why some groups who are ordinarily antagonistic or unfriendly, find it necessary to cooperate. It's the only game in town."

"But how do you know what the parties stand for?"

"What they stand for? What do you mean by that?"

"I mean you choose a party or a candidate because he wants to do things that are better than the other guy. But if they say the same things, you have no choice."

"That's true—if they say the same things. But, if you look closely, you will find they rarely do promise the same things exactly and the closer you look the less alike they are. But I will agree about one thing. The similarity of parties almost everywhere in the world is as important as their differences. The choices they provide everywhere are limited. It has one especially important limitation, except for revolutionary parties."

"I always thought that political parties agreed too much about everything. You have to know a lot about politics to know what the differences are, though, don't you? And now you tell me that they're both different and alike. That's even harder to follow. What's this similarity you're talking about now?"

"It is the very thing we've been talking about here for a while. There's only one game in town. In other words, parties and followers, otherwise very antagonistic, agree to abide by the election results and agree not to start another game of their own. If they didn't agree they'd be revolutionary parties, in principle anyway. You should expect that similarity and you should look for the differences as well. The fact that they're sometimes more difficult to find than at other times may tell us as much about who's looking as what he is looking for. If one insists on very clear-cut choices, one has a view of party politics which is rarely fulfilled. Alternatives in politics are rarely that clear, you know. Ambiguity may be a political virtue when your supporters are divided, and if, as a political leader, you take sides in disputes between your supporters for the sake of clarity you may destroy your capacity to act because you may lose your position from which you can do things."

"That's a terrible argument, I think," called out a new participant. "I think that it just takes choice away from people when politicians don't say clearly what they are going to do."

"I don't disagree," replied the teacher, "but I'm not sure that there's a lot of help for that, given the nature of political democracy."

"But if there's no choice, how can you control the government?"

"I'll just register an opinion that in many matters government is controlled by the registration of displeasure after things turn out badly. You vote against how poorly things turned out, not for how well the government will do them, since that is very difficult to tell."

"But that's very hopeless," said the new speaker who had identified herself as Vivian Bailey.

"Why is it hopeless?"

"It means that you can't control what they're going to do ahead of time."

"Yes, it does, but a large part of partisan sentiment is based on past performance of parties, leaders, and of the political system, isn't it? In general, people know the line of policy parties are committed to and which they are trying to effectuate. But it may not work out that way, or they may have bad luck, or the leaders may be inept. In addition, the problems of government can change very suddenly. In all of those cases, you can't predict the outcome. You hope for the best, and when it doesn't work you punish the incumbents and substitute another team. The major point of my answer is this: as long as the only game in town has to be played by the kinds of rules that make competition possible, the competition for the support of the game players is expected to act as control over the leaders. I don't expect you to appreciate this next point as yet, but I'll make it, anyway. It's probably true that in democracies leaders and parties tend to be cautious rather than daring because they always have elections to face, and in politics a lot of things can go wrong from day to day which followers in the party system can punish leaders for. That makes them fearful some of the time."

Miss Bailey, for whom this interpretation was very hard to bear, returned with one of the vital questions of party politics.

"But how do people make sure that the government, I mean the party people in government, keep up with changing conditions, then, if their control over them is so limited, and they are so timid?"

"Your own question will reveal that there is probably no way of making sure of that in the sense you mean it. There are a lot of contingencies in the way people organize themselves for political action, and many of them make politics seem somewhat hazardous and unpredictable, Miss Bailey. The answer, if there is any, is that followers register their discontents by either granting or withholding support in all sorts of ways, including the act of voting or other forms of political participation. From that point of view, you may look at political parties as antennae of the political system. They're keeping the system in operation by spotting trouble and responding to it. At least they try. So, part of the life of politics is conflict over what should be done. As long as that conflict is carried on within certain bounds, it is the life blood and the nervous energy on which politics moves, so to speak."

Realizing that he had been speaking for relatively long periods, the teacher waited for further responses. He was about to resume when John Mason, the first student to speak during the hour, raised his hand again.

"Professor," he said, "what about our dirty pillow—are we ever going to get back to it?"

The question was asked gently, but with insistence just the same. The teacher had to join in the general laughter and, when it had subsided, replied.

"Yes, Mr. Mason, I am intending to get back there. Do you think we have dealt with your elected representatives to the point where we might get back to it?"

"I'm satisfied," the student answered, "but I thought you had gotten us into this discussion just because you wanted to show us something about how dirty pillows are prevented by government."

"You thought right, Mr. Mason, but it's your elected representatives that got me to make a large detour. After all, we did conclude that the consumers' right to complain of having been cheated depended on what the law stipulates about the rights of buyers and sellers of goods. We came to the conclusion that it was the province of lawmakers in the first instance, and depended on their willingness to listen to appeals for help from people and from groups who are, or think they are, in need of help."

"But do you think that the regulation of the content of pillows, which is actually a health law, is controversial? Why should the legislators not be willing to pass it, when so many people would be benefited by it? That has nothing to do with party differences, does it?"

"Don't you think that the pillow manufacturers and feather merchants, and the wholesalers and retailers of pillows have any friends in the legislature, or that one of the political parties is more inclined to defend the interests or point of view of that group than of those who are asking that pillows be inspected?"

"Is that what you meant when you said that the parties represent different classes in society?" asked Mason. "I can understand that this argument makes sense about some things, but clean pillows don't really represent such a powerful economic interest, do they? It seems such a simple matter."

"Yes, it does now," agreed the teacher. "But don't forget that the law we are speculating about has in fact been passed long ago. Many people at the time must have been wary about the new obligations it imposed on the sellers of goods and upon the government, and a lot of them must have fought that tooth and nail, if only because it would hurt them economically or it would cost money to administer."

"But they had to admit that it's a lot safer than it used to be, didn't they, though?"

"Yes, except that people have goals other than safety, and values other than their health, hard as that may be to believe at the present. Are you satisfied that politics and government touched you significantly before you came to class today?"

"Yes, but I'm puzzled about it. I always thought of the government as some bunch of people sitting in offices, or in special places, doing things that have to do with international problems, or with conflicts between labor and management, and crime and the police. I really don't think about pillows and stuff like that, at all."

"And that, Mr. Mason is, in and of itself, a very important part of our problem of thinking about politics. We need to include in our discussion the awareness or unawareness on the part of the population that they are being governed. Is it possible that the manufacturers of pillows and the wholesalers and retailers are more keenly aware of the presence of governmental regulation of their product than are the buyers of pillows?"

"Yes, because their . . . ah . . . freedom, or ah . . . right to make whatever they want to make and sell is being limited. They are being restrained in some way but I'm being benefited. If I get something like that out of government, it's a pretty good deal and I'm prone to forget about it. It just doesn't grate on me all the time as a burden."

Teacher and pupil regarded each other for a moment in silence.

"You're a good witness, Mason," said the teacher.

"It's an interesting problem," said the pupil.

"Professor!"

In the last row of the room up against the rear wall and just below the little interior window used for projecting an occasional movie, a new participant seemed eager to be heard.

"Yes?"

"There's a problem in the discussion you were just having that bothers me. Don't the pillow manufacturers sleep, too? I mean, why would they deliberately want to get out from under a regulation of a thing which they, themselves, benefit from? They have families and friends and so forth whom they don't want to hurt by dangerous pillow stuffing. It must be in their interest to have healthy pillows, too!"

"We appreciate your reminding us of that, I'm sure. I am impressed by your raising this point at this juncture. Especially important is the fact that you use the word 'interest' here and that you speak of a balance of benefits and burdens which seem a bit more complicated than the portrait we just put together. Does it suggest that the individuals subjected to a regulation against their interests may have more than a single interest and that some interests run counter to others?"

"Yes, I think so, but that might be true of everybody."

"What do you mean?"

"Well, the user of the pillow, for example."

"Yes?"

"He might want a cheaper pillow, for example. When the government can tell a manufacturer what he cannot put into the pillow, it might be forcing up the price of the approved materials. Besides, in order for them to be able to tell the manufacturers what they can use, they have to have civil servants and a whole bureaucracy and that costs money, and everybody I know is against higher taxes."

"The hell they are!" The exclamation had come from a new participant in the discussion.

"Welcome to the discussion," said the teacher. "Your name, please."

"I'm Stephan Light, and I disagree. Taxes are not opposed by everybody. A lot of people like the idea that they can get healthier pillows and other things with their tax dollars, even though they complain about it. Dirty pillows are worse than higher taxes and that's the choice here. I am against some kinds of taxes and some of the things they do with the money, and against some of the people who spend the money, but I'm for a lot of it."

"What do you say to that?" the teacher asked the previous speaker.

"Nothing. I've had my say."

"Are there other contributions?"

"Yeah, I'm Tom Bowen, and I say that taxes stink except for those things that we absolutely have to have, like national defense and police and things like that. When it comes to paying for pillow inspectors, that's wrong because it makes the government too big and powerful and it interferes in the natural laws of economics. If you don't trust the pillow merchants who cheat you, you let honest people compete with them so that the best pillow manufacturer can win, and we won't have some nosey government inspector poking around in the business telling people what to do."

The professor surveyed the class. "It seems to me," he said, "that some members of this class have well developed views about politics. I am somewhat surprised, therefore, that my initial question received so little response. The positions you have just heard espoused are, in fact, quite sophisticated in their implication. They diverge very sharply and are connected to what might be called fundamentally different and opposing views of political relationships. I'm glad that they emerged so early in the discussion. It teaches us a particularly important lesson about politics, and it is this: Among the elements of political life are what are called values, or preferences, or philosophical assumptions about the good life. In other words, political activity, like other human activity is value laden, oriented towards some definition of what is good. It is a matter of the greatest consequence for you to understand that this ingredient of political life tends to make for controversy for the reason that men do not, basically, agree, on these definitions. One of the functions of politics is to find a way to organize human activity in the presence of such controversies."

John Mason, the original respondent, reentered.

"And all the time I thought," he said, "we were discussing pillows."

"It strikes me, Mr. Mason, that you protest a lot. When I directed you towards pillows you resisted because I said we'd be talking about politics and now that we are, you resist and want to go back to the pillow."

"I guess I'm confused because we keep changing the subject."

"Are we? What is the subject?"

"Politics, I thought."

"And what else?"

"The way we are all in touch with it directly."

"Excellent. We thank you."

3

Power for the People

"Perhaps," the professor resumed, "we can find someone else who might be willing to discuss another matter with me. How about you, young lady, third row, last seat, by the window?"

"Well—all right. I'm Pat Panello. I'll go along for a while, even though I really don't know anything about this business at all."

"Thank you, Miss Panello. You'll find, just as others have, that you know quite a lot, even though you've never really thought about it carefully or politically. Would you be kind enough to tell us how you manage to awaken in the morning? Do you just wake up, does a family member call you, or is there an alarm clock by your bedside that does the dirty work?"

"Oh, I have an alarm clock."

"Lucky for us, if you'd given another answer we'd be having complications now. What kind of an alarm is it?"

"Well, you set it at night and it makes a noise at the right time and you have to get up to shut it off."

"All right. That's a definition of an alarm clock. But what makes the machinery go around?"

"It guess it's the electricity."

"Electricity?"

"Yes, you plug the cord into an outlet in the wall and it makes it run."

"The outlet?"

"Yes, the stuff that's in the outlet, electricity."

"Where does the outlet get it from?"

"Well, there's an electric line out in the street and it comes into the house and there are a lot of wires connected to it and one of them goes to the outlet."

"Good. Now where does the electric line in the street get the electricity from?"

"From the power company, I guess."

"The power company? How so?"

"Well, they manufacture it and sell it, don't they?"

"Yes, they do. How do they manufacture it?"

"I'm sure I don't know, exactly. Something about generators and transformers and stuff like that. I don't really know. I'm majoring in fine arts and drama. I really don't know about these things at all."

"All right. Let's settle for it then. The power company makes and sells the electric power and transmits it through wires to the customers, where it is used for running alarm clocks, television sets, trains, and all kinds of other things, right?"

"Right."

"Now, Miss Panello, why did your household choose a particular company to buy its power from? Why not some other outfit with cheaper electricity or a better delivery system?"

"I didn't know that there were any other companies selling the stuff where I live than the one we get it from. Are there?"

"My guess is that there aren't. Why not? You can buy candy or furniture or gasoline or even courses in political science at a great many different places in the same area. Why not electricity?"

"I don't know. It seems peculiar. It looks like it might be a good business."

"Wouldn't you think that among the tens of millions of customers, even hundreds of millions of them, actually, there would be a lot who are eager to invest their money in a business which, like the delivery of electricity, is so universally needed? Imagine, if you will, the profits to be made from a commodity which is indispensable to modern life."

Miss Panello was about to respond when a hitherto silent onlooker could restrain himself no longer. During the preceding discussion he had become increasingly agitated. He had groaned once or twice, fidgeted in his chair and, towards the end, had slapped his open palm against his forehead in consternation. Unable to clear his stress any longer, he finally spoke up.

"Excuse me for butting in like this, but this whole discussion reminds me of an elementary school class. I'm surprised you didn't get into the business about what electricity is and so forth. I'm an economics major and I'm taking this course because it's required for me. I sure hope it'll get better than this. Hasn't anybody ever heard of a public utility, or a monopoly, or things of that sort? Why do we have to go through that whole business? I thought that everybody knew you can't have competition in electric power distribution because it would cost so much money to have multiple electric lines that it would drive up the costs to the point where most people just couldn't afford to use it."

"That was timely and useful intervention. Your name?"

"I'm John Diner. If you had a lot of electric lines, miss what's-her-name would have to wind up her alarm clock by hand, I bet. Can't you assume that most of us know simple things like that, professor?"

"Did Miss Panello know?"

"I guess not. I wonder why?"

"How many people in the class knew what Mr. Diner has just contributed to the discussion?" asked the professor.

About three or four hands went up, including Mr. Diner's.

"Wow," he said. "Am I surprised."

"Should I be surprised, too?" asked the professor.

"Well, I don't know. I guess you must have taught this course a few times and you have some sort of an idea what to expect."

"I do. I can't say that I've ever gotten over it, but I'm willing to do the work. I'm glad you're here to help us along. Miss Panello, are you willing to resume with me?"

"I'd rather not. There are people here who know so much more than I do about that, and I'd rather not be embarrassed."

"How about all the people here who are in your shoes rather than those of Mr. Diner and his friends?"

"Well, why don't you just lecture to us, then? I'm satisfied with that. If I knew the things I came here to learn I wouldn't be here."

"You're not suggesting that Mr. Diner leave, are you?"

"Oh, no, I don't really care what he does. Let him complain to you after class that the course is too simple for him. We can't all be as smart as he."

"Did you feel the sting, Mr. Diner?"

"I'll say I did. But I'm sticking it out. I figure that you don't really want to teach us anything about electricity, or alarm clocks, and I'm waiting to see what it is. I think I know. Besides, I know that chicks don't know as much about this stuff as guys do. If you'd picked on me we'd be much further along in this discussion, anyway."

A low, but audible hiss was heard in class, most of it coming from assorted female students, resentful of the sexist slur.

"Did you hear that?"

"Yeah, I did. So, I'm a male chauvinist. I can't help knowing what I know."

"If you were in my place now, Mr. Diner, what would you do right this minute?" asked the professor.

"Well, I'd keep right on going."

"Without apology?"

"If they want an apology, I'll give it to them, but I'm just—oh hell, I'm sorry, girls."

"Do you accept, Miss Panello?"

"On behalf of all the women in this class, and on behalf of all women everywhere I accept, and I'm warning him and any others that I will resist similar attempts to put us down in the future."

Loud laughter, punctuated by a round of applause, joined in by all, including the teacher.

"Now then, Mr. Diner, since you've earned your admission into this dialogue, what do you suppose the point of that question about electricity was?"

"Well, I suppose you were going to say that a commodity like electricity poses special problems, some of which are political. Somebody has to decide how to distribute the stuff and to enforce the decision. Otherwise, we'd not have enough electricity, or it would become too expensive, or it wouldn't be the right frequencies, or it would be d.c. instead of a.c., or it might get turned off and on at odd hours and so forth. Some people's economic interests have to give way to the general interest of the whole society in having a steady supply of the right kind of electric power at the right price. Only the government has that much power."

"That much what?"

"Power."

"Electric power?"

"No, I mean power, you know, being able to push people around."

"Is that the point you think I was getting at, political power?"

"Sure, it's obvious. You were showing us how, without political power applied to the problem of making the alarm clock go, some people, I'm not saying who, now, would have trouble getting up in the morning in time to go to school or to work."

"All right, sir. That was excellent and you are right. Still, it cannot be said, excellent as the summary you have just given us is, that the problem of the supply of electric energy is well enough described by it. In fact, it has ramifications larger than those just covered, as you know."

"I'm not sure what you are driving at now, sir."

"Well, your description dealt with the way in which governmental regulation of a private business is justified. In fact, there is a very serious public controversy over electric power at a point different from the one you touched upon. Supposing, instead of living in an area where public authority regulates the flow and price of privately owned electric power, you lived in a place where the power you use is sold to you by a government agency? Would that change your analysis of the relationship between electricity and politics?"

"Yes, I guess it would have to. I didn't take that into account."

"Well, how would it be altered?"

"I suppose you'd first have to explain why government is in the power-producing business, wouldn't you?"

"Why would you have to explain that?"

"Well, it isn't usual in this country for government to be in business, is it?"

"What do you mean by usual?"

"Why, the economic system in the United States is called a private enterprise system or a capitalist system or other things like that. It means that people are free to buy and sell and invest on the basis of their own decisions and because they want to or because it's profitable. The government interferes when there's some public interest like the case we were talking about, but it's rare for it to actually be in business for itself as a profit maker, isn't it?"

"The factors resulting in the uses of public power in the United States are, actually, quite unusual. We can examine them briefly. Supposing, Mr. Diner, you lived in a section of the country that was being very poorly served by private electric power companies. That happens for a variety of reasons—especially the fact that population is thinly distributed—and that private power companies were unwilling to invest in electrification. What would you do in such a case if you still wanted electricity priced at competitive levels?"

"Are you suggesting that the government could deliver cheaper power than private enterprise?"

"I'm not sure, but is it possible? If it is so, why would that be the case?"

"Maybe they wouldn't have to show a profit for their stockholders, like private companies do, would they?"

"Yes, that might be a factor. What else?"

"They might not have to buy the property, you know, the land and the rights to the uses of the water, that private companies would have to acquire in order to do business either."

"Why not?"

"Don't they own them already?" responded the student.

"Are you asking me, or are you telling me?"

"Well, I know that there is a lot of public land in this country and also that the rivers are regarded as part of the public domain."

"So?"

"Well, if you need rivers and land for making electricity and you don't have to buy it, you could make it cheaper, couldn't you?"

"Yes, to the extent that the purchases wouldn't have to be made, that's true. But it would still cost something, wouldn't it, to construct the machinery and the wires for delivering the power? What, then, is the difference between using public and private means for doing it? Money alone isn't the answer, surely, but what is it, if not that?"

"Well, I'm not sure, but it's political somehow, isn't it? I mean, when you have something like electricity that a lot of people need and want so they can live better you have a kind of political thing, don't you?"

"What makes it political?"

"The fact that a lot of people want it."

"A lot of people want to eat cereal, or drive cars, or drink beer, or live in houses. Does that make these things political?" The teacher pressed.

"Well, yes and no. I mean most of these things you just buy in a store which buys them from some factory that's in business to make money. They can satisfy the want. But somehow I don't think that's all there is to it."

"Well, why not?"

"I mean there are some things that are political about beer, and homes, and cereal, aren't there?" asked Diner.

"There are? What are they?"

"Well, I mean, there are laws against drinking for minors, and there is rent control, and the cereal is inspected. I mean, that's political. The laws had to be passed to protect people against something they were helpless against, and so the law was used."

"Good," the contented teacher said, "even if you *are* a little ahead of the story we're trying to develop here. Now, how does that logic apply to electricity?"

"It's possible that people in electricity-poor areas made demands for power which private power companies wouldn't fill, isn't it?" asked the student.

"Whom would they make these demands upon?"

"The people who are in charge of the government and who own all that property that can be used for making electricity."

"All right. But why should those people in charge of government be any more willing to furnish the power than the private electric companies?"

"Well, they have to do it, don't they? That's the idea of having government—to serve the public."

"But, what are the means to compel them to do it?"

"Well, they have to get reelected, don't they?"

"And so, to preserve their control of government, which comes as a result of elections and other processes like that, the governmental leaders promise to use public money for the construction of hydroelectric dams from which publicly owned and produced power can be distributed at lower prices."

"Right," replied the student.

The teacher, who had been pressing a little harder for responses than heretofore, agreed with the student, and added, "In a very rough way, of course, that's a correct picture, although many of the details of how public power came about in particular circumstances, are missing and they vary from place to place and time to time. Let us just say that analytically, the picture is correct as far as it goes."

"Professor, can I ask a question now?" asked a voice from the side of the room.

"Yes, of course. You're . . . ?"

"Oh, I'm John Wise. Well, isn't it true that a lot of public power has to do with war?"

"War? How is that, Mr. Wise?"

"Well, for example, during World War II, the United States government developed atomic power through fission of uranium for the purposes of building bombs, didn't they?"

"Yes, and . . . ?"

"Well, after that succeeded, people started talking about using atomic energy for purposes of supplying electricity, but it was all owned by the government. They had to do it because of the war, and also because it cost a lot of money that no one else could raise because there were not immediate prospects of using it for anything but war at that time."

"Yes, Mr. Wise," the teacher responded. "That's an instructive example, because it shows that the supply of public power is partly a matter of the government's unique capacity to command the wealth of the society for certain purposes."

"Well, isn't war one of those purposes?" asked Wise.

"Yes, it is," replied the teacher. He turned away from the new questioner to face the entire class, and continued.

"You might be interested in knowing that, in point of fact, it was as an indirect result of World War I, that the United States Government got into the public power business in the Tennessee Valley. The government operated a munitions-making plant with a small power plant down in Tennessee during that war and, when proposals were made to sell it to private interests, several congressmen resisted the sale for many years. They attempted to persuade the public and the Congress to enlarge the power-generating capacity of the whole valley with public money. It was one of the most interesting political struggles of the 1920s and 1930s, and it finally succeeded with the building of the Tennessee Valley Authority in the midthirties. Only the determined opposition of a few men prevented the sale of the plant, and in time national and local sentiment changed to favor public power. By now, of course, federal, state, and local publicly owned power production accounts for a good share of the entire power output in the country."

The short lecture concluded, the teacher surveyed the class briefly and asked, "Now, are there any other questions from any of you about the relationship between being able to operate the electric alarm clock and other sundry appliances, and being in politics?"

The hand of John Diner arose again, while he asked, "A lot of people think that when the government owns something it's being socialistic. Is that true?"

"Is it true that some people think so? Yes, it is."

"No, I don't mean that, I mean is it a fact that that's socialism?"

"That's a more difficult question to answer, don't you think?"

"I don't see what makes it hard. It's a matter of definition, isn't it?"

"Precisely, so, and that is what makes it hard."

"I don't get it," said Diner. "I mean, either something is socialistic or it isn't, isn't that right?"

"Well, I certainly would not agree to that solution so quickly," replied the now somewhat amused teacher.

"But, why not?" pressed the student.

"I'm not quite sure that we can satisfy the question in the present situation, but we can try," the wary professor replied, and continued. "To begin with, it is not hard to see that there are many public enterprises in the United States, operated by federal, state, and local governments. In fact, the entire government itself may be called a public enterprise, and is often referred to just that way. These enterprises include schools, roads, power stations, railroads, the post office, universities, and a lot of other things like that."

"And you still say that it's not socialist?" asked the student.

The teacher pressed on without responding to the question directly.

"The better way of distinguishing these enterprises from others which are not public is to call these private. They respond to this definition best because they are in fact owned, by title and right of legal possession, by individuals and groups of persons for reasons of private economic gain. The other enterprises are public because the title to them belongs to government in a custodial fashion, that is to say, on behalf of all of the people governed by the political system. They are financed with the public treasury which comes from taxes, through fees, as in the case of the post office, or in both ways, as in the case of public transportation, in bus, train, or planes."

Diner interrupted again. "Are you saying, professor, that when there is private enterprise and public enterprise together, the public part is not socialist?"

"I was, in fact, trying to keep from saying that for a particularly important reason, but since you press me so hard, I guess I have to give in. The difficulty here is that the term socialism usually is more than just a description of whether one enterprise or another is publicly owned, but it is also a statement of intention, so to speak, of a kind of social program or a purpose. This purpose has it that all or most of the means of production and distribution of goods in society *ought to be* owned by all for the benefit of all. Socialism proper is, in short, anticapitalist in *purpose*."

"Well," responded the student, "isn't that confusing? I mean our government owns enterprises for the benefit of all, doesn't it?"

"Yes, it does, but is there a general purpose of destroying private enterprise as a system of economic production, or of substituting for the present methods of governing these public enterprises new methods of government and control?"

"I don't understand all that."

"All right, that's fair enough. What I'm really asking is whether the reasons for having public enterprises are a result of a general belief that they are to be preferred on moral grounds or for general political reasons, to private enterprises."

"Well, but how do we know that?" asked the student.

"Isn't there a way of finding out?" responded the teacher.

"How do you find out?" pressed the student.

"Well, Mr. Diner, don't you think one can ask certain questions that will tell the answers?"

"For example?"

"Let's begin by your naming a public enterprise."

"All right. Let's see. Well, I know that in the big cities like New York, and Chicago, and San Francisco, the mass transportation system is public."

"Good. Now what are the reasons for that? I mean, what motives are at work for choosing public enterprises for those purposes?"

"Well, I don't know. Somebody once told me that the New York City subway system was first built by private companies. Is that true?"

"Yes, it is the case, but it answers our question only in part. Were the public transit systems in all of these cities built by city governments which wanted to establish a socialist economy and therefore kept private interests out of it?"

"I don't know," replied the student.

"Well, but without knowing that you can't know what the reasons really were for using public methods, can you?"

"No, I guess not."

"Mr. Diner, is it possible that there were some other kinds of reasons?"

"Well, yes, I guess so, but what kind?"

"How much money does it cost to build a mass transit system and what kind of return on their investment could private enterprise obtain?"

"I'm sure I don't know," replied the student.

"Would it surprise you that many mass transit systems are not paying their way from fares and have to be supported by tax dollars?"

"No, I guess I knew that."

"So, public ownership is used here because private capital is not interested and because the general interest in effective transportation is very great, but not so readily convertible into cash value which can be collected by private investors."

"I didn't understand all that," said Diner, "but I'll let it go. I think you said that there's not enough money in that business and that it takes a lot of capital. Also, I think you said that mass transportation is indispensable. For those reasons the government is used.

"Very good summary. Now, with regard to our main inquiry, are any of these reasons directed towards the establishment of a general system of economic and social management that could be called socialist?"

"No, I don't think so," replied the student.

"There is a case for public power which is difficult, but it may illustrate the point with some merit. The business of producing electric power in private enterprises is a rather peculiar one, economically speaking. As we discovered, the markets of these firms are protected against competition by being given governmentally guaranteed monopolies. Naturally, some of these businesses are very large because they serve marketing areas that are either very extensive, or very densely populated, as in the case of major cities or metropolitan areas. The defenders of public power have always argued that private power companies escape the need for competition and tend to become inefficient for that reason, and that public power production can be used to provide a kind of yardstick of comparison for determining whether the cost of private power is reasonable. Of course, they also make the point that the presence of a substantial supply of public power places government in a position to restrain excessive profiteering by the private companies."

Diner stayed with it, and so did the rest of the class. "But didn't you say that the price of electricity is regulated by government? Why can't it be regulated to the point where no excess profiteering can be made?"

"I wish," replied the teacher, "that we had time to go into that question. For now let me just say that it is an important issue of public policy over which there is a lot of controversy, and that the advocates of public power have never been satisfied that the regulations have worked well enough. They also say that private power companies are not sufficiently venturesome economically and that they tend to retard growth of facilities, especially in areas of economic underdevelopment, where profits are bound to be low for long periods because of the absence of a sufficient number of customers. And now, we can return to the question which began this particular discussion. Did this description of the problems of public power in the United States show any evidence that it is a part of an attempt to make the economic system into a socialistic one?"

"Well, no, I guess not," agreed the student, "but you could have such cases, couldn't you?"

"Explain yourself," asked the teacher.

"I mean, you could have public ownership of enterprise because people were convinced that socialism is a better economic system."

"Yes, of course you could. In fact, there are some countries in the world where such reasons are very important. In some cases, entire economic systems are socialized, so to speak, and in others only certain kinds of enterprises. Conditions vary a good deal, and the reasons do also, of course. If you don't mind, I'd like to return to the problem we started out with in this discussion, and that is, as you remember, the general problem of the supply of electric power in a modern social and economic system."

But Diner was not satisfied. He returned to the discussion by saying, "So far we have only looked at the good reasons why you should have publicly owned enterprises and why some things like electricity are natural monopolies. I mean even I think so, and I'm generally for free enterprise. I'll even accept the TVA idea, you know, although that was in part accidental. But still, there must be some problems with that, aren't there?"

"Problems?" the teacher inquired.

"Well, for example, when you have a business which is run for the general benefit, supposedly, you could have influences in it that wouldn't be good for its operation. When something is privately owned, it has to make money or to compete against some other business. But when the government does something, as you said when we talked about political parties, they're irresistible. You could have people take advantage of the public nature of a business and have it maintained for political reasons, couldn't you?"

"For political reasons?"

"Well, yes. I don't remember it exactly, but in one of my economics courses we studied public policy and there was some case about the U. S. Navy owning a very old rope factory that the President of the U.S. wanted to close down because the Navy could buy rope more cheaply from manufacturers than the factory could make it, but it wasn't closed anyway. Do you remember that?"

"As it happens, I recall it quite well. The ropewalk, as it is called, was not closed down because the local congressman was a very powerful figure in his political party and was able to have a special bill passed to keep it open. It was widely agreed at the time that his reasons were political. A couple of hundred of his constituents were employed there, or depended for a living on that rope factory, and he thought he had to preserve their livelihoods. Is that what you meant by political reasons?"

"That's right. It seems to me a wasteful expenditure of public money to have a thing like that happen."

"In my opinion, you're right about this case and perhaps also about the more general difficulties of political reasons that operate in public enterprises. There are other cases which have raised questions in the minds of even the most impassioned defenders of public enterprise. One of them is the United States Post Office, as it was called until recently. It was one of the biggest departments in the government. The mail service became public mainly for the reason that it was the most effective way of insuring the safe delivery of mail at reasonable rates. As the service grew very large, other things began to happen that made its efficient management difficult. Appointments for postmasterships and even mailmen were used for the purpose of satisfying the needs of the political party in power. Patronage appointments made the department a rich source of rewards for loyal political service. That hurt efficiency. When the department became locked into the civil service, it may have added to the difficulty of using personnel policy for the purpose of improving efficiency, since civil servants are usually safe against being fired from their positions. Furthermore, since the Congress of the United States was in control of the rates to be charged for postal service, the prices charged for the mail service were very heavily influenced by political considerations. Politically powerful groups were able to persuade Congress to fix mail rates at such low levels that they amounted to a public subsidy of business which depended on having available cheap rates for mailing. Consequently, individual mailers of letters and post cards had to be charged a disproportionately large price for mailing, and Congress had to make up, year after year, the deficits created by the Post Office Department because of their inability to charge the rates which would have wiped the deficits out. So, the department had become a virtual public subsidy of private business, such as mail order houses and their customers, and mass circulation magazines. There seemed no way to break into that kind of difficulty until recently. Is that the kind of thing you had in mind, Mr. Diner?"

"Yes, that's right. The case of the post office is very interesting, I think also for another reason. That allowed some of the people actually to be supported with tax money from the whole population, which is supposed to be used for the public good, and to make use of their political power to keep their businesses alive. If they would have had to compete, they might not have made it. Maybe that's not even good for those businesses. Anyway, why should the public treasury support such businesses?"

"But don't you think that there is some problem here, Mr. Diner? After all, there is some public interest in maintaining an effective mail system, isn't there? It's important to everyone that it be safe, speedy and reliable, isn't it?"

"It is, I know, but don't you think that the customers of the mail order houses or the subscribers of the magazines could be asked to pay the real prices of carrying that stuff through the mail instead of having the taxpayers who don't even want to see those magazines, or people who never buy through the mails pay for it, pay for it through their hard earned money which was taken by the government? You know, if you carry that logic much further, the politically most powerful people will have their upkeep paid for by the poorer people who get nothing out of it at all."

"Well, it's very hard to disagree with that, on logical grounds. Some of the critics of that kind of policy have in recent years been saying that this is called 'socialism for the rich'. Isn't that an ironic term?"

"You make it sound as if both private and public enterprise are impossible."

"I don't recall having said that," the teacher replied.

"But you described both as full of problems that are almost insoluble."

"Most of those things proceed by trial and error, rather than by design and principle. You solve problems as you come to them. You do the best you can with what you have. Obviously, both public and private enterprises have their difficulties. But I doubt whether these are soluble as matters of principle alone. Most of these principles, so-called, are tied in with questions which are very hard to apply to the problems of running railroads or post offices or mass transit systems, be they private or public."

"Yes, but people are all the time talking about them anyway, aren't they?"

"Oh yes, that's quite true, and that is another one of those problems that you have to meet as you go along."

"But don't you have to choose between one way of doing things or another, according to some principle?"

"Well, I will acknowledge that the vast majority of mankind certainly seems to think so, and that is quite a problem for people who want to run railroads as well as those who want to ride on them. They all the time have to choose between their principles and their convenience or their pocketbooks."

"That sounds as if you didn't think those principles very important," Diner answered with wry amusement.

"Quite the contrary. So far as I'm concerned, they may be the most important problems of all. Imagine what life would be like without them," the teacher replied.

"I can't imagine that. I thought that most people, maybe everybody, thinks of his life by way of principle."

"I agree, and what is important for us is that individuals living together in communities, such as political systems, are bound to do that, because those principles are a way of sharing the common life."

"So there's no help for that either, according to you?"

"Help for it? I should hope not. How would you know that you're human and living among other human beings if it weren't for conflicts over principle?"

The teacher, who had become intensely involved in the argument with the student, paused to survey the class. There was considerable division in attention. The one-to-one discussion had moved to a track on which the teacher and student were highly sensitized, but where many of the rest of the class had been left behind and puzzled. To verify his impression, he called on one of the students sitting nearest to him in the front row, before which he had been pacing back and forth, and asked him, "What principles do you think Mr. Diner and I are talking about here?"

"I was beginning to wonder about that, myself," the candid student replied.

The teacher turned toward the class, asking, "Is there anyone else here who's lost? Hands, please."

Some hands rose, but before they were all up, one of the students contributed, "Well I think you're talking about whether private rights and privileges come before public interest. That's sometimes a matter of principle. When someone is convicted to die because he took a life, that means life is valued very highly, but not so highly that it cannot be taken for violating the principle that life is sacred."

"Do you think that socialism versus capitalism are matters of principle?"

"Well, I'm not sure, but a lot of people think of them that way. They say that socialism puts the individual in second place and the community in first place, while capitalism places the individual first and the community second."

"How do you mean that?"

"I'm really not so sure of my ground here, but I know there is a lot of controversy over things like that. A lot of the time I don't even know what the principles are that people say they're arguing about. It's very hard to tell because they don't say, or maybe it's not even clear to them."

"But a minute ago you delineated the capitalist-socialist controversy very sharply, didn't you?"

"But that's just what they say. Don't they give some reasons for believing in these principles? I don't know what they are, and I have the feeling that a lot of people don't either. I'm not even sure that's a good distinction. It could be something I just picked up from somebody."

"That's careful thinking and I applaud you for it. The so-called reasons at the base of these two divergent ways of looking at society and economic life are too complex for us at this point, but let's just not underestimate their importance in the modern world. Some time later, when we will be talking about the relationship of work and politics, we'll explore the matter more deeply."

At that point an agitatedly waving hand became visible, accompanied by a demand to be heard:

"Can I ask you something before you go on?"

"Yes, but we must keep it brief. We've got to close the discussion," replied the teacher.

"Well, when you mentioned the reasons why mass transportation systems and electric power plants were publicly owned, you said that it was done mostly for economic kinds of reasons, like the kinds of profits that could be made and so on. But isn't it true that when you take all of those reasons together they show that public ownership of an enterprise might really be a better way than private ownership?"

"Yes, in some cases we might be entitled to say that it's a better way."

"No, I don't mean that. I mean that it might show socialism in general is a better economic system than capitalism. Many of the reasons you gave are just good reasons. Well, don't the socialists prefer their system for the very same reasons? And doesn't that make their preference sensible?"

"So far as you have reraised the question we have already examined, I'll not go over the ground again, but I must reply that socialism as a political and economic and social program is based on an analysis of relationships that include moral considerations and considerations of the distribution of power in society which are not included in the reasons for establishing public enterprises in a so-called free economy. Economic and administrative advantages alone are at work in those cases."

"Yes, but don't you think it's possible that the economic and administrative reasons might result in making so many enterprises public that one can no longer tell whether everything is socialized for those political reasons or whether things are done because they are economically and administratively more convenient?"

"May I know who you are, before I answer that?" asked the teacher. "I'd like to remember you. That was a very sophisticated question, and I sincerely hope to be able to cope with it. I wish, in fact, I'd thought of it myself."

"Thank you. We've been arguing about things like that in my house ever since I was a kid. I'm Dick Bundy."

"Well, Mr. Bundy, I suppose one has to agree that there is the possibility of such a trend. In fact, there are groups and people who are opposed to public enterprises just because they represent what is sometimes called 'a foot in the door for socialism,' to which they are opposed on moral and political grounds."

"Well, that's what I was coming to. I think its possible that you could get socialism by the back door, so to speak, even when most people wouldn't want to have it if they had a chance to vote on it."

"I regret I can't give you much help with the problem, since it's in the future, and I don't know. I'll say that the number and variety of public enterprises seem to be increasing with the complexity of the society and the density of the population, but I would like to add this thought-provoking item before we conclude. In a few countries with officially socialist economic systems, private enterprises are not unknown and seem, in a couple of cases, to be increasing. In addition, socialist economies, so-called, are often only partially socialized, and some of their public enterprises are managed in ways very reminiscent of free enterprise competition. In those kinds of settings it is sometimes alleged, of course, that free enterprise activities represent a 'foot in the door for capitalism,' which are to be feared for moral and political reasons."

Bundy returned to the point. "That's pretty funny, don't you think? I mean, it sounds as if the socialist countries and the capitalist countries are getting more like one another."

The teacher's response was restrained. "I'm certain that such an analysis is not warranted on the basis of the few facts we used in our discussion so far, even though you may be right for other reasons. Ideological socialism, to use a short phrase for it, is deeply rooted in social belief, as is the free enterprise or capitalist system. It would be an error to assume that changes in social philosophy are as easy as that, even though the untrained eye might perceive them that way. Economic systems are not purely matters of efficiency and administration. They are part of ongoing social systems which include structures of power and authority as well as ways of looking at the world that are quite distinct, and difficult to change."

The teacher let a brief pause interrupt the flow of the conversation and when he resumed, he said, "We have traveled a long way from the motive power in the alarm clock which awakened Miss Panello, and if in the process we have become fully awake, I propose to take another look at that piece of machinery. It's full of a number of other things connected to politics. Let us do that next time we meet."

4

The Alarm Clock

The class was assembled again and the professor prepared to lead the discussion through the mazes of the politics of international trade, as revealed by looking again at the alarm clock, whose motive power was the subject of the previous discussion. He began: "That electrically fed alarm clock of Miss Panello's was manufactured someplace, distributed to a wholesaler and then to a retailer, and then sold to customers. On the face of it, it looks like a simple series of economic transactions. Somebody makes something other people want to buy. Other people resell it and the last person purchases it for the use it was intended to fulfill. To do that a lot of buying and selling takes place, in turn. Materials, transportation, labor, capital, etcetera, etcetera. The whole thing depends on price mechanism of some sort. You buy what you can afford in keeping with what you sell things for, including your labor. Now, to make a long question short, what do you suppose an alarm clock costs?"

"Oh, I'd say about seven or eight dollars."

"Who said that?" asked the teacher.

"I did," responded a new participant. "I'm Stephan Hardy. I bought one of those things a few weeks ago when the old one gave out. I paid about $7.50, I think."

"Couldn't you get a cheaper one?"

"Oh, I don't know. I didn't do a lot of shopping around. Most of these things are about the same price. Most of the time you really pay for decoration or a fancy box. All I wanted was a thing that wakes me up and keeps the time."

"Did you buy a brand-name product."

"Yes, I think it was a Sears & Roebuck clock."

"Was it made in the United States?"

"Sure, I think so."

"Didn't you try to buy at a discount house, or look for a product made in Japan, or Hong Kong, or Switzerland to get the benefit of lower pricing?"

"No."

"Did you consult some comparison shopping guide, such as Consumer Union Reports, on prices, quality, performance, guarantees, and so forth?"

"No, I'm not too familiar with those, but I hear that a lot of prices of appliances are the same as in discount stores. They used to be different, but that was before the law changed."

"The law?" asked the teacher.

"Yes, there used to be some sort of law against merchants lowering the prices of things which the manufacturers printed on the boxes. Something like that, I think. I'm not too sure."

"Without going into detail, I'd say that we have identified another aspect of governmental interference here. You're right. Suppose you'd gone into a large retail store with a great many differently priced clocks on the shelves, and that many of the more attractive ones had been imports from a foreign country, which each produce goods at lower prices than American industries. Would you have chosen one of them?"

"Sure, if I liked it."

"Do you suppose that most people, when they buy things like that, consider that the price is paramount, providing other things are satisfactory?"

"Well, money's money. The more you can buy with it, the better. Some of the Japanese or German appliances are pretty nice. In some places they have things from all over the world at ridiculous prices. Some places have nothing made in this country at all."

"Now then, if the manufacturers in the foreign countries can undersell their American competitors that way wouldn't you say that the demand for such less expensive things would be high?"

"Yes, of course. There would be a lot of people interested in getting cheaper goods. It's happening with automobiles. Volkswagens, Renaults, Toyotas and all sorts of makes, and with cameras, watches. . . ."

"It's a wonder that anybody buys anything made in this country when imports can save him all that money," interrupted the professor.

"A lot of people don't like to buy foreign stuff. They think it's unpatriotic."

"Unpatriotic?"

"Yes, they say that when you buy an American manufactured car, it helps other Americans, workers, dealers, and like that, but you hurt them when you buy imports."

"Do you think that's true?"

"I don't know. It sounds all right. I don't know a lot about this stuff. I remember in high school there was a lot of talk about that. How this country and others prevent foreign goods from being sold by putting tariff or quotas on them. That way they wouldn't compete so much because the tariff would reduce the difference in price between the imported and the domestic item."

"How is it," asked the teacher, "that you can claim you don't know too much about the business when you can explain it very well indeed?"

"I'm sure there are a lot of things I don't know about it," responded the student. "For instance, I don't know how much these tariffs amount to, and I don't know how you decide what kinds of things you put a tariff on, and so forth."

"Do you sense that the tariffs may have the effect of keeping up the domestic prices of things?"

"No, I can't say that. How does that work?"

"Well, if the foreign import was permitted to be sold at its actual price rather than the one inflated by the tariff, the domestic manufacturers would have to scramble to meet those prices by coming down a little, or even quite a lot, in their own prices. Without the competition, they don't need to do that and they can worry less about competition. So that this alarm clock you bought might well be less expensive than the seven or so dollars you paid for it, had the maker of it, or the sellers been allowed to compete."

"Well, then," said the puzzled student, "why doesn't the government let them compete with each other, instead of stopping it? Is the government trying to make us pay more?"

"What would you say if I told you that, in a certain way, the answer is yes?"

"Are you trying to tell me that?"

"Not directly, I am not, but what I need to get at here involves a policy which, in fact, has the effect of making people pay more than they would otherwise have to pay."

"It seems very odd," said the student. "I thought the government interfered in economic matters to help the people."

"Isn't this policy helping them?"

"How can it help if it costs more money?"

"Are there no other ways of helping people except making things cheaper?" the teacher retorted.

"That is just confusing the whole issue, I think. You can't have it both ways."

"Is it possible that the object of a tariff policy is to help some people in preference to others?"

"How so?"

"If cheaper imports were allowed to displace native alarm clocks on the store shelves, would anybody be harmed thereby? If Toyotas and Volkswagens and Renaults and Triumphs were to displace Chevrolets and Fords and so on, would anybody be harmed by it?"

"The automobile business and the alarm clock business in this country would sure go to hell."

"That means what to people? Sales decline, right?"

"Right."

"Manufacturing is reduced?"

"Right."

"What results for people? Salesmen lose jobs?"

"No, they'd sell the other stuff."

"Good."

"Workers get laid off in the factories and in the raw-material plants and the places that do the shipping and so forth."

"That's right, but not in Japan, Germany, Italy, or all those other places. They'd really go to town, wouldn't they?"

"Nice thinking. Add to that two more complicating elements. There are also some people in this country who'd benefit from increased imports. The shippers of goods—railroads, ships, planes, trucks, the importers, and so forth. But the domestic workers and the factory owners would not. Perhaps even banks are involved. They furnish capital to domestic manufacturers, but would not be able to do so quite so easily in other countries. But financiers whose investments abroad are their main business, or foreign bankers, would obviously profit."

"All I can say," said the student, "is that the price of alarm clocks is complicated business."

"And we haven't even scratched the surface," said the teacher.

"That's right," offered another participant in the classroom. "I'm Bob Sheldon. You know you've just presented the so-called protectionist side of it. Actually, people who think like that are wrong. All they can see is that their own incomes disappear, or their jobs. There's another side to it that's also very important, I believe. When the industries in the other countries get prosperous with money earned in the American market, they become customers for the stuff we manufacture and you have a case where everybody benefits from free trade. The prices can be kept down because different countries can produce different kinds of things cheaply. That's a much better policy than artificial price levels as a result of tariff policy."

The teacher, turning to the class, thanked Mr. Sheldon for the contribution, and continued. "I had not anticipated that Miss Panello's alarm clock would take us so deeply into the subject so quickly, but I'm pleased. If we focus clearly we can see that we're dealing with very complex matters, indeed. There's no denying the so-called free trade principles espoused by Mr. Sheldon have a lot of merit. Our task right here and now is to see what the conflicts are over this policy and how they are dealt with. You have noticed that there is fear of imported goods on the part of some people. These fears are justified by facts. Jobs do disappear and the people interested in protecting themselves against it have, of course, access to the people who can protect them against it. Those are congressmen and senators, the President, and many others, and organizations like pressure groups, labor unions, and manufacturers' associations. They're powerful, as are the people interested in foreign trade and in imports, but many of these are in foreign countries and do not have the same kind of access to the American political system."

"Does anybody in a foreign country have influence in American politics?" The question had come from a hitherto silent girl. "I'm Tillie Knight. How would that work, that somebody from another country had influence here?"

"Oh, come on," shouted a voice from the rear of the class. "They've got embassies and consulates and they're always going around promoting their countries. They come on trade missions and are always trying to get a piece of the American buck. First, we give them foreign aid to build their factories and then they produce stuff to undersell American manufacturers who pay the taxes with money the foreign aid comes from."

"You're who?" asked the teacher.

"I'm Fred Carpenter. My father works in a place that makes electronic testing equipment and they have to compete against gauges and things that were built in factories in Europe which were rebuilt with American money after the second World War. It really gripes me. Sure, they hire big money representatives in this country who go around the Congress and other places pleading for a free trade policy."

"All right. We have at least isolated some of the major reasons why the alarm clock must be regarded as directly connected to government and public policy. The economic well-being of its citizens or inhabitants is a central concern of political institutions and processes."

Without asking to be recognized, a tall and lean young man seated right in front of the teacher spoke up by saying, "You know this whole discussion was really way over my head. The fellow back there said you gave a protectionist argument and you agreed and then you said something about a free trade argument. I mean that I don't really understand what any of you are saying. I remember something about tariffs that was taught in high school, but it was never really explained to me how it works, and all. I mean that whole business I just heard was like a conversation in some kind of language I hardly understood."

The teacher, taken aback, replied gingerly, "Well, didn't anything at all come through to you?"

"Oh, sure," the student replied. "I know what you were talking *about*, but I hardly understood what you were saying, if you know what I mean."

"I'm not too clear about the distinction," said the teacher. "Why don't you show us what you mean."

"Well, all right," agreed the student. "For example, you said something about how the tariff raises prices but you didn't say exactly how that works. And then you said that the people who want tariffs to be put on imported goods have a lot of friends in the government, or something like that. I don't know how that works, either. That's what I mean."

"I see," replied the teacher, slowly. Here and there in the classroom he could hear the suppressed snickers of the better-informed students. He turned to the owner of one of the grinning facades and asked, "Do you suppose you could help in laying this out a bit more plainly?"

The surprised student said, "Who, me? Gee, I don't know. Doesn't the government pass laws, or something like that."

"Are you asking me about it?"

"Yes, well, I'm not too sure myself, actually. How it works is that Congress passes a law that the importers of certain articles, before they can import something into the country, or before it can be sold here, have to pay a percentage of their price to the government."

"In general, that's right. Now then, how many different kinds of articles do you suppose are imported into the United States?"

"How many?"

"Right. How many?"

"How is it possible for anybody to guess that?"

"Why would it be so difficult?"

"There must be zillions."

"If you mean a zillion to be something in excess of a million, you may be right, but that's not very precise, is it?"

"No, but at least we have a working number of some sort."

"Now why would it be of interest to know how many different articles there are, in order to know something about how the tariff is applied?"

"Well, first of all, it shows that it's a very complicated business."

"Good. What else does it show?"

"I don't know what you mean. Isn't that enough?"

"It's a big part of it, but not enough, no."

"But what else could it show?"

"Does it indicate how many different kinds of articles are brought into the country, too?" asked the teacher.

"Well, sure it does."

"Now, how do you suppose the Congress of the United States decides on which of these many varieties of goods it is necessary to impose a tariff in order to protect domestic businesses from being economically undercut in the American market?"

"Don't they have committees, or something like that?"

"That doesn't change the question, does it? The committees also have to have a way of knowing which imports should be discouraged and which should not, and how much of a burden to impose on some as distinct from others."

"Don't the people who want to be protected against some import or other tell their congressmen or their senators?"

"All right, how do you suppose they do that?"

"They could give them lists of things they would like to have kept out of the country."

"Yes, they could, and I suppose here and there individuals might do that. And what would the congressmen do with those lists, do you suppose?"

"Well, they could give them to the right people on the committees, and then they would take all of them and figure out the best way of dealing with the items on the list."

"First of all," said the teacher, "that is a very simple, and therefore mistaken picture of the process. It is a good deal more complex, in actuality. The Congress' general authority over tariffs has, of course, from the very beginning, made it the target for appeals for protection against foreign competition. But the demands come only rarely from individuals or firms and corporations, except the very biggest ones. They come, first of all, from groups of producers or manufacturers. In that way, the Congress receives information about entire groups of products against which the tariff protection is sought."

"But doesn't that still mean that a lot of people have to tell Congress what they want?" the student asked.

"Yes, but it cuts down the number quite a bit," the teacher responded, and continued, "Another aspect of the policy is that large numbers of congressmen are, of course, very familiar with the needs of their constituents from frequent contact with them. Important industries or enterprises have good access to the national legislators in the districts and states in which they're located. Moreover, the groups or associations of which these industries are a part are highly skilled in informing congressmen or senators in whose districts the same kinds of economic interests are looking for protection. So there are nationally connected legislators from similar places. Moreover, there are some kinds of economic interests which are represented directly in the Congress. For example, the well-known farm bloc consists of legislators who are very well informed on the intricacies of agricultural economics, including the kinds of protection from imported goods their constituents are looking for."

"Well, in that case," replied the student, "it should be simple, after all. If the Congressmen know what their constituents need they shouldn't have any trouble putting some kind of law together that satisfies them. In that case, why all the fuss? I mean, you shouldn't even have to raise the question about the many different kinds of items that need protection, should you?"

"You raise several difficulties," replied the teacher. "In the first place, the Congress used to spend many long hours and weeks, often the better part of whole congressional sessions, setting rates for literally thousands and thousands of items. They don't do that any more because they gave over to the President, through the Tariff Commission, the power to set import rates within certain limits. In the second place, you are assuming that the rates that would satisfy a manufacturer of automobiles would, for example, cause no difficulty for the consumers of them, and that they would not object in some way. The problem is that there are deep disagreements over some of the specific items in tariff bills. Another problem is that the rates set for groups of items raise grave problems of international economic relations. The Congress or the President don't just have the job of satisfying domestic industries but they have to find a point at which consumers will not complain about high prices, and a point at which foreign countries, especially friendly ones, will not complain bitterly about the effect of high tariffs on their own economies. In fact, the struggle between high and low tariff advocates is carried on all the time, largely out of the public view, but it's not hard to find out what's going on. Readers of the business pages of major newspapers are well informed about those things, and every once in a while one of the controversies breaks out into the open."

"I don't remember anything about that in the newspapers recently," confessed the student.

"The teacher turned to the class. "Is there anyone here who does remember reading about a foreign trade controversy?" he asked.

The hands of several of the participants in the previous discussion went up. Sheldon, who had previously defended free trade, was first. "I guess it depends on whether you're tuned in to things. Not long ago there was a whole flap about Japanese objections against the high rates on imports of textiles that they need to sell. It went all the way to the President, who sent a special mission to Japan to plead with them not to be too unhappy. The President got caught between domestic politics and international relations with Japan, which is one of our allies in the Far East, and a big textile exporter. If the Japanese can't earn dollars in our country they can't become customers for our goods. So that American exports to Japan can be hurt a lot when we raise the tariffs against their goods. Also, when that happens, Japanese politicians have to protect Japanese domestic manufacturers against imports and they start putting tariffs on their imports and that hurts American exporters."

The teacher returned to the student who earlier had complained of not understanding the operations of the tariff and asked him whether things were any clearer now.

"Well, yes, in a way. At least I know why the fellow over there didn't think it made a lot of difference whether he bought an imported clock or an American one. The tariff laws make them cost about the same. It doesn't make a lot of difference to the customer, after all."

With a yell, Bob Sheldon was on his feet.

"My God," he said, "What does it take to get through to you? I was just telling you that it makes a lot of difference to the consumer. It means that he is forced to spend more money than he would have to if there were no tariff. Then he could get the advantage of more cheaply produced articles from other countries."

"Yeah, but if he works in an industry that is protected against foreign competition, he has a job and the money to buy things, but he might be out of work if his employer had to compete with cheaply made goods, isn't that right?"

Sheldon had resumed his seat. The teacher turned to the class. "There you have it, in a nutshell. The arguments for and against tariff laws."

"Well, isn't it true that people would be out of work if the protection were ended?"

"At least," said the teacher, "it's an important enough argument to make a lot of political difference. It's true to that extent, yes."

"No, I don't mean that. I'm asking if it isn't actually true?"

"I regret," the teacher replied, "that I cannot tell you the answer to that. I don't believe the government would be permitted to experiment sufficiently to find out what the truth is. Politically speaking, that is an important fact. As long as the risks of free trade policies are as high as they seem to be to so many people, we don't stand much chance of finding out the truth of the matter. All we have a right to ask of politics is that it manages to satisfy enough people to make them willing to continue to abide by the rules. But, I suppose I'm philosophizing again. Let's just assume that Miss Panello has finally found the turn-off button on the buzzing alarm clock so that we can go on into the rest of the world, where other kinds of politics await us. When we meet next we'll talk about the bathroom."

"The bathroom?" asked an astonished girl nearby. "That's not political, is it?"

"We'll see," said the teacher.

5

The Bathroom and Beyond

At the end of the last hour the students had been dismissed with promises of bathroom talk. In the memory of any of them, no teacher had held out such expectations. When they assembled again the instructor, after a brief greeting, went to the blackboard and wrote out in large block letters, THE BATHROOM AND BEYOND—A VOYAGE OF POLITICAL DISCOVERY. One or two newcomers turned to their neighbors and asked in loud whispers, "What the hell's been going on here?"

"What's been going on here" said the teacher, "is that I've been trying to show your dependence on politics and government. Today, we'll go from the bedroom to the bathroom. Last hour's stay in the bedroom proved disappointing to some students here in some ways. They hoped or feared—whichever the case may be—that I might appeal to their prurient interests. I'll do that when it is educationally sound, and when the subject matter calls for it. By then we'll be on more familiar terms, of course, so it'll be easy. Now then, we'll proceed as we did during the last hour. I'll frame the questions and keep the discussions moving in the proper directions and you may feel free to interrupt when there's something you have to contribute. Having gotten out of bed with the help of international trade policy and the local electric company, protected by a solicitous government during a peaceful night, let us now take the first few brave steps into the new day. Upon rising from bed, most urban Americans, and many rural ones, move to the bathroom, there to fulfill a number of missions which have become urgent during the night. Mr. Berrigan, what's the first thing you do when you get into the bathroom?"

53

Berrigan was surprised. He had waited for someone to be examined but had not seen himself in that role.

Recovering from the shock, he said, "I guess the first thing I do is to brush my teeth."

"Come on, now, Mr. Berrigan," retorted the teacher, with more than a shade of doubt in his voice.

"Oh, ah, well, all right, I guess it isn't the *first* thing, either. First, I, well, use the bathroom."

"Use the bathroom? In what way? Don't you want to say?"

"Well, no, it's just not the kind of thing I'm used to talking about publicly in the classroom like this."

"What is?"

"You, know, using the bathroom, ah, eliminating."

"Are you embarrassed, Mr. Berrigan?"

"Yes, I am."

"I'm sorry. It was not my intention to embarrass you but, at the same time, we've got to get clear what we are talking about here. We use the bathroom for a lot of other things, don't we? To shave, bathe, wash, powder our noses, to store medicine. We have stumbled upon a cultural inhibition. Urination and defecation are not fit subjects for polite and academic discourse, apparently, but in the present context we are simply obliged to give them their proper names. So, Mr. Berrigan, there's no need to be embarrassed. It's going to be a purely academic and political, rather than medical or personal discussion. All right?"

"OK, if you say so."

"Now, could you tell us a little about the way the mechanics of the toilet are arranged? You see, we've come from this foreign planet where we don't have such things and we need you to induct us into the uses of this important cultural artifact."

"Well, after your bladder and your bowels have been emptied into this bowl. . . ."

"Admirable language, Mr. Berrigan, just admirable," interrupts the teacher.

"Thank you, well, anyway . . . after you do that, you trip this little lever on a water tank that sits just above the toilet bowl, and that releases a few gallons of water. In that way, the waste is flushed out of the bowl and down a pipe out into the street."

"Into the street?"

"Yes, well, I mean into pipes under the street."

"And from there?"

"Well, I guess it goes to a bigger pipe somewhere and then into the nearest river or maybe the ocean, if you live near it, as we do."

"Hmm." The teacher waited for elaboration and correction, slightly impatient, one foot tapping ever so little, arms crossed at chest level, his chin in one hand.

"I didn't expect to find a polluter in any of my classes this semester," he finally added. "Unfortunately, Mr. Berrigan is not too wrong in his description. Now, Mr. Berrigan, you've established that the waste enters a pipe under the street or sidewalk and is carried away. Whose pipes are these?"

"I guess they belong to the village or the city."

"Right. What would happen if they weren't there?"

"Well, I don't know."

"Is it an important question?"

"I guess so."

"Why?"

"Well, you have to get rid of the stuff, somehow, don't you?"

"Why?"

"It smells."

"OK. But is that the only reason to get rid of it, and is it the only way?"

"Well, I guess there might be others."

"Such as . . . ?"

"In some places they have cesspools."

"What are they?"

"I'm not really sure—I think they are basins in the ground with sides that let out the water and the solid stays in there and is destroyed by bacterial action, and it flushes out into the surrounding soil when it is deteriorated."

"For a guy who's not really sure, you do all right, Mr. Berrigan. What happens when you really know your stuff?"

"I do even better."

"Good. Now are there other ways of getting rid of human waste."

"I suppose you could let it run out into the street or the gutter. They did that after the middle ages."

"After the middle ages?"

"Yes, a history teacher once told us that in some cities there was a gutter in the middle of the street and the waste just sort of flowed down."

"Some of these cities still exist, Mr. Berrigan. How did the 'stuff' as we've been calling it, get into the gutter? Were there water-flush toilet bowls with pipes?"

Berrigan mused silently. "I don't know."

"Have you ever heard of chamber pots, sir?"

"Yes, I have. We have some around the house. We bought them at some auction or other and my mother uses them for flower pots."

"Are they pretty?"

"Yes, they are. I think it's funny that they should be sitting right out in the open in the living room, like that. They make nice conversation pieces."

"How recently in this country were they used, do you suppose?"

"Hell, I wouldn't doubt if they still used them in some places."

"You wouldn't? Why not?"

"Not everybody lives in cities with water toilets and sewers, I guess. There are a lot of people living in the country."

"I thought those people had outhouses. Shacks out back with simple holes in the ground."

"Yeah, but what do they do in the wintertime?"

"As I recall," said the teacher, "that was not too bad a problem. It must be that the bacterial action provides a certain amount of heat in the place. The one I remember actually had a concrete-lined pit and it required emptying every so often. It was a favorite job for the children, including myself. There was a bucket attached to a pole. You'd stick it down into the pit and come up with it full. You emptied it into a couple of pails, carried it carefully into the garden and poured it gently into the small ditches on either side of the vegetables, peas, spinach, tomatoes, and so forth. It wasn't a big job, or even particularly disagreeable. I guess country people have somewhat different attitudes towards that sort of thing. City dwellers simply flush it down and—out of sight—out of mind—away it goes and where it stops, nobody knows."

The class had been attentive to the narration but seemed puzzled why the teacher would indulge in this recalling of his personal history. He sensed it and sought to bring the discussion back to politics and government with another question: "At which point or points do you suppose elimination becomes a government problem, and why?"

"Yes, young lady." This to a girl who identified herself as Emily Andrews.

"Well, you said there was a pipe under the street. That's public and so are the outlets into the water. But a lot of waste is treated chemically, and that's done in public plants. I think I read someplace that they now have ways of converting the liquid waste into drinkable water. Didn't the President visit one of those places in Chicago last year and wasn't he offered a drink of it? He refused it, saying he never took a drink until late afternoon, or something like that."

"Right, Miss Andrews. Now what about the rest of the question?"

"Oh, I'm sorry, I forgot what it was."

"The whole question was, 'At which point do you suppose elimination becomes a governmental problem, and why?'"

"Oh, I see. Well, if you want to get rid of a lot of human waste you have more than just an individual problem, I guess, and that's when some general solution is required."

"How much is a lot?"

"I don't know, but it must have to do with the size or the density of the population. Imagine everybody in New York City with chamber pots and outhouses!"

"Well, why not?"

Laughter from the class.

"But there are people who live in fifty or sixty story buildings. The outhouses would have to be colossal."

Laughter from the class.

"Good answer. But couldn't you have catchbasins in each apartment house which you empty into tank trucks and which you then ship to the country for fertilizer? A sort of fair trade in return for all the food we get from there."

"I don't know. It would require a whole industry to do that, wouldn't it?"

"Well, don't we in fact have a whole industry to do something like it? Pipes, sewage lines, disposal plants, recirculation plants, large-scale bureaucracies, a whole technology, tax money given over to support the operation?"

"I guess so, but it seems to be a public industry. Aside from the problem of volume, isn't there also the matter of cost? I mean, it costs a lot of money to set all this up, doesn't it? And there are the health reasons. Didn't a lot of diseases come from open sewers and toilets in the old days?"

"Yes," replied the teacher, "open sewers are disease breeding places. One of their gifts is typhoid fever. So there are cost problems, health problems, and technical problems combined. Installation of sewage lines in previously unserviced areas is, typically, an expensive undertaking. Usually, the owners of the property along the sewage line are assessed some portion of the cost and as a result there is a great struggle against doing it by people who don't want to spend the money for it. But in some areas there's no other choice. For example, where there are cesspools and the population density rises beyond a certain point, the excessive human waste seeping into the ground may have an adverse effect upon the water supply, or perhaps even on the water table, itself. Besides, the cost of sewage lines has to be offset against the cost of maintaining cesspools. They need repairs and frequently even replacement at high prices. In addition, the mere presence of sewer lines makes possible the development of population growth and industry. Not only human waste, but industrial waste can be flushed and that's a gain on the side of economic development. From that point of view, sewage lines are a boon because they represent a good investment, increasing the value of the land and of the houses and other properties adjacent to them. Of course, they also present a problem of deciding where they go, who should pay for them and why, and as we all now know, what should be done with the waste. Thoughtless dumping into rivers, lakes, and oceans seems especially wrongheaded. Our lakes and rivers as well as portions of the adjacent oceans are terribly polluted from the dumped wastes of open sewers. We need to spend billions of dollars for conversion plants and we have to find ways to reuse presently polluted places. Now all of these pressures for dealing with the problem call for political kinds of remedies. And that's what your first use of the bathroom has had to do with government and politics this morning. Any questions?"

There were none. The class sat silent. They'd had enough.

6

Water, Water Everywhere

"Having disposed of our waste, we have of course made only partial use of the bathroom, regardless of the euphemistic conventions. We live in a culture in which cleanliness is regarded as next to godliness. I hint that the next step has to do with the elixir of life—water. Do I have someone to argue with? The question, broadly speaking, is the same as the others. What is the political significance of water?"

The teacher saw a wary, cautious hand being raised by an unusually youthful looking male student. "Yes," he beckoned the student.

"Do you want my name?"

"If you don't mind. That way we'll get to know each other."

"OK. I'm Jed Conklin."

"Hello, Mr. Conklin. You were a little cautious raising your hand. Is that your way, or was there a reason?"

"Neither, I was just wondering who else might want to talk about water, that's all."

"Fine. Now, how about that water."

"Of course, you expect me to say that I get water from a tap, and then you'd lead me on to show me that it really comes from a reservoir which you'd then prove conclusively is a government installation. I'm a jump ahead of you. By now everybody in this classroom should be catching on to the game, so I've caught on and I'm saying the water comes from a publicly owned reservoir."

Sharing in the amusement of the other students, the teacher responded, "Are you sure that it does?"

"What do you mean?"

"Well, how do you know that it comes from a public reservoir?"

"I thought all of our water comes from there."

"No, Mr. Conklin, not all of it. Even in metropolitan areas, much water is drawn from wells. Some of these are public, others are private and personal, and still others are private and commercial."

"I'm surprised."

"That's a real benefit. It makes your tuition dollar rise in value."

"Well, how do we know that we're getting good water from private wells?"

"How do you suppose?"

"The government again?"

"Why not, don't you like the government?"

"I don't hate it, except for some things they do."

"But as far as water is concerned, you think they do well, if you will pardon the slight pun."

"Yes, I think so."

"Quite correct. There's little reason to think otherwise. We go to the tap in the morning and thoughtlessly turn it on, we fill our glasses and without even once looking, drink it down without worry. Needless to say it was not always thus, and it is not that way everywhere in the world nor everywhere in the country. In fact, a steady, healthful, plentiful, and tasteful water supply is one hell of a governmental problem. Without water nothing can happen in civilization. It just dies. Let the supply be problematic or scarce or absent and human habitation becomes impossible. Look at a water resource map of the world and try an overlay map of flourishing countries, cities, and civilizations. Water may not be a sufficient condition for the expansion of human civilization but it is a necessary one. Now, Mr. Conklin, what kind of conditions must be met to put a water reservoir together?"

"Well, I suppose you have to find a place where you can put a dam and let the water collect behind it. Then you run some pipes from there to the places where people want the water and that's it."

"Fundamentally, that's right. Now, supposing that the land you've found for damming is not sufficiently within the rain belt to give you enough water?"

"Oh, you have to make sure that there is enough rain or enough river water, I guess."

"All right, now supposing that you've found the properly located land with the right topographic conditions, but you notice that the ground is too porous. It won't hold the water."

"Well, I don't know."

"All right, you find out about that by taking some borings and testing the soil. It's not, I think, a serious problem, but there is another one. Supposing you find out that the land you need belongs to private owners —farmers, hunting lodges, summer camps, lumber companies, etcetera, what then?"

"You can always buy it with tax money."

"Supposing the owners believe that it's worth so much to them that they refuse to sell?"

"You take it away from them."

"Take it?"

"Yeah, the government can do that, can't it?"

"Can it?"

"Sure, I learned in high school that when the government wants to build a road and it's being blocked by private land, the owners can be compelled to sell. It's called predominant domain, or something like that. You just have to give it to them or go to jail."

"Does it ever come to that?"

"I don't know, but I once saw a movie about an old lady on an island in the middle of a lake that was going to be made into a reservoir down in Tennessee. They bought her out but she wouldn't budge. It was a whole long story."

"So, the government pays a going price for the land which the owner has to accept eventually. The federal Constitution speaks of 'just compensation.' These cases tend to be settled in courts which judge the fairness of the price. You are right. The right to refuse to sell to the government does not exist in the same form as in private transactions. I wonder why such a principle is thought to be important in a political system?"

"How would the government do anything for the public if it didn't have some sort of right like that?" asked Mr. Conklin.

"I can't imagine it," replied the instructor, and continued, "not that the right of eminent domain is the major problem with water. Much more serious is the problem of supply, and its proper distribution. In certain areas of the United States, water is scarce. The California-Arizona-New Mexico controversy over the uses of the Colorado River waters is especially serious and has been the source of great political and legal conflict. Who has the right to the water from a river forming interstate boundaries? Who within the state may have the use of it and at what price? Indeed, you will find that the question of water rights is one of the most ancient of controversies in all civilizations and there are many interesting principles of use which have been evolved in different countries at different times. In addition, there is the problem of which level of government has the proper authority to distribute the water and who has the final say when conflicts between governmental jurisdiction arise. The literature is especially rich here, even though the general public rarely gets wind of these problems. Can any of you think of some very widely publicized controversies about water?"

The student, who had been paying close attention, spoke up. "Yes," he said, "last year there was a big thing about fluoridation."

"Fluoridation?"

"Haven't you ever heard of fluoridation?"

"Oh, I have, I have, Mr. Conklin. I'm interested that you explain it to the other people in class here. This conversation is after all not just a personal matter between you and me, is it?"

"OK," said Mr. Conklin, cheerfully. "Fluoride is a chemical which can help reduce tooth cavities and it can be taken in water. A lot of people want to add it to the water supply to prevent cavities, especially in children. A lot of other people protest against it because they say it's harmful medication for people with heart ailments and other troubles. It was interesting because some of the antifluoride people accused the others of a communist plot to poison the water, and the proponents called them reactionaries."

"All right. An interesting object lesson in the ideological aspects of political controversy. How did this controversy come out?"

"I think there was a vote in this North Shore Long Island village that has control over some water supply and the fluoridation people won: the ones that were for it, I mean."

"Do you suppose that will end it?"

"I don't know. I read in the paper a few months ago that there are some places where the water has enough fluoride in it that nobody in the community has any cavities to speak of."

"Yes, as I recall, it was a place in Texas. Do you suppose that the chemical content of water is everywhere such that the stuff is drinkable as it comes out of the ground?"

"No, I know that in some places things have to be taken out of the water and in others stuff has to be added. I vacationed in a place last year where the water tasted like chloride. The hotel manager told me that they had to add it to kill other harmful bacteria."

"Now we need to move on somewhat. My question suggested that the only thing that water is really good for is drinking. As you know, the famous W. C. Fields thought it wasn't even fit for that and restricted himself to gin and other medications. We need water for washing, for industrial processes, for cooking, for recreation, and for plant irrigation, and for heating homes and other places in the winter and for cooling them in the summer. That means there is a possibility of using water unfit for human consumption but useful for other things. This expands the possibility of the useful sources from which it may be drawn. Already we are working on desalinization of the oceans. We have covered quite a range of problems in this discussion and I wonder whether there are any questions Mr. Conklin and I have not touched upon which may have occurred to some of you and which may be pertinent before we move on."

There was a short silence, followed by the raising of a single hand.

"Sir," the questioner asked, "what seems to you to be the principle of the relationship between the water problems and politics and government?"

"That is a very fine, if difficult question," replied the instructor. "It is marvellously designed to speculate, I think. I want to thank you for it, Mr. . . ."

"Stark. . . . Harry Stark."

"Mr. Stark, do you want to work with me on the question for a while?"

"Sure, I'm interested."

"All right. Now suppose, Mr. Stark, that we lived in a place where the water was fabulously abundant. Water everywhere and all of it fit to drink, so to speak, in contradiction to the Ancient Mariner. Never so much as to cause floods, but never so little as to give anyone the thought that it could be a problem. You take it from there, Mr. Stark."

"As you put it, there would be no problem. Everyone could drink, without anyone else feeling threatened. There would be no need for government to get into it at all, I think."

"Are you saying that if there is no scarcity or threat of it no regulation is needed, and if no regulation is needed there is no need for compulsion and therefore no need for an agency such as government to exist?"

"I didn't say that, but I'm sure that's what it means."

"Are you sure?"

"Well, I was a second ago, but the way you ask if I'm sure, I'm not so sure, after all. You must have some reason for asking me if I'm sure. Right?"

"I do. Could anything go wrong with the water even though it is plentiful?"

"Let's see. It could get polluted, or dirty, or smelly."

"Right. Then what would happen?"

"I guess you'd have to filter it."

"Filter?"

"Yes, you spray dirty water up into the air and let it come down and pass through filters of all kinds to take out the impurities."

"Right, and that means resources have to be collected, technical methods have to be invented, people have to be trained and supervised, and the water has to be redistributed after processing. What it means is that organized, and possibly coerced, relationships have to be introduced. At least some sharing of the costs among consumers, even if they are not willing, has to be arranged. The unwilling must be coerced and the necessary means for doing that have to be produced. That is a form of regulatory action requiring a social apparatus and a justification. The ordinary definition of government—which I'm not now prepared to give—would fit it pretty well, I think."

"So, what's the principle?" asked Mr. Stark again.

"Why not try to state it yourself?" suggested the teacher.

The student regarded the teacher thoughtfully for a while, shifted in his seat, scratched his head, smiled hopefully a couple of times and said, "It's damned difficult."

"Is that the principle?"

"I never thought of that, but if you're satisfied with it, I'm willing to let it go at that."

"Now, wouldn't I have to be ashamed of myself for being willing to let you get out of it so soon?"

"That's soon?"

"How many centuries, Mr. Stark, do you think men have struggled to find the correct principles of interpreting the various relationships between natural and social phenomena, or between natural events or social events? Don't answer that, please. It was rhetorical in nature. No, I think we'll stay on the hook for a while longer. In a preliminary way, would you settle for this, Mr. Stark?" offered the teacher. "Whenever some kind of control or regulation of a supply of a natural resource is thought proper for the common good, men will employ some sort of a socially coercive mechanism to accomplish the purpose."

"I'll buy it," said the student.

"I'd advise you to be careful of what you 'bought' just now. It has all kinds of problems in it. I'll point to some of them, if I may: What is the common good? How does it get defined and who defines it? What purposes are being served in doing so? Is there a possibility that men will disagree over it, and what is the meaning of their disagreement? The point is that we have hold of formulations that are essentially philosophical and disputable. Some of these disputes go to the very core of social philosophy and are, in their nature, not capable of satisfactory solution, as long as men disagree over definition of the good."

"And all that just for a drink of water," responded a hitherto passive student.

"Yes, all that, and more," answered the teacher, continuing to the new participant. "Do you have a question, too?"

"Sure. I'm Bob Phillips. A while ago, when you and that guy over there talked about the perfect water situation and then changed it by polluting the water and said that for the common good taxes would have to be collected to clean up the water—well, I have a question about that. Suppose somebody in that situation decides to dig a well of his own, on his own land, and he gets enough water for himself and maybe enough to sell to other people, what would be the matter with that? Why should he be compelled to pay taxes? After all, he's got water of his own."

"I'm impressed by that question, Mr. Phillips. You picked out one of the critical problems in theory and fact. Are you sure that the well digger had the right to dig the well?"

"Why, yes, it's his property; he can do with it as he pleases, can't he?"

"Can he?"

"Sure, that's what I always thought. That's what having private property means, doesn't it?"

"Does it?"

"Every time I ask a question I get a question back in return," said the irritated student.

"And every time I ask a question I get an answer in question form," responded the delighted teacher who, by all appearances, had had such encounters before. "Look here, Mr. Phillips, having private property does not mean what you said it meant, because there are restraints of public policy upon all owners with regards to some things, including also the digging of wells. You may devote your private property only to those uses permitted by the law, by custom and other such arrangements. The water derived from the well might be considered beyond the legal uses of private property. It depends on the circumstances, can't you see?"

"No, I can't. Either land is yours or it isn't. If the law says what you can't do with it then it isn't yours."

"If the law said you could make no use of it, it might not be yours, of course. There are some societies, ancient and modern, where private property does not, in fact, exist that way at all. But supposing the law specified those matters in which you have only limited or restricted choices and left other matters up to you? What could that mean?"

"Well, then it would be yours to do with as the law allowed. But what the law forbids is out of your control, and whatever is not in your control isn't yours, even if you have the deed."

"Now, Mr. Phillips, can you imagine living in a desert?" asked the teacher.

"Yeah, I can imagine it, but I don't like it."

"OK. Now, suppose in that desert you dug a well to get water, and suppose there is some kind of lawful government there or that somebody rules. Do you think that you would be allowed to keep other people from drinking because they did not have enough money to pay you, because that well was yours?"

"Well, it's my well, isn't it?"

"Is it?"

"Sure, if they don't like it they can dig their own."

"If they did, yours would be worth a lot less to you."

"That's all right. All I want is water for myself. How else can you survive in the desert?"

"Maybe there would be less water for everyone if everyone had his own well."

"How's that possible?"

"Hydrostatically speaking—imagine my sneaking in a word like that —there'd be more evaporation at the surface of the water and there would be less pressure on the underground water veins and consequently the water table would drop and greater water scarcity for all would result. Besides, can't your thirsty neighbors do anything besides dig their own wells?"

"What?"

"Nothing?"

"I can't imagine what."

"Do you recall that I said there was a government of some sort in the territory?"

"I remember you said that, but I didn't know what you were driving at."

"What I meant to suggest by it was that there are people who exercise authority on behalf of the whole society who can be counted on to defend the major principles of established law in the area. Also, I meant to suggest that the tribesmen who want water have some place they can turn to for help other than to ask you for it or to dig their own wells."

"Oh, I see," the student replied and added, after a moment's reflection, "but don't you think that the government has to defend me? After all, it's my well and that means I have a right to it and the government has to protect me."

"What do you suppose the tribesmen who appeal to the government for help against you would do, if the government placed the protection of your private rights ahead of what they deemed to be the most vital necessity of life?"

"What could they do? After all, the government is the final authority, isn't it? That's what it means to have a government."

"Yes, it does mean that. But does it follow from that principle that people are helpless against government?"

"Well, I thought so," replied the student.

"Don't you think that the desert tribesmen's sense of loyalty to established authority would be affected at all by the decision not to intervene on their behalf?"

"Well, I guess so, but they would have to take the law into their own hands to do anything about it, isn't that right?"

"I think, Mr. Phillips, you're beginning to see something, aren't you?"

"Well, yes, I guess they could always come and kill me and take the well away, but that would be murder and theft."

"Yes, it would be. Would you be around to complain of it?"

"No, I guess not, but the government could punish them for that, couldn't they?"

"But could they?"

"Do you mean they wouldn't let the government arrest them? But that means they would have to fight them, or even to overthrow them."

"Well, haven't you ever heard of that?" the teacher asked.

"Yes, but that would be revolution."

"So it would be," the teacher replied. "Doesn't that ever happen? Don't you think your killers have a good case for revolution? Couldn't they argue that the principle of private ownership of wells and water is practically and morally inconsistent with life in the desert, that a government defending such principles does not deserve to be obeyed, that, far from having committed murder and theft against you, they have merely executed you and expropriated the well under a new system of law which makes water the common property of all, that the old government has forfeited its claim to obedience, and that all right-thinking desert people should join the revolution?"

"But wouldn't that lead to civil war?"

"Yes, it might, and do you suppose the revolutionaries might win it?"

"Well, I guess that depends on who has the most support and the most guns."

"It might depend on that, yes. Or perhaps even on who has control over water wells, right? But on the other hand it also might depend on who defends what the desert people think is the right set of principles and practices about the use of water, might it not? The whole thing is all about life in the desert after all, and how can a government expect to endure there if it doesn't give authoritative expression to a common sense of what is right?"

"And all that just for water," mused the student.

"Why not for water?" the teacher asked.

"I really don't know," the student replied.

"Perhaps if you were thirsty more of the time you might have seen it more quickly," the teacher suggested.

"Yes, I guess so. It's a lucky thing I'm not."

"So far as water is concerned that is certainly true, Mr. Phillips," the teacher agreed. And turning to the class, he concluded by saying, "I think that the discussion about water and politics is now complete."

7

A Healthy Body

"I am very tempted," the teacher began, "to summarize for you the importance of the discussion of water. We touched upon a great many diverse matters and if my guess is right, there must be many of you here who are waiting with poised pencils for the summary statement from the authority. I will resist the temptation, however, because I sense that it would violate the spirit of what we must first do in this classroom before we enter into the proper study of politics itself. You should be keeping a sharp ear open, however, because the dialogues we have already had in this classroom have dealt with problems of a fundamental sort. A few times during the last hour our discussion was so good that I heard myself silently wishing that you would remember what was being said here for a long time. Now I am saying it aloud. I hope you will remember both the substance and the method of this introduction to our course work."

The brief pedagogic exposition concluded, the instructor returned to the proper work:

"It is apparent that in this culture our bathrooms are not merely devoted to cleanliness and to the disposal of human waste. They are also the ordinary family dispensary and contain the supply of medicines, bandaids, thermometers, ice bags, tourniquets, antiseptic soaps, eyedroppers, elastic bandages, bedpans, etcetera. Who among you here has had need of some sort of medication from your own storehouse of drugs and pharmaceuticals today?"

A few hands went up. The teacher took them in turn, to get a quick medical census.

"We'll start at the rear of the class. Yes, sir . . . include your name, please."

"I'm Jack Freebert, sir. I woke up with a terrible headache and took two aspirins right off the bat this morning."

"How is it now?"

"All right, thank you."

"Good. Now, next case, please."

"I've been taking antihistamine tablets for a few days so I could come to class . . . Oh! I'm Evan Paul."

"All right, Mr. Paul. You want to watch the dosage, especially if you're driving."

"Yes, doctor."

"Don't tempt me. Some of the medicine we professors prescribe is hard to take. Next case."

The next student, a young woman, unbuttoned the sleeve of her blouse and rolled it up, revealing a tightly wound elastic bandage extending from her wrist to her elbow.

"Laurel Hammer," she said. "I've strained my forearm muscles playing tennis and I thought a bandage would help me. I'm also doped up a little."

"Doped up?"

The class leaned forward, waiting.

"Yes, the doctor prescribed some pain-killing pills while the strain gets better, and I'm taking them."

"Are we developing a sick call list here?" asked the teacher. The reporting of the minor ailments had encouraged others to raise their hands. "Yes," he continued, pointing to the next student.

"I'm Bill Raymond," he said, "and I'm a diabetic. I have enough insulin on hand to keep me going, with all the equipment necessary to administer it each day. Also, I have to be very careful in my eating habits, so as to maintain the proper sugar balance in my blood."

The teacher, sensing that the student had revealed an aspect of his private life he would rather have kept to himself, decided at that point not to continue the medical reports and said so, giving his reason. "I suppose it might not be wise or even necessary to continue this kind of participation. We all ail from time to time. How many of you here are aware that your medicine cabinets at home contain medication beyond the aspirin tablet or cough syrup stage of seriousness, especially those which have to do with organic ailments like diabetes, or painful disorders, such as skin diseases, or respiratory trouble like asthma—the kinds of ailments that require a special store of a certain kind of medication which are taken by you or another member of the family?"

A fairly good proportion of hands arose. One student, without identifying himself, asked, "Does migraine headache qualify?"

"I'm not drawing any lines about it. If you want to raise your hand, do so."

It was an impressive showing. Very few hands were not up. "Look around," said the professor, "and regard the frailty of mankind in microcosm. Thank you. Now let's ask our question. What has all this stuff got to do with government and politics?"

A small pause, followed by a few hands in the air.

"Don't medicines have to be registered with the government?" offered a student.

"Are you asking us or telling us?"

"A little of both. I think they have to, . . . yes, they do. I remember that they can't be sold without having been approved as safe."

"That's good, Miss . . . ?"

"My name is Hyde, Dorothy Hyde. Yes, now that I think of it, there is an office in the federal government checking on drugs. A few years ago, one of their chemists thought a certain drug had not been sufficiently tested before it was allowed to be sold in this country. It was thalidomide and the European manufacturers had passed a government test which was not as rigid as the American tests, and when pregnant women took the drug they gave birth to malformed children without feet, hands, arms, or legs. It was a terrible scandal. There are still hundreds of lawsuits in the courts in Europe about it, and I think that it's now forbidden. So I guess the answer is that govenment gets into the drug business to keep harmful substances from being sold and used."

"Why do you suppose it needs governmental authority to establish what is harmful? Are physicians and drug manufacturers not able to tell that by their experiments with drugs before they sell them to the public?"

"Maybe," replied the student, "it's because of the money they can make. It is very profitable business, after all. Oh, that reminds me, there's another reason for governmental control, the money they make. There have been some suits brought into courts and there have been some congressional investigations about the cost of drugs, I think."

"Yes, and . . . ?"

"Well, I read the other day that drug companies had taken a common chemical compound and given it a commercial name which was registered and sold it at several times the price at which the chemical could be bought by its regular name, and people are suing. In one case the suit was brought by the state government which had bought the drug for its own use, claiming they had been made to overpay."

"The state government bought drugs for its own use? How does that work?"

"Doesn't the state run hospitals for people with mental sickness?" asked the student.

"Yes, it does," replied the teacher.

"Well, I think that's what these drugs were for; the treatment of mental patients."

"Could we get back to the business of drug testing, please?" encouraged the professor.

Miss Hyde, warmed to her subject, resumed. "Well, I think that the drug firms do test their products but they might be tempted to put them on the market without applying a good enough test, for example. Some drugs have side effects that would be serious for some people and they might not turn up in the test. Sometimes, a physician prescribing a drug might not know enough about it and make a terrible mistake because he didn't have enough information."

"So, we have established that there is a safety problem with certain drugs, which consists in part of the incompleteness of scientific knowledge and in part of the possible temptation to offer a drug for sale, though it is unsafe, in order to compete commercially. We have also the observation that the government's proprietary interest is involved. Not only does it maintain hospitals for the mentally ill, but municipal hospitals for general purposes are widespread, though not as widely as in other countries. The government's economic interest is at stake, of course, and it battles to save money. Part of the story has to do with controversy over the unusual price structure of the drug-manufacturing business, which a congressional investigation of some years ago unearthed. It showed that there are extremely wide differences in the prices charged by different firms for the same drugs, and that there are extremely large profit margins in the manufacturing of some kinds of pharmaceuticals."

"Aren't there some other ways the government is in the drug business, too?" asked another student.

"How?"

"I thought drugs were patentable."

"Are they?"

"Well, yes, I think so. And if that's true, it can prevent some manufacturers from offering the same drugs others are making, except if they agree to pay a price for the use of the patent."

"Good," said the teacher. "You're right, Mr. . . . ?"

"Hawlett."

"Yes, the patent problem is especially interesting in pharmaceuticals. Much of the currently offered pharmacopeia is, in fact, made under licensing processes to the big firms capable of managing large laboratory facilities. That presents a special, and fairly sophisticated, economic problem in which government is involved, but for which we have too little time at this moment."

"I just thought of a whole new angle on this," called out yet another student. "I'm Barbara Palmer and what about all these inoculations we got when we were children, and even when you travel to other countries, they don't let you in unless you first get a lot of shots for all kinds of strange diseases?"

"Yes, a good angle indeed. What do they reflect about the political aspect of health?"

"I suppose that some kinds of sicknesses are problems for the general community as well as for the individual who has them."

"Excellently put, Miss Palmer. How about some examples?"

"Well, typhoid, for example, or anything that could be an epidemic—even influenza. If enough people got the flu, it could stop the whole economy. Some diseases are very easy to communicate."

"That's certainly a clear case justifying governmental intervention, isn't it, even if you believed that medical matters were the private business of each individual. But, of course, it is also the case that in a lot of places in the world, and in some kinds of matters other than public health in this country as well, the belief in private medicine, so-called, is being seriously challenged, isn't it, Miss Palmer?"

"Yes, our local paper last week had a series on socialized medicine in other countries, like Sweden, England, Russia, and so on. It was very interesting."

"Was it about politics?"

"Well, yes, in a way."

"In what way?"

"In some of those countries they introduced socialized medicine after one of the political parties adopted it as part of their program and when they won elections they passed laws which changed the whole system of medical treatment."

"A very good answer. Now, is not having so-called socialized medicine or public health laws also political?"

"I don't see how that can be. It either is or isn't."

"Well, what are the medical practices in the United States?"

"You couldn't call them socialized, could you? I mean, doctors are in private practice and patients pay their own bills, mostly, don't they? The government has nothing to do with medicine, does it?"

"Nothing at all? You've heard of Medicare and Medicaid, haven't you?"

"Oh, yes, that's right."

"Anyway, what does 'socialized medicine' mean?"

"I think it means the absence of private practice, and free medicine and treatments. Like they have in Russia, where nobody pays anything for hospitals, or doctors, or medicine."

"Are you sure that that describes Soviet medicine?"

"No, I'm not sure, but that's what people say. Anyway, in England medicine is free."

"Free?"

"Yes, it doesn't cost anything for the patients, the government pays it all, I think."

"The government?"

"Yes, it comes from the general taxes."

"Most of it does, and where if you please, does that come from?"

"Oh, the taxpayers, of course."

"And who are they? Are they the same people who get medical treatment?"

"Well, I guess some of them are and some of them are not. Not everybody gets care, I'm sure. So that they would be paying for the rest who did."

"Well, Miss Palmer, what are we doing now?"

"I suppose we're trying to establish what socialized medicine is."

"All right, you think you can say what it is now?"

"I don't know, let me see . . . I guess it is when health is treated as a public rather than a private problem. But isn't there any private practice under socialized medicine?"

"That was a good definition, incidentally, and the answer to your question is, of course, that it depends entirely upon the case. In some countries yes and in some countries no. I suspect that even in the cases of a completely public system, there may be some people who go to doctors privately and pay for it on their own. In England, there is a mixed system, and I suppose there are a great many possible variations, actually. In the United States, there are some wholly public parts, some wholly private ones, some mixed ones, some insurance systems, and so forth. At any rate, the difference between public and private systems is not the absence of costs or of politics. It costs money, whatever the arrangement. The distinction is who pays for it and in what manner it is paid for, and in what manner medical care is dispensed, either in public institutions or in private ones, or in a mixture of these two and, it is in this that politics plays a role. The decision to have one or another kind of system, or one or another way of paying for it, or one or another way of administering it, is political, even though the medicine itself or the administration of it is, strictly speaking, not political."

"Could you have private manufacturing of medicine and still have socialized medicine?" asked the student.

The teacher, resuming his old stance, replied, "That's fine as a question, but what do you suppose the answer would be in the context of this whole discussion?"

"You mean that that is a political question?"

"Might it not be?"

"The answer you want me to give is yes, but is it?"

"If you had a law specifying that health is an entirely public matter, bringing all aspects of it under governmental control, that would be political. And, if the law exempted the production of medicines and medical supplies from that control, it would be a politically defined exemption, would it not? What possible answer can I be left with?"

"You could say that there are some things that are political by the very nature of them and others are not."

"You could say that, but you would have to produce the evidence for such an assertion and what would the evidence be?"

"Well, aren't there some things that are by nature not political?"

"By nature? What does nature mean here?"

Miss Palmer leaned back in her chair and replied, "I don't seem to be getting anywhere in this. I've always heard that medicine and politics don't mix, and I still think so, but now I see that some medical matters are political. At least, that's what you just showed to us, but now the problem is this: if medicine is political, is there anything that is not political?"

The teacher, who had been watching the approach of this question, was having some difficulty in restraining other students from entering the discussion. He saw the eagerness of the other possible contestants in this crucial moment and decided to keep the discourse flowing. He paused for a moment before he responded and, trying to include the whole class in his response to the single student, said, "Young lady—and pardon me for being slighlty pompous at this point—you have moved us very swiftly into deep waters. Your question requires extremely careful analysis and has been the subject of considerable literature in antiquity as well as in our time. It is, in a manner of speaking, the central organizing question of political life and of political inquiry. No brief response can do it justice, but in the present context some answer is clearly required.

"If one defined everything as political, the term politics would lose its ability to distinguish some kinds of relationships or facts from others and would come to mean nothing at all. One deals with this by saying that politics has to do with ruling or governing a community of people or that political relationships are those which have to do with the exercise of the authority of the whole community in which men live. According to that definition, it is not necessary that everything be regarded as political, only that it be possible to choose whether some thing, such as medicine may be made subject to public authority and the degree to which it may be made so. However, at the present time, we are mainly concerned with a kind of empirical question—a question of evidence. That question is whether you have had anything to do with politics and government today. With regard to medical matters, it is fairly clear by now, isn't it, that it is the case. Without saying that medicine is political, we therefore must conclude that it may be and is subject to political management. Let that suffice for the moment, even though I would urge you to keep that question of definition resting in the back of your mind."

Miss Palmer, who had been listening intently was not ready. "I don't see how it is possible to talk about anything if you don't first define what you mean by it," she resisted bravely.

"But aren't you satisfied that we have defined politics? Didn't I just say that it is the relationship involving the exercise of the authority or the power of the whole community in which men live?"

"Oh yes, that's right. But that won't tell us whether medicine is political will it?"

"As a definition it won't, but neither will it exclude medicine, will it?"

"But don't you think that if we wanted to know if medicine is political or not, the definition of politics should do that?"

"I'm certain," the teacher replied, "that you are not using the term 'definition' properly here. Perhaps you are really looking for something else."

"Well, now I'm thoroughly confused. I thought you could settle the whole thing with a definition."

"On the other hand," replied the teacher, "I am certain that one cannot logically do that. What can be done is to see whether in any given case the processes of medicine—activities having to do with healing of human ailments—are subject to politics and to what degree. But that doesn't define politics, it merely describes whether, in any given case, it is more or less concerned with medicine."

"Are you saying that you can make anything in society into an object of politics without changing the definition of what politics is?" the student demanded.

"Yes, I am saying that. If it involves the making of rules or of decisions on behalf of the whole community, it is political. One of the problems of politics consists of deciding how many and what kinds of activities and social relationships are to be managed by means of politics, or of authoritative rule-making. Factual observations about that may be made, but these don't change the definition of politics itself."

"In other words," the student replied, "The question of whether medicine is political is a problem of political decision but not definition?"

"It's somewhat awkward, I suppose," the teacher replied, "but I'd go along with it."

"I'm still not sure that's right, though," the student persisted. "I always thought that the things that government did were political by definition, or that a lot of them were. I can't seem to work my way out of that, somehow. I'm sure there must be more than that to it."

"What makes you so sure, though?"

"Well, it's like this," the student responded. "If politics is defined as making rules and having authority, then the reasons for having rules and authority are also political in a way, because if it weren't for those reasons there wouldn't have to be government. Now most of those reasons seem to have to do with conflict over one thing or another. I mean, for example, medicine. If it hadn't been for the fact that a lot of people were fighting over getting better medical attention, government might not have had to get into it at all. I mean you showed that to us also when we were talking about water, and about some of the other things like the regulation of the content of the pillow, isn't that right? So the whole idea of the conflict that makes people want to settle their differences by having government make laws is also political. And if that's true, then you could call any conflict that involves people political, couldn't you?"

"Some of your logic is very difficult to argue with," the teacher responded." To the extent that it is true that conflict gives rise to government activity, or even to government itself, that conflict could well be thought of as political. But there are so many kinds of conflicts that don't have that consequence, aren't there? Or do you imagine that the mere existence of differences among people about anything at all is at the bottom of political life, or of the politicization of life?"

"Well, but do you think that government would even have been invented if it weren't for those conflicts?"

"I don't know the answer to that," the teacher replied carefully.

"But isn't it important to know that?" the student demanded.

"Yes, very much so. Still, I don't know it as a matter of fact, even though I know how people have speculated about the question, and not a few argue, just as you do, that the need for politics is an outcome of the presence of conflicts that require settling. But I think it is a problem of knowing for sure. There are other ways of speculating on the invention of politics, some of them very famous. These speculations have always been a very significant part of thinking about political life, of course, and many of them have become included in a body of thinking called political philosophy or political theory. That's what we're doing right now, you know."

"But hasn't politics always been part of human life?" the student persisted.

"Scholars differ on questions of that kind, and so do philosophers. Some say that one cannot have human society without some kind of system of ultimate rule, and that this is by definition political. Others say that one can have such rule, but as long as one doesn't differentiate among magic, religion, family, or tribal rules, one does not have politics. In other words, as long as one does not separate the business of ruling and power from other kinds of social relationships by definition, one does not have politics as a distinct function."

"That's confusing, isn't it?"

"If not confusing, it's certainly very difficult intellectually as well as in terms of the evidence by which one establishes such claims. For us, living at the present time, it is, of course, possible to distinguish between political and nonpolitical matters—partly by definition because we are accustomed to knowing where to draw the lines between them and we customarily do, even though the drawing of the lines is often a matter of hot political dispute. We generally say that nonpolitical matters become political by being included in the conflict system involving government or politics, or the authority of the entire community in which we live. So that even a discussion about whether something is political or not, or whether it ought to be, is a political discussion in the sense that it seeks to find a way to draw the line on one side or another."

"Do *you* think it's possible for human beings to live in society without rules or authority?" the student mused.

"Would you mind if I didn't answer that just yet, Miss Palmer?" replied the teacher. "We have many a mile to go in our work. I'm glad the question came up. It's the hardy perennial of all political philosophy, but let us continue to explore some other, perhaps more mundane, matters before we deal with it."

The teacher offered no further comment and asked for none.

8

The Clothes We Wear

"As I look about in the class," began the teacher, "I notice that we have all fallen victim to the conventions of wearing clothing of all kinds. With some notable exception, for some special occasions, most people in most places in the world wear clothes. They need protection from the elements, and they are interested in adornment and in expressing some sense of themselves in what they wear. In addition, clothes are a convenient way of denoting one's status in life, both as to social class, occupation, age, or even special roles played in the society, such as in the case of uniforms or other special occupational garb. So, we leave the bathroom and return to the bedroom to get dressed. Now, it might be of some interest to some members of the class if I proceeded in the usual fashion here this morning by asking some student to enumerate specifically the items of clothing he or she is wearing today. But, as you know, that would cause too much of a commotion in the classroom. Some of these items are regarded in our culture as having symbolic significance and are associated with feelings of an intimate and sexual character. I don't want to put anybody on the spot about wearing brassieres, for example, or other kinds of supporting equipment. From experience I know that one can be sidetracked into all kinds of irrelevancies that way, and I must ask you therefore to keep your minds strictly on politics, if you can, or upon the clothing itself, without anybody in it or, as the case may be, out of it."

The appreciative chuckles eased the atmosphere somewhat.

"We can get started by asking rather what kinds of materials are used for the making of the clothes we wear. Are there any sons and daughters of people employed in the making or selling of clothing here who could help us to expedite the work?"

There were several hands and their owners identified themselves in turn as the sons and daughters of clothing salesmen, textile converters, an importer of silk, a cotton broker, and one daughter of a seamstress in a garment factory.

"I suppose," said the teacher, "we could at least observe that, were it not for the activities of at least some of your parents, you'd be wearing different clothing than you are. A respectable proportion of our population in this classroom gets economic sustenance from the business of clothing. I'm sure that, if we were to look more closely at the occupations of the rest of you, more people would, in fact, turn out to have economic connections with clothing the population. That is one of the clues to its political significance, of course. What we are now concerned with is the stuff that clothes are made of, and the possible significance of it to you in terms of the political processes. Could some of you describe the main components of the most prominent kinds of clothing we wear, first of all? Yes, young lady?"

"Oh, yeah. Well, there is really quite a lot of stuff that clothes are made from, isn't there? I mean, there's cotton and wool, and silk and nylon, and a lot of other synthetic kinds of stuff like orlon, or polyester, and so forth. And leather, and all kinds of plastic coatings."

"Good. Would you introduce yourself, too?"

"I'm Maureen Jamison. My family has been in the clothing business for a long time, several generations, I think. I'm pretty sure what you're driving at, I think. There's a lot of international complication about the exportation and imports of textile goods because the prices are very different in different countries, and there is a lot of competition for markets among the different countries. Even now the Japanese are trying to get more access to the American market, but this country is resisting."

"This country is resisting?"

"Yes, well, the government."

"Is it like the business of the price of the alarm clocks?" asked the professor.

"Just like that, I believe. The competition is very keen. American textile manufacturers are influencing the government not to give in, because their businesses would be hurt. Even the Textile Workers Union of America is trying to keep imports out because their jobs are at stake, just like the clock manufacturers, I suppose."

"Good, Miss Jamison, but you will recall that I asked about the relationship between the material itself and politics. Have you any information about that to give us?"

"You mean like wool or cotton?"

"Yes, I do."

"Well, I don't really know much about it. I think I heard my father talk about the competition between Australian and American wool growers but I thought it was just ordinary economic competition without any politics in it."

"Miss Jamison, do you know very much about the laws governing immigration into the United States?"

"No, I don't."

"Does anyone here?"

Several hands rose quickly into the air.

"Yes, in the back to the right. Name, please?"

"I'm Al Lampert. Yes, I know something. Until 1920 or so, there were very few immigration laws except for the Chinese Exclusion Act. After the first World War, they passed the so-called nationalities law. It limited entry to a certain number of people annually and it also put a ceiling on the number of people from any one country that might come here."

"Good, Mr. Lampert. Now how did they get to those so-called nationalities quotas?"

"I don't know exactly, but I think that the Congress decided that some kinds of nationalities were more desirable for American civilization and they gave them a bigger share than the others."

"Fairly close. The claim was that the mix of nationalities in the country at the time was desirable and the quotas were adjusted to maintain the same kind of mixture. So, northern and western European immigrants were given the edge in the quotas and southern and eastern Europeans were disadvantaged. But, look here, why did I raise the question of the immigration law in relation to Miss Jamison's answer on competition in wool growing?"

No one knew.

"Well, it's this way," said the professor. "In that immigration law there is an exception to the quota of immigrants admissible into the United States, provided they are trained sheepherders. These may exceed the quota, if the attorney general certifies that they are employable. Is that interesting?"

"Yes, but what does it mean?" asked Miss Jamison.

"That law, made in 1952, was called the McCarran Act, in honor of a late, powerful senator from the woolgrowing state of Nevada. Does something click, Mr. Lampert, or Miss Jamison?"

In unison, the two students said "Yes," while their hands went up.

"What clicks, Miss Jamison?"

"I'm sure that that senator must have gotten a lot of pressure from a special group to get shepherds from abroad."

"Right, and the countries producing shepherds were low-quota countries, especially Spain. I don't know the extent to which Senator McCarran was satisfying some interests in Spain. Perhaps he wasn't, but the home folks sure wanted shepherds. Now, Miss Jamison said this benefited a speical group of people. In an earlier dialogue, Mr. Stark and I worked it out that political interference arises out of common concerns of one sort or another, as in the case of water. Does this case conform to that definition?"

"Isn't it possible," interrupted Miss Jamison, "that a special interest can be served without hurting the common good?"

"That puts the eternal question in the smallest nutshell," opined the professor. "We must grant that possibility, of course. The question is, whether in any given circumstance it is the case, or whether it is even possible to tell from the evidence which is the case. We would need to know something about what constitutes the common interest, wouldn't we? That's easier to tell in the case of water or, let's say, public health, or electricity than it is in the case of competition between countries over wool."

"I don't think the common interest is even considered in a case like that," said Mr. Lampert, and continued, "the special interests have a lot of muscle with a powerful senator who is willing to give them what they want."

"And that, Mr. Lampert, makes it necessary to ask what this thing called special interest really is, doesn't it? Actually, we should have been asking it some time ago, but this is a good point because we don't seem to be able to talk about this problem without considering it. So, let's get cracking on it. What do you mean when you use the term 'special interest,' or what do you think I mean by it, or other people, when the matter is discussed?"

"Well, there are groups of people who are trying to protect their interests by getting the government to help them, just like you mentioned a while ago. It seems that we've talked about them quite a few times already."

"You say that special interests are groups of people. What kinds of people are groups made of, though?"

"I don't understand the question that way!" the student responded.

"What holds the people who are in that group together as a group? I gather you don't mean that these are just accidental or random gatherings of individuals who happen to come together, or are they?"

"Oh, I see. I don't think that, no. I guess what holds them together is that they're interested in the same things, like their economic protection of wool, or of cotton, maybe."

"All right, that's good, so far. Now, Mr. Lampert, how many different kinds of groups do you think there are in the United States?"

"How many? Gee, I don't know that. There must be an awful lot, though."

"Why must there be an awful lot?"

"Well, there are so many different kinds of interests, aren't there?"

"Could you name some?"

"Well, labor unions, and farm organizations, and, well, the NAACP, and CORE and SNCC, and the White Citizens Council and. . . ."

"Let me interrupt, Mr. Lampert. I simply have to stop you. What do you suppose would happen if I gave out a class assignment right now, requiring every student to give the names and the nature of the interest of at least three groups, without mentioning any group already named? Do you think we could manage that?"

"I'm sure we could. Probably we could do it a couple of times around without difficulty."

"Why is that?"

"Well, once you start thinking about it, you all of a sudden discover that the whole society must be made up of them."

"Does that surprise you?"

"No, not exactly, but it's damn interesting. I mean it's true even on college campuses. There are dozens of them, maybe more, and they come and go in all kinds of ways."

"Do you have any idea what kinds of groups would be mentioned by the students in this class if we went through with that assignment?"

"I guess the big ones I mentioned, like labor or the farmers, you know, the ones you always hear or read about."

"All right, why do you always read or hear about them?"

"They're the ones with a lot of political power. They're always running around the government, or negotiating with employers, or lobbying for one thing or another. Also, a lot of the local news in politics usually has to do with one kind of group or another, so I guess they would get mentioned, too."

"Well, that was quite interesting, wasn't it, Mr. Lampert. I wonder if anyone else in class has any question about this."

There was another questioner, as it turned out. He spoke after the professor had nodded in the direction of his upraised hand.

"A while ago Al Lampert said that there were some big powerful groups like the unions and also some groups on college campuses. Just because you call them groups doesn't make them all alike, does it? I mean, they look different to me."

"What's the difference?"

"Some are very big, and the others are very small. Some of the big ones would be a lot more powerful than the small ones, wouldn't they?"

"I don't know," the teacher said. "Perhaps so, perhaps not."

"But isn't it obvious? I mean the labor unions must have millions of people in them, right?"

"Yes, but they are deeply divided internally between industries and trades and crafts, at least in this country."

"But with that many people they must have a lot more power than, say, some group of students on a college campus or some group of faculty members on a campus, for that matter. That's what I mean."

"Don't you know that quite a few campuses have been set on their ears by very small groups of people, sometimes less than fifty, in a college or university of thousands?" the teacher asked.

"But a labor union can paralyze the whole country with a strike, can't they?"

"A few of them. They can at least try, can't they? So, some unions are as powerful in the country as students may be on a campus. Now tell me this: could you guess the difference in power between labor unions and the American Medical Association?"

"I don't know. How could you tell?"

"The AMA has about seven hundred thousand members and the combined unions about twenty-two million."

"That's easy, then. The unions."

"But the AMA was able to stop the unions from achieving major legislative goals for many years, nevertheless. And they forced them to accept major compromises in the field of social legislation, particularly about medical insurance. The U. S. Congress did not give in to the unions, despite what you think are superior numbers. What seems to count here is cohesiveness, superior organization, higher social status, and greater wealth rather than numbers."

"So what you're saying is that the power of a group depends on what they're trying to accomplish and where."

"At least in part, yes. One further factor is the degree to which the group is concentrated. For political purposes, being widely scattered across the country in small minorities, is a disadvantage if you're interested in elections, as black groups have been finding out. But there are some groups that are territorially concentrated, like the farmers, and they can pursue election politics in whole states and many congressional districts, far in disproportion to their numbers. Mostly, however, interest groups are not noted for wanting to elect their own people to the government. They'd rather influence the ones that get elected. In that way they don't have to compromise their interests with other groups, and they can let the Congress or the state legislature do it."

"But," Al Lampert returned, "wouldn't they be better off getting into office? That way they would have direct access to and control of the machinery."

"Remember the rule about the only game in town, though, Mr. Lampert. What was it?"

"You mean majority rule? So what?"

"Can anyone else answer that? Miss Peretti, you are our resident expert on election politics; how about it?"

"I guess there aren't many places where an interest group has enough membership to make sure of a continuing majority of votes," said Miss Peretti.

"And . . . ?" encouraged the teacher.

"Well, that means they have to get together with other groups to make up a majority. In a lot of places maybe even more than two groups, maybe three or four or even more than that. So they would have to compromise their interests, and the group members might not like that, because I think they are more interested in getting what they want from government and wouldn't waste their time and money on caring who gets in."

"Nicely done, Miss Peretti. Very good indeed. The process of compromising interests among groups, which you identify, is actually the process called political party, isn't it?"

"That's right, that's just what happens. Also, you know parties have to be kind of vague on what they promise just because there are so many different groups in them. That explains a lot of the ambiguity that somebody was complaining about when we talked about parties. I don't think there's anything ambiguous about what most of the groups want. I don't think most of the members of groups would belong to them if that were so. They know exactly what they want, down to the last detail, and they go after the people in government to get it. Political parties have to be careful not to lean too far in the direction of some groups, and interest groups can't lean too far in the direction of other groups."

"Miss Peretti, you have a good way with words. That was succinct. Parties, interested in elections, compromise interests to produce reliable majorities. Interest groups, in order to maximize their influence with elected and appointed officials of the government, specialize in sharpening or differentiating their interests as sharply as they can."

Peretti's hand was up, waving back and forth.

"I have a question. Most of the people who vote and belong to parties also belong to interest groups, don't they?"

"I'm not sure about most of them, but of course very many do. What is your question?"

"Well, don't the members of some of these groups prefer the same parties, where members of other groups prefer another one?"

"Right again. The affinity between labor groups and the Democratic party and business groups and the Republican party is well known, and there are many other good examples of that. Why do you ask?"

"Well, that would make the groups much more influential with their own parties than with the opposition, wouldn't it?"

The teacher hesitated for a moment before replying, and then said, "In general, that is true. The interests of labor and of business groups are central interests for Democratic and Republican parties, but only central, and not complete. Neither party can win national elections on that basis alone, Miss Peretti, even though in some states and in some districts that may be enough. But parties are coalitions of groups and electoral politicians differ from others because they must be coalition builders in most cases."

"But that means that pressure groups are none too happy as party members, doesn't it? They probably don't think of them as very reliable."

"Yes," the teacher agreed, "and that's why they keep a small distance, enough to be able to go to both parties, wherever they're in power, to go after what their members need. But you see they need the parties very badly, because they are the ones who play the only game in town—that is, the winning of elections."

Lampert reentered the argument. "But in the case of wool growers, the political parties from the states where they are important probably have to listen carefully, don't they?"

"Yes, they do," the teacher agreed, "and that goes for both of them, probably. But, I suspect it is because wool growing is the dominant economic activity and it ties together many interests which tend to converge because in those states there are relatively few competing economic and political groups. It's more like a one-crop economy, as for example in the old South. Here cotton was king because the bankers, the farmers, merchants, transporters, in other words *all* of the dominant interests, were tied together by that one crop. Consequently, there was little conflict about what cotton needed, even though there was some mild conflict between the groups. In most modern industrial systems, there is much greater diversity and consequently also much more conflict between groups."

"So, getting back to wool, or even cotton, the government protects the special interests for reasons of making sure that they're not too dissatisfied, right?"

"Do you mean that the maintenance of a healthy wool-growing industry is not necessarily in the national, the public, or the common interest?" asked the teacher sharply.

"What difference does it make where the wool is grown?" replied Lampert.

"Difference to whom?" replied the teacher.

"To the country as a whole or to the people."

"And to Nevadans, Montanans, and Idahoans?"

"Well, maybe to them, that's possible. They have a lot invested in it, after all, but that's still a special interest."

"At what point do special interests become common interests?"

"I guess when they affect enough people."

"In Nevada and Montana, sheep and wool represent a substantial segment of economic activity, by your own admission. Are you saying that, in national terms, such special interests may not be served without hurting the common interest?"

"I really don't know. It's pretty confused. I don't know whether it makes any difference to the country."

"Would you be willing to concede that there is more to the problem than the simple assertion of special interest protection?"

"Not really, no. There's something odd here."

"Odd?"

"Yes. The Congress makes laws for the whole country, not for just a few people. In this case, the law gives special benefits to wool growers and shepherds, but I can't see what the general benefit is, for the life of me."

"Could you at least see that a lack of shepherds might imperil the wool growers?"

"That's what I said. Yes, I can see that."

"What would be the consequences of a decline in the ability to grow wool in the United States?"

"That's what I can't understand. If an industry like that is in trouble, why should the rest of the country be called on to bail them out?"

"In this case, what does bailing out really amount to?"

"Oh, I guess just a few extra specially trained immigrants. But I object to the whole idea of the thing. I don't think it's right for the government to rescue such interests."

"Why not?"

"I just don't think there are enough people being served."

"All right. Now can you imagine that there are a lot of people out west who look at the matter very differently because their interests are directly involved?"

"Yes," Lampert replied, "that I can understand."

"Can you see that there might be a whole regional bloc of legislators from the wool-growing states who might also think so, as well as the legislatures and governors of these states?"

"Yes, that's possible and I guess it must be true."

"Now, imagine if some of these legislators insist on protecting the interests of their constituents by adding so-called special interest amendments to existing laws, such as the McCarran amendment. Will that be a popular thing back home?"

"Of course it will. They probably even campaign on the question. But what should happen to such proposals is that they should be defeated by other legislators because they affect so few people and such an insubstantial interest."

"The point I was driving you towards, is that practically every legislator has such special constituent interests which, for political reasons, he must advocate if he is to retain the support of voters in his state or district, and that many of them have these in common."

"What does that have to do with it?"

"Only this. In order to get enough votes for their own special projects, legislators help others in the protection of their specialties. The name of that game is logrolling."

"But that's pretty terrible, isn't it?"

"For whom?"

"For the country."

"Why?"

"What about the general interest? I mean, who takes care of the people who have nobody to represent them in the Congress so nobody can roll their logs?"

"That's a hard and a fair question. But, assuming that everybody did have somebody to roll their logs, so to speak, would you think that kind of trading of support for mutual advantage is a bad policy?"

"I'm just not sure. I'm very uncomfortable with it. I'm sure there's something wrong with it, but right now I don't know what."

"All right. Suppose we risk letting you be somewhat dissatisfied on that, and go on to cotton, Mr. Lampert. In contrast with wool, cotton is a plant fiber and, as you know, it has been the subject of extremely serious economic and political conflict in the United States. The sectional conflict from 1820 to 1860 was centered on cotton. The Civil War would not have been quite what it was had it not been for the so-called Cotton Kingdom. The institution of slavery in this country and all that followed in its wake would have been very different, save the peculiar nature of the cotton economy."

"But, there isn't any more conflict now," offered another student, "is there?"

"If we were in a classroom in Texas, or Alabama, Mississippi, South Carolina, or other cotton-producing states the discussion would be different, wouldn't it?"

"Yes, but that's no reason for the government to bother with cotton. I can understand water, medicine, or the sewage problem, but cotton I don't, or wool."

"Well, let's see about it. Incidentally, we never did get your name, did we?"

"No, you didn't. It's Miles, Tommy Miles."

"Right. The government is still hip-deep in cotton. Since the early 1930s, there have been laws limiting the production of cotton in order to stabilize the price, also surplus cotton is stored with government help to keep it off the market so as to prevent serious depressions in the world price of the fiber. Government sponsors research in the improvement of the fiber, studies in the prevention of harmful insects or diseases, in the increased use of cotton seed and so on and so forth."

Miles was amazed, but seemed to find a contact in his memory bank. "This reminds me a lot of the farm programs the government has where it restricts production to keep prices up and pays subsidies to buy up surpluses, and also pays for the improvement of crops so that more can be produced on less land and so forth, and all the time the food prices keep going up. It has always seemed stupid to me, I must say."

"Well, Mr. Miles, where does the cotton come from if not farms?"

"But I don't see how it can be in the common interest to keep prices up by means of government subsidies. That means we pay tax money to keep the prices of the things we buy higher than they would ordinarily be. Consequently we get taxed twice, right?"

"You aren't getting taxed twice, exactly," said the teacher, "though you are paying twice, that's true enough. But that is fairly simple thinking, in economic and political terms, isn't it? The question is how the government gets into programs of this sort, why it stays in them, and what the explanation is for the apparently contradictory character of the policy. We do have some kinds of answers for that, but they are complex, I fear. First of all, why do you think farmers want the government to restrict their production of cotton? Don't you think they would want to produce as much as they can on land they have under cultivation so as to get the most out of it?"

"That's what I would think. The more they grow the more they sell, and the more money they make."

"How do you know that's true, though?"

"How is it possible for it to be any other way?"

"What would happen to the price of automobiles if the manufacturers produced many more than they could sell?"

"They would probably go down. That's why they don't produce any more, right?"

"Right. How do they find out how many cars they can sell at the prices where they can make a profit?"

"I really don't know. I guess they take market surveys."

"Right, and check on the number of obsolete cars, and produce only enough at a time to prevent a backlog from building up. When sales slow down, say in April, compared to last year or the year before, what is likely to happen to the May production schedule at Ford?"

"Well, they might slow down."

"How?"

"Lay off workers, or reduce the hours, send home the night shift and so forth."

"Very good. Your future at General Motors seems assured. Shrewd man. Now watch. What happens when there is a fantastic bumper crop of cotton one year—exceeding by a large margin what the growers know to be the level of possible world or national consumption of cotton?"

"I guess the prices go down."

"And cotton goods become cheaper, right?"

"Yes, but that's not bad, it's good."

"For whom is it good?"

"For the consumer, because he gets his clothing more cheaply, and maybe he can buy more cotton goods, to take advantage of the lowered price."

"You don't think the consumers would rather save the money and buy things other than clothing with it?"

"Probably, yes."

"Why?"

"How many undershirts and stuff do people really need. And besides, they might go out of fashion, if they are women's dresses."

"Now, meanwhile, back at the farm, what happens?"

"Well, the farmer just sells more of his cheap cotton and makes out all right."

"But selling more cotton at lowered prices will drive him against the wall."

"But why?"

"Think about it. The farmer paid money for labor, for machines, for fertilizer, for other materials in anticipation of the crop. That money he got by borrowing and the loan is predicated on a certain return on the price of the cotton. Then the price collapses, and the loan can't be paid back. What happens?"

"He might get an extension on it."

"If you were a banker, would you give it to him?"

"Well, I don't know."

"I do. I wouldn't."

"Why not?"

"How do I know that the price of the cotton might not further decline next year as a result of bumper crops, or new methods of fertilizer, or the elimination of the boll weevil, or the sudden collapse of the market for cotton as a result of the introduction of new and cheaper synthetic fiber, made out of, say, decayed bayberry leaves?"

"So what can you do?"

"You ask him to pay up, go bankrupt and give you as much on the dollar as he can."

"But why would you want to do that? If I were a banker, I'd want all of my money plus interest, not some settlement for less."

"Nice work, Mr. Miles. Now can you add the bankers' interest and the cotton growers' interest to one another, instead of subtracting them, as we have been doing?"

"You mean that the bankers are also interested in high cotton prices?"

"Eureka, he's got it."

The pace of the discussion, and the voice level of both participants had been increasing steadily.

"Now, sir, who else might be interested in high cotton prices? Machine manufacturers?"

"Sure."

"Railroads?"

"Right."

"Cotton pickers?"

"Maybe, if it means work and jobs and better pay."

"Fertilizer manufacturers?"

"Yes."

"In fact, the whole cluster of businessmen whose goods and services can be sold to prosperous cotton farmers, but not to poor ones. Do you suppose that this makes a powerful political combination nationally?"

"It must."

"How do you know it must?"

"Otherwise, how could they ever get a law like that passed?"

"I trust you never forget that lesson."

The class had been paying close attention to the quickfire exchange of the student and the teacher. The discussion seemed finished. The teacher felt compelled to add what he thought might be a grace note. "You see," he said to the class, "in technical terms, the difference between the car manufacturer and the cotton farmer is that that farmer can't shut down the factory. He can get wiped out by a flood or by a catastrophe of good weather. Or, he can get rich from the unexpected increase in demand for cotton that comes from war or from the destruction of crops in other parts of the world. Let the war end and the government stops making clothing for soldiers and the cotton piles up in the sheds and on the docks, piers, and loading platforms. So his case for a stable price structure is very compelling *and* he has a political advantage: The cotton section of the country is a large territory represented by legislators and political leaders whose agreement for the making of national policy on matters large and small is indispensable and who, in return for that agreement, must be sure that their interests, like those of others with representatives at the decision-making table, are protected against these great economic risks."

Another question followed. It was Tom Miles coming back for more.

"Are you suggesting," he asked, "that the point about government interference in the cotton is just political?"

"Just political?" asked the professor, with an emphasis on the first word.

"Well, I mean that anybody can get help from the government if he is politically powerful enough to insist on it."

"If that's what you mean, you are right. That is at least one of the points about cotton. What is objectionable about the arrangement, Mr. Miles?"

"What about the rest of the people? Who represents their interests?"

"Well, who does?"

"For example, what about the poor?"

"Isn't there government help for them?"

"You mean welfare?"

"Yes, there is that, and food stamps, and minimum wages, maximum hours, social security with Medicare and Medicaid, and so on, and so forth, and more coming, I suspect."

"But the poverty continues and nobody seems to be doing anything about that."

"We come back to an earlier question, Mr. Miles. Are you objecting to the fact that the diversity of interests represented in the making of policy is not great enough and that certain interests are ignored, or are you saying that this way of deciding what the common interest consists of is the wrong way to do it?"

"Well, I know that some people get much more out of the government than others and that's not right in principle, especially when the ones that get little or nothing aren't represented."

"That's of course factually correct, in essence, though there'd be some disagreement about details between us. But, what about the question of how you discover what the common interest is? Would this bargaining and logrolling seem objectionable to you, even if it were more perfect?"

"I'm not sure I understand this quite yet," responded the student.

"In the literature of political thought," replied the professor, "the question is usually rendered in this fashion: Is the common interest merely the sum of all of the particular interests, or is it substantively and qualitatively different from any distinct interests, concerning itself with those matters which all men truly have in common?"

"If that is the question, what is the answer? After all, that's what I came here to find out."

"Is it?" asked the teacher.

"Of course, it is."

"I didn't realize that; I thought there were other reasons more important."

"What could they be?" the student wanted to know.

"To think," answered the teacher.

And that took care of the clothes we wear.

"Next," said the professor, "we eat."

9

Give Us This Day Our Daily Bread

"In the discussion to come, we shall examine the political aspects of our daily bread. It's possible, of course, to dispose of the problem by simply asserting that a sufficient supply of healthful food is the central problem of survival for man and that, considering its importance, the whole apparatus of societal organization, including that of politics, can be expected to be mobilized for the purpose of securing it. But such generalizations are extremely broad and, in the present context, somewhat elusive. What we need to show now is the relationship between the vital activity of eating and political life in a direct way. Let's begin it the way in which we talked about medicine.

"Having gotten dressed, we move into the kitchen, there to prepare our first meal of the day or, if we're lucky, to sit down to one which has already been prepared for us. Let's get a list of typical breakfast foods into play. I'll start over here in the corner and ask each of you to name at least one food item you consume at breakfast time."

Pointing to the first student, the teacher requested that the listing begin.

"Milk," was the first response and it was followed by:
"Sugar,"
"Bread,"
"Butter,"
"Margarine,"
"Eggs,"
"Orange juice,"
"Bacon,"

"Cereal,"
"Jam,"
"Tea,"
"Pancakes,"
"Muffins,"
"Cream."

"A well-fed, suburban group," opined the teacher.

One hand went up in protest. "You didn't call on me."

"I'm sorry, what's your contribution?"

"I just wanted to say that I never have breakfast."

"Well," replied the instructor, "if you can show us the political significance of that, we might be able to turn it to some use here. What do you suppose it is?"

"I guess," said the student, "that way I get away from having anything to do with politics. I just don't eat anything."

"You never eat?"

"Oh, no."

"Well . . . ?"

"I mean, I could say that a reduction in the volume of food intake also reduces the political aspect of one's life."

"I must say that I am tempted to pursue the line, but why don't we return to the eaters, since they constitute the mainstream of humanity, foodwise, anyway. Still, there are possibilities in your argument. For example, the volume of food available for each individual living in a political system, or the variety of foods available to him might become a problem to which political solutions may be sought and applied. One obvious case of that occurs during wartime when the supply of food constitutes one of the weapons of war, and when the resources available for producing it may be limited. Therefore, rationing and reduction of special foods, such as delicacies, are common aspects of modern warfare.

"For the present, let's concentrate on the political implications of what happened to you this very morning. If I recall correctly, the first commodity mentioned was milk. What political implications could that have, do you suppose? Would it surprise you if I said that where milk is concerned, the United States is not a federal union of states but an arrangement of state and federal milk-marketing districts?"

"What's a milk-marketing district?" asked a student in the front row.

"Has anyone here ever heard of milk-marketing districts?" responded the teacher.

No one had.

"Imagine that, and you've been drinking milk for such a long time," replied the teacher again, and continued. "A milk-marketing district is an area marked out by joint state and federal action in which the supply of milk is regulated so that neither scarcity nor surplus occurs. One may not be a producer of milk in such an area without a license."

"I'm surprised," opined a student. "I guess I never thought about it much at all, but I really don't understand. I can see that some of the things about milk should be regulated. I remember that a while ago they stopped requiring that milk containers have dates on them, but now they're doing it again. I remember that the mayor of New York City once said that we didn't need dating on milk any more because we now have good refrigeration and that the milk doesn't spoil like it used to. So, I don't know why they started dating it again. It made sense to pass a law forcing the milk processors to put a date on a container so that you could know how many days it was in the store before you got it. That's obviously a protection of the consumer and it's also a health regulation. Babies can get pretty sick from spoiled milk. So it also makes sense to me to remove the law when conditions change. But I'm afraid I don't understand milk-marketing areas. I thought this was a free enterprise economy and the government could not decide whether you can go into a certain business or not."

By the time the comment was complete, the student had become somewhat agitated.

"You will remember, Mr. . . . . did we get your name?"

"It's Sampson, Jim Sampson."

"Well, Mr. Sampson, you'll recall the discussion about electric power, and water, don't you?"

"Sure I do," said the student, "but I don't see the connection."

"Well, you raise a theoretical question which I thought we had already examined. Economic activity may obviously be regulated, regardless of the theory by which the system of economic enterprise operates, supposedly. The problem is the reason or the grounds upon which the regulation is justified and what, in actual fact, it does regulate. The mere existence of milk-marketing districts, for example, does not in principle prevent people from going into the milk business at any level they desire, but it does lay down conditions under which one may enter and puts limits on what one may do in it."

"What I don't understand," interrupted the student, "is the reason for trying to regulate milk production, I mean, the volume of it. I can see that you'd need regulations about some of the things in it, like freshness."

"What about the content of butterfat—do you think that might be important enough to justify public policy?" asked the teacher.

"I don't know why, but maybe there are reasons," responded the student.

"What could they be?" asked the teacher.

"I said I don't know."

"All right now—what is butter made of?"

"The cream from milk."

"Where does the dairyman get the cream?"

"I said from the milk."

"So you did—I meant what is done with the milk from which the cream has been separated?"

"I guess they sell it as skimmed milk, or maybe use it for making cheese."

"Or glue?"

"Glue?"

"Yes, glue. You've heard of casein?"

"Oh, yes, sure. I'm sorry."

"Now then," asked the teacher, again, "how do we know that the milk processors don't skim off some of the butterfat from whole milk and sell the rest as if it were unskimmed? For that matter, how does one make sure that milk processors don't add water to increase the volume of the whole milk a little? Or that they don't say that the milk is processed free from bacteria when it is not? Or to sell milk as cream when it is not really as creamy as it should be?"

"I understand all that," said the student, "but what I don't get is the reason for controlling the volume of production somehow. I think the reasons you just gave are all fine with me. They're just to cut down on cheating, like in the case of the pillow that we talked about or maybe even in the medicine. But why bother with the volume?"

"Is it possible that the volume of milk produced has some relationship to the quality?" asked the teacher.

"How can that be? If they produce too much milk they just can't sell it and that's that. They take a loss, and start cutting down on the production, or they just throw the stuff out."

"Isn't there another way to deal with oversupply of a commodity than to take a loss? Can't you cut down the price so that people will buy more milk or milk products?"

"That's right, I would do that if I were a milk manufacturer or processor."

"So, I guess you'd be prepared to say that people would drink more milk and use more milk products if the prices were lower, wouldn't you."

"That's right," replied the student, firmly.

"How do you know that the consumption of milk products varies with the price?"

"Well, doesn't everything? I mean, the cheaper things are the more you can buy of them and the more expensive they get the less you can buy. That's only logical, isn't it?"

"Yes," replied the teacher. "It is only logical; but it isn't true, all the same. How much milk do you drink in a day?"

"Oh, a couple of glasses, I guess. Sometimes less, sometimes more."

"Suppose we'd cut the price in half—would you drink four glasses?"

"Probably not—how much of that stuff can you take?"

"I appreciate that answer," beamed the teacher, and asked "Why am I smiling so broadly?"

"I guess you must be happy for some reason."

"Well, not exactly happy, but I am pleased. But why?"

"I really don't know, but I'm glad, I'm glad you're pleased."

The teacher turned to the class. There were a few smiling faces among the witnesses to the exchange. He picked on one of them.

"Miss, you seem to share my pleasure. What's the cause?"

"Well," the girl replied, "it's obvious—you trapped him and you're enjoying it."

"Trapped him? How?"

"First you got him to say that the price of milk would influence the consumption of it and then you got him to say that it wouldn't. You trapped him."

"I never said those things," interjected Mr. Sampson.

"Yes, you did," replied the girl. "First you agreed that a reduced price of milk would encourage greater consumption and then you said that you wouldn't drink any more milk than you now do even if the price were cut."

Sampson sat stunned. "I'll be damned," was all he could muster.

"It's not so terrible, Mr. Sampson," the teacher said reassuringly. "It is quite common to miss the connection between some sweeping generalization about how other people behave and the way in which we behave ourselves. But the fact is that you are not likely to drink any more milk than you do now even if the price dropped, and it's probably also true that you're not likely to cut down by much if the price went up."

"Yes, I can see that," replied Sampson, "but very poor people drink less milk than people with more money."

"I suppose so," granted the teacher, "but you don't need to increase the income of poor people by much to enable them to buy more milk, do you? It's fairly inexpensive, after all. The point is that the consumption of milk is a matter of personal and even cultural habits and does not change much with changing income or changing prices. Probably poor people, who are unaccustomed to drinking as much milk as you or others in this class, would do other things with increased incomes before they increased their milk consumption. They'd buy shoes, or clothes, or better housing, or more of other kinds of food. At any rate, it appears that the consumption of milk is relatively inelastic."

"Inelastic?"

"Yes, inelastic."

"You mean it doesn't stretch?"

"Something like that. It's relatively unchanging compared to the consumption of other goods or commodities."

"Professor, can I ask you a question now?"

"Yes, of course."

"What does all of that have to do with what we're talking about?"

"What were we talking about?"

"How government regulates the supply of the milk volume."

"You mean *why* it does, don't you?"

"Right."

"I'll try to answer it simply," replied the professor. "It seems we've demonstrated that the price of milk has only a limited effect on consumption. That means overproduction of milk cannot be remedied by price reduction, in general. Therefore, the producers of the milk, the farmers, trucking companies, processors, wholesalers, advertising companies, grocers, and others would have to pay the costs of having purchased milk they cannot sell at the usual price. They would therefore try to avoid that. One of the ways to avoid it would be to reduce the price of producing the milk by giving the farmers less money per pound for it, or by using less expensive methods of processing the milk. But that would make it more dangerous for the consumer of the milk and less profitable and economical for the farmers to produce milk. And now comes another wrinkle, so to speak. Milk is produced by cows who've just calved. It costs money to raise cows for milking and to maintain dairy herds in prime milking condition. A sudden reduction in the price of milk would have to threaten the economic structure of the dairymen who plan for the production of milk for some time in advance and have much money invested in it. They are therefore interested in price maintenance. So are consumers who demand safe and healthy milk. In short, we have a case where the limitation of production to a level approximately in keeping with consumption is an economic advantage to all as well as a method for maintaining health standards. Too much milk on the market would endanger the economic *and* physical health of the people concerned with the production and consumption of milk. It doesn't take a lot of governmental power to achieve what most people think is an acceptable goal. Resistance to milk regulation is low."

The summary complete, the teacher paused for questions. He asked, encouragingly, if there were no questions. There were none. The mechanics of the problem of licensing milk producers, or of inspecting them, did not seem to be very interesting. But there was still something missing. Some level of generality had not been accomplished and he tried again to raise the issue:

"Even if there are no questions, I think we are not finished with the topic. I'll violate the spirit of our discussions a bit more by pointing out that in the case of milk we have government play an interesting dual role. On the one side it regulates conduct by laying down requirements for the marketing and processing of milk and its general quality. On the other hand it operates as a promoter of the economic health of the productive relationships by which milk is brought to the consumer. Such a policy imposes a few burdens, but compared with the benefits it confers on all concerned, these are very slight. It illustrates very nicely one of the conditions of political life: Regulations seem easier to bear when the benefits are quickly visible. Perhaps it suggests something deeper about the relations between benefits and costs which make politics a possibility in human civilization."

The teacher stopped, and looked out over his charges. Some were thoughtful, others bored, some very interested and alert. None seemed in the mood to question the sweeping conclusions which had just arisen from the breakfast table. He hoped that more than milk had been served for breakfast, and picked up the thread again.

"In some ways the discussion of food and politics tends to be repetitive," opined the teacher. "Public policy on food is not designed to deal with each of the thousands of edible foods separately, but tries to accomplish certain general purposes which affect different kinds of foods in different ways. So the politics of food is rather complicated. We have already shown, for example, that in the case of milk, government acts as a maintainer of safety and of quality and that it gets involved in the control of the amounts of food produced. Other food products become subject to governmental control for very different reasons. For example, the United States, because of its climate, grows only a portion of the sugar consumed by the population which, incidentally, has one of the all-time great sweet tooths in the history of mankind. That means sugar has to be imported. So, the business firms looking for out-of-country sugar sources shop around for the cheapest and most suitable kinds. They go to nearby countries which grow it in abundance and buy their supply there. But they run into a problem. On the one side, the domestic manufacturers of sugar want to limit import so that their own prices aren't destroyed."

One of the listeners interrupted. "Is the control over imports of sugar brought about in the same way as some of the controls you talked about in the importation of cotton, and stuff like that?"

"Would you briefly state how that happens?"

"A group of people from industry, like landowners, workers, manufacturers, etcetera, go to the right congressman and tell him that foreign competition is destroying them or endangering them economically and the congressman helps them by getting protective legislation introduced."

"Roughly speaking," replied the professor, "that's how it works. It is of interest that these limitations on imports can get through Congress at all when they are apparently designed to protect the economic stake of relatively small numbers of people. How does that happen? After all, one needs majorities of Congress in both houses as well as a presidential signature to make a law."

"Doesn't it have something to do with pressure groups again?" asked the student.

"Again?"

"Well, they turn up everytime we look at a policy in which somebody's economic advantage is threatened, it seems."

"For example," suggested the teacher.

"Well, let me see. There was that pillow stuffing, right? And then the wool growers and the shepherds and the cotton growers, the doctors and patients in the medicine argument, and maybe even in other policies we haven't even looked at."

"Nice work, Mr. . . . ."

"Mauro, Tony Mauro, sir."

"Now, do you suppose, Mr. Mauro, that the policy on sugar importation can be explained in terms of the pressure group alone?"

"I'm not sure what you mean here, professor."

"Where does the congressional majority for the sugar import limitation come from? It cannot just be the sugar growers' friends in Congress, can it? By what means are such majorities produced?"

"I'm not sure of the answer," replied Mauro.

"Let's reason it out together, then. What are the steps by which a law is adopted in the Congress?"

"That's complicated, isn't it?" answered the student, somewhat hesitatingly.

"Yes, it has its intricacies, but the fundamental idea is not too hard. Bills are introduced by individuals or groups of congressmen, referred to committees with appropriate jurisdiction, and studied there. If they survive, they come back to Congress altered or not and are voted upon in some sequence ordered by a variety of procedures. Both houses must agree; therefore they confer and, if they can make agreement, they re-vote the matter and send it to the White House where the President signs it and it becomes law. Short of complications, of which all laws have plenty, that's the process. Our question remains: How does one build majorities for laws?"

As happened when controversy heats up a little, a number of hands were now in evidence. Calling on one of them produced a time-saving response, as it turned out.

"Why do we have to go through that? I thought Congress has majorities built right into it because all of the members are either Democrats or Republicans and there are always more of one side than of the other. That makes it simple. When a party is in the majority its bills get passed and the minority can get only what the others are willing to let it have."

"As far as it goes, that's accurate, but of course it doesn't go nearly far enough," replied the professor. "Most of the regulatory activity of Congress is of such a character as *not* to produce majorities along partisan lines. In fact, strictly partisan majorities are rather the exception than the rule in the American legislatures. Most majorities and minorities in legislative votes in this country tend to be composed of segments of both parties."

The student, who identified himself as David Chaffee, persisted, however:

"One of my high school teachers told us once that you couldn't hope to make laws if you had to put together new majorities for each piece of legislation, and that's what political parties do in Congress. That's what I meant."

"That's a very sound observation, Mr. Chaffee, but didn't that teacher also say that on most legislation party members don't stick together completely, and that there are some kinds of controversies which can split both parties almost right down the middle?"

"I don't remember that, maybe I was absent the day he said it."

"Have you no memory of a recent case when Democrats and Republicans split very markedly?"

"No, I can't say that I do."

"My suggestion, sir, is to pick up tomorrow's newspaper and watch out for it. Better yet, our library carries the daily editions of the Congressional Record, in which roll call votes are listed. Take a good look."

"OK, I will."

"Good! Now what does all this have to do with sugar? Let's be sure that we don't forget about our food."

Chaffee replied, "It means that the domestic sugar-producing interests have to go to Congressmen tied up with political parties, to get help from the government against too much sugar importaion."

"Good! Now, are these interests the only ones asking for help in this, Mr. Chaffee?"

"Well, I guess not. Probably the people who want to import sugar because it's cheaper for them or of a more suitable quality also go there to keep the domestic-sugar people from getting everything *they* want."

"Good! Do you think there are others involved? How about the representatives of foreign sugar producers, including, perhaps, diplomats from the sugar-producing countries who are competing for a piece of the American market?"

"As long as you show it so plainly, I suppose that must be the case. At least, I don't know of any reason why that shouldn't be true."

"You're a good and easily instructed pupil, Mr. Chaffee."

"Well, that's because I like it here."

"All right now, there we have it. Congressional power to regulate imports is used partly on behalf of sugar importers' interests for a sufficient supply of sugar, partly on behalf of domestic producers of sugar to keep them from suffering economically from competition, and partly as an instrument of American foreign policy in allocating the tonnages of imports among countries friendly to the United States, within the range of prices which make the import feasible. In order to make a satisfactory law allocating these goods and interests, Congress must know how to balance the effective political power of the various claimants so that enough sugar is supplied, so that prices don't get out of hand, and so that nobody goes away mad, including foreign countries who depend heavily on access to our markets and might go elsewhere to sell their stuff if we didn't buy it."

"Why couldn't we, I mean the United States, just go ahead and grow enough sugar to supply ourselves without having to worry about foreign countries?"

The voice was that of a previous participant whose name the teacher had not yet grasped. When he turned in her direction she continued, considering that she had been invited to do so.

"I mean," she said, "that would simplify it. Then we wouldn't have to have any sugar politics and countries like Cuba wouldn't be a problem for us, right?"

"I doubt if that's possible, even theoretically," replied the teacher. "Where could we grow the stuff, do you know?"

"No, I don't."

"What kinds of conditions does it take to grow sugar in abundance and at low prices?"

"I guess it has to be hot and humid, like in Cuba and Santo Domingo."

"Couldn't we just suppose that the conditions aren't good enough within the domestic borders of the United States to make that possible, and go on from there? The international relations problems don't seem so difficult that they can't be dealt with, after all."

"But that means we are at the mercy of other countries for our sugar."

"Yes, that's true. But it is equally true for some other kinds of things which we need very badly and which we cannot produce enough of in this country, including stuff more vital than sugar. Do you think that kind of economic interdependence is bad?"

"Well, it complicates everything so much. I mean the United States could get rid of all these problems by just taking care of itself."

"Don't you suppose," replied the teacher, "that if it were possible to produce enough sugar domestically at the right prices, investors would long ago have promoted the growth of domestic sugar?"

"Well, I don't really know enough about it," responded the student.

"I'm not too sure what you are objecting to," the teacher persisted. "Does it trouble you that some small countries, such as Cuba or Santo Domingo, are dependent on big ones, like the United States, for their livelihood, or are you bothered by the reverse—Uncle Sam's need for Santo Domingan sugar, or are you put off by conflict between nations?"

"Well, don't you think that the whole thing wouldn't be so full of problems if the country could produce its own sugar without having to go abroad?" responded the student.

"What do you mean by 'the whole thing'?" asked the teacher.

"Well, isn't it very complicated to have to work out just how much sugar can be imported from each of the foreign producing countries?"

"Yes, in some ways, but it's a manageable problem."

"Doesn't the United States act like a colonial power towards the sugar countries, and doesn't that keep them from modernizing their own economies?"

"Yes, at least it's true that in the countries which depend heavily on sugar export there is, in some cases, resistance to the dependence."

"Isn't there a lot of anti-American sentiment which wouldn't be there if they weren't so dependent on us?"

"Yes, we know that a lot of turmoil in economically dependent countries does occur and that it's sometimes related to the economic dependence on the United States. Do you think such turmoil would cease if we withdrew our business and made our own sugar, so to speak?"

"It seems to me that it would, yes."

"I see," responded the teacher. "It's the turmoil of international relations you're seeking to prevent."

"Yes, that's right, and also the economic suppression by big countries of the smaller ones."

"And what about the economic dependence of the big ones on the small ones?"

"That too, I guess," replied the student.

"Perhaps you are not aware of the fundamental nature of the political question you have raised here, Miss Hyde—that's the name, isn't it? In the present-day world there are serious and interesting differences between the political boundaries of nation-states and the physical extent of the economic relationships required to sustain the populations in each of the countries."

Miss Hyde looked somewhat puzzled and asked, "Is that what the whole thing is all about?"

"Well, try it on for size," suggested the teacher. "The United States is certainly not an economically self-sufficient country, is it? It needs raw materials from everywhere in the world, and it needs customers for its goods elsewhere, also. The portraits of these economic boundaries would look very different from the typical map of geopolitical boundaries around the territories of nations, wouldn't they?"

"Yes, I guess so," answered Miss Hyde, "but if each nation were self-sufficient, the pictures would be the same, I think."

"Don't forget the other techniques, however. Instead of adjusting the pattern of economic sufficiency to the pattern of political control, you could reverse it and adjust national boundaries to economic boundaries. That would mean for the more powerful nation simply to take over any country that possesses needed raw materials, and make it part of the more powerful nation. But, as we know, this has never happened, of course."

The last sentence was pronounced in mock seriousness by the teacher and the class, especially Miss Hyde, didn't quite know what to make of it. Finally, she replied:

"Yes, but that would be imperialism, wouldn't it?"

"Oh, yes, that's right," replied the teacher. "How did you know what to call it, Miss Hyde? You didn't just invent the term, did you?"

"No, but that's the word used when you describe the taking over of weak countries by strong ones for the advantage of the strong, isn't that so?"

"Yes, of course that's so. What I wanted to know from you was whether you thought that it happened a lot in recent centuries."

"Yes, it has. And I think even the United States acted like that now and then in Latin America, Asia, and other places."

"Right. Now, Miss Hyde, our problem is very interesting. How much of the tendency to enlarge the political boundaries of countries can be attributed to the desire to secure a more adequate supply of food?"

"Gosh, I don't know."

"Actually, I don't either, but it seemed to me a very interesting thing to speculate about. At the present time, for example, some very important international food marketing schemes are being developed in Europe and some people are saying that these will eventually have the result of making Europe into a single political community."

Miss Hyde sat reflectively for a moment, and before she had a chance to put her thoughts in order another student intervened.

"I think there's a much simpler way than either nationalism or imperialism," he said. "If you just eliminated the boundaries between nations altogether there wouldn't be any international conflict anymore of the kind Miss Hyde is so worried about. People could buy and sell without being bothered by tariffs and stuff like that."

"Certainly an interesting idea," responded the teacher. "You seem to suggest that as a logical extension of the principle that there are no economic conflicts within nations, however. Is it, in fact, the case that trading in goods within nations is free from the kinds of conflicts which appear in international exchange? For example, do you recall our discussion over the politics of cotton?"

"Oh, yes, I do."

"Well, do you remember that I suggested that the Civil War of

1860–1865 was an outcome of political controversies in which cotton was the central commodity?"

"I do, yes, and I guess that's true. So, are you saying that there would be conflict over sugar even if it weren't an international commodity?"

"Yes, and I hope, much more. I was hoping to show you that political conflict is not just the consequence of the international character of sugar production any more than conflict over cotton was the result simply of there being a nation. Instead, I would say that nations are, themselves, ways of managing internal conflicts over a whole lot of things. And more than that, I hoped to provide evidence for the idea that politics is a technique for managing conflict within as well as among nations, and that it can be applied to a great variety of subjects, including our daily bread."

"Maybe the best way to avoid the conflict over sugar then would be to stop using it. Then nobody would care what it costs and how much of it there is, and where it came from, and so on," responded the student.

"Yes, quite so," agreed the teacher. We would have a right to call that a solution, but it wouldn't be a very sweet one, would it? A problem can be solved by making its causes, in this case the use of sugar, disappear. Moreover, your idea is an admirable model for what can be done about having to use politics as a method of accommodation of conflicting interests and desires."

"But the most complete way of doing that," suggested the student, "would be to eliminate the people who have those conflicting interests and desires, isn't that so?"

"Indeed, it is," the teacher agreed, with wry amusement at the turn of the conversation. "Barring such drastic solutions, one might, of course, try to get them to have the kinds of interests or desires that do not conflict with one another."

"Do you really think that's possible?" asked the student.

"The question is the stuff great dreams are made of," replied the teacher. "We're back at utopia again."

The class sat silent, waiting for more.

"In my humble opinion," said the teacher, "we have gotten quite a bit out of sugar. I don't think we could learn much more than that about politics from a single item of food, do you?"

No one seemed in the mood to quarrel with the opinion and the teacher was satisfied with the condition. Yet, he knew that the uses of food for the purposes of instruction about politics were far from exhausted, and he continued.

"Even in the land of milk and honey," he continued, "it would not be sufficient to end our discussion here. We have squeezed a good deal of political savvy out of sugar and milk, but there's more than that. So I propose to go to one more item of food to display yet another corner of the relationship.

"One of the most common foods eaten by all of mankind is bread in one form or another. Do you suppose that we could, together, find some political ingredients in it? Will those of you who think you may know of such elements please raise your hands so that I can call on you for a short list?"

Several hands arose and the teacher began to call on the students by pointing to them and nodding his head briefly in encouragement.

"Well, there are chemicals in the dough from which bread is made that are added to it and they're supervised, I guess, by some kind of agency, aren't they?"

"Yes, that's right. Next case."

"I suppose that when a bakery or a bread factory says its products weigh a pound or two, or whatever, that must be the real net weight. No cheating."

"Good! Weights and measures standards are public and governmentally enforced through inspections, fines, and the rest of the machinery. Next!"

"Don't they also have to tell the truth in describing the kinds of flour they use, like wheat, or rye, or barley, and so forth?"

"That's true, and it also applies to statements about the way the flour has been treated as, for example, in the case of bleaching to increase the appearance of whiteness in bread. Good, so far. Who's next?"

"Couldn't you have bread rationing for political reasons?"

"Political reasons?"

"Yes. I mean, you could have a shortage of food or a famine and the government could try to limit everybody to a certain amount each day."

"Right, and you might add to that the case of war in which, as we said at the outset of this discussion, food becomes part of the arsenal, or the weaponry, and is therefore controlled."

"Can I ask something about that?" inquired the student.

"Yes, of course. What is it?"

"I never understood why people say that food is a weapon of war. Do people eat more during wartime than they do in times of peace?"

The teacher paused. The question was not within his plan for exposing the subject's political side. But the vicissitudes of dialogues are unpredictable. He yielded to the student's inquiry.

"I'm not sure that they do, though they may. My impression is that they eat less perforce, that is, because there is less food to be had and because the prices of it are higher than usual."

"Yes, but why is that?"

"In modern war, at least, it may be explained in two ways, to begin with. First, large masses of men are fighting the war, including many who worked in food producing industries and therefore less is being produced for eating. Second, one method of fighting a war is to destroy or threaten the sources of food of one's enemy by burning off the wheatfields, killing animals, or destroying crops in other ways. If you face a starving army in the fields, backed up by a starving population, you may be on the way to winning. In other words, war reduces the food supply on two counts. Rationing is a defense against some of that since it lowers the general level of consumption of food *and* also reduces the variety of available food. In that way it may keep people from eating caviar or ladyfingers and get them to help make bread, which is more useful, generally."

"Yes, but that's not what people mean when they say that armies travel on their stomachs, is it?" the student continued.

"I don't suppose so," agreed the teacher, "but what is meant by it that has to do with your original question?"

"Maybe that you can't fight a war without feeding soldiers, or that the food supply for the soldiers is an absolute limit on their fighting ability."

"Those are both nice formulations of the problem, but what have they to do with that question you first asked?"

"Well, maybe that's all the answer I need now. I mean, if you can show why food is in short supply during wartime, and why eating and fighting have special relationships, that's sufficient."

"I suppose so," agreed the teacher again, "except there may be additional reasons that have political relevance which add to the explainability of the question you posed. Don't you want to know any more about the subject?"

"If you don't think it's too hard for me to learn, OK," replied the student.

"Well, how have we been doing up to this point," the teacher asked.

"OK. So far."

"All right, then—let me add a word or two here. Among the reasons for food shortages in wartime is the well-known habit of hoarding. When war threatens, farmers don't sell their produce but tend to save it as a defense against starvation and as a way of taking advantage of the rapidly rising prices caused by the scarcity of food. Consumers of food tend to overbuy things like sugar or salt or flour or other staples which can be easily preserved and which may become very expensive later on. Society has, after all, a lot of experience with war and these practices are probably transmitted from generation to generation without benefit of special teaching."

"So, one of the important political problems of wartime is to devise workable food policies. They have to be directed towards feeding the population, towards fighting the war, towards preventing profiteering and sundry other purposes. Food production is one of the great strains of the conduct of war, even if the food itself were not actually a kind of weapon in the agressive and the defensive sense as well. I don't actually know a lot about it from the technical side, but it seems plausible that what is meant by the metaphor about armies fighting on their stomachs is that wherever they are they must be fed and that they cannot go where they cannot be fed. That is, I think, as much as we can fairly do at the present to answer the question. I'm pleased that you raised the issue; it gave me a chance to expose an aspect of the politics of food I had not planned on. Now, we do need to get on to other matters about bread and politics.

"I was beginning to show, before the discussion turned to war, that our daily bread is one of the many articles of food which is literally full of political characteristics, some of which have already been listed by some of you. The politics of bread, if one wants to call it that, begin with the recognition that the basic material from which it is manufactured is a product of agriculture and that the economics of agriculture in an industrial society present some special problems. Now, is there anyone in this classroom who, from personal experience, can help us in understanding at least some of the ramifications of that?"

The teacher and several of the students cast their eyes over the members of the class, waiting for hands to rise. None did. It was a startling demonstration of the sectional-regional character of the student population in the college and, unavoidably, it had to be called attention to.

"Supposing," said the teacher, "I had asked this question of students in a college in Kansas or Texas or the Dakotas—how many hands would have been raised?"

Full of smiles, one of the suburbanites replied, "If this school were in Kansas you wouldn't even have to discuss the problem and you wouldn't even have asked the question, isn't that right?"

The teacher had to agree. "Yes, that's most likely the case. So, my question may have been useful in some other ways. Even in Kansas and the Dakotas, the proportion of college students whose families earn their living by farming has declined, though not to the point evident in this school. The difference is very instructive, and may be brought into play as one of the factors at work in the politics of bread—the economic and social interests which make bread production a political problem are regionally based in the United States—the population in some parts of the country have a much higher stake in the economics of wheat production than do people in the cities."

"How is that possible?" called out a student whose chair was firmly propped against the side wall of the classroom. "When we all eat bread? At least, I'm interested in what it costs to buy bread, aren't I? I think it's just a matter of being on different sides of the same business. We're the consumers and they're the producers."

"And, who might you be, Mr. Consumer."

"I guess you forgot. I'm John Diner. I got involved in the discussion about electrical utilities, remember?"

"Yes. All right, Mr. Diner, welcome back. Now you were saying that the farmer's interest in bread is no greater than yours, but that it is just a different kind of interest—right?"

"That's right."

"Fine! We'll let that rest for a while and come back to it a little later in the discussion, if you will. Would you concede that the politicization of wheat and other grains are in strong measure the result of the peculiar pattern of growing crops, however?"

"I'm afraid I don't quite follow you."

"I guess the question was a bit concentrated," agreed the teacher, and began to rephrase it:

"Mr. Diner, since you seem familiar with certain economic problems, what do you know about the economics of wheat or other grains and their relationship to politics?"

"Well, not too much, I guess, but are you talking about farm subsidies and things like that?"

"Yes, things like that."

"The government pays farmers not to produce more than a certain amount of crops, isn't that right?"

"In a very generalized way, and with regard to some things, that's right. But, we need to be more precise. Why do you suppose there is a public policy limiting the production in foodstuffs?"

"Well, isn't it like the case of milk, where overproduction would be economically harmful to the producers?"

"There's some comparability, yes, but there are larger problems involved than just the case of a single crop like milk. The use of public money to compensate farmers for economic losses is an unsual policy in a free enterprise economy and it requires extended explanation. First of all, what were the reasons farmers and their organizations began to claim that the government needed to help the farm economy in such a direct way?"

"I think it had something to do with the great surplusses of food that were produced, didn't it?" replied Diner, questioningly.

"Yes, it did, but what did it have to do with it?"

"When the supply of crops increased beyond the needs of the food market the farm prices would drop very sharply, and farmers would not be able to repay their debts because of the declining income and would be threatened with bankruptcy."

"Good! Now, don't you think it would have been a good idea for those bankrupt farmers just to quit the business and do something else? In that way there would be fewer and fewer farmers and less and less likelihood of surplus food production. So, the bankruptcy of the farmers could be regarded as a good indication that they were in the wrong business, to begin with. Too much food was being grown."

"Well, I guess that's right. I really don't know why they didn't look at it that way."

"Would you, had you been a farmer?"

"I don't know, but what's the use of staying in a business that's bankrupt?"

"Maybe you keep hoping for better times."

"But you can't keep hoping forever, can you?"

"But sometimes times are good and food prices are on the rise. Besides, there's a flaw in my question of a few minutes ago. I don't think farmers thought, by and large, that they were in a business in any simple way. They treated their whole relationship as a part of a way of life or a civilization which was constantly embattled by the difficulties of a business civilization, much of which they cordially hated and feared and against which they felt, in any case, fairly helpless."

"But how could they feel helpless? After all, they were in the food-growing business, weren't they? Everybody else had to depend on them to eat, didn't they?"

"That's true enough but, like other kinds of dependent relationships, it was mutual. The farmers were, in turn, dependent on a lot of other elements of the economy. They needed to borrow money for purchasing machinery and seed and animals, and for making the land more fertile. That means dependence on bankers, on industrial products, and on scientific progress. But bankers charge interest, and that costs money, machinery prices keep rising because of inflation and because of increasing labor costs due to unionization of workers, and so labor becomes an economic antagonist. And farmers are dependent on railroads for transporting their produce to market, but railroads charge high prices for their freight, and *they* become an enemy, too. All in all, that's a formidable collection of antagonists to have. And, when prices fall because of overproduction, the burden of all of these dependencies becomes very heavy, and the antagonism and helplessness increase."

"Well then, if it's that tough, why not get out? That way you wouldn't have to battle all those enemies."

"Good point, Mr. Diner. Well, of course, a lot of farmers did get out, so to speak. But that is an especially tough problem for individuals and families who believe in agriculture as a way of life and who don't have the skills, and other habits required, to live in an industrial society. Farming has no equivalent or counterpart occupation in industry, and people who have been reared in the country and believe in the virtues of country living find it extremely difficult to move into cities. Most of the agricultural population, after all, believed cities to be the incarnation of evil, and the source of most of what was wrong with their societies. So, the explanation for the political intervention in agriculture lies in these kinds of factors. But most of all it lies in the discovery by the farmers that they did not have to battle their enemies directly, that they could get at them by using the government as their defender, just as other groups in the society had done before them. And that is the basis of my question about the political results of farming as a geographically concentrated activity a while ago."

"I still don't quite get it. Do you mean it has to do with farmers living in the same places in the country?"

"Yes, I do," replied the teacher.

"What has that got to do with the government getting into agricultural economics?"

"Think about it a minute. What kind of influence is required to get the government interested in people's troubles."

"You have to get politicians to listen and do something about what you want."

"Good! Now, how do you get them to listen?"

"Well, they have to listen if they want to be part of the government because you can vote them into office and out of it, can't you?"

"That's correct, and how does it work out in the specific case of the farmer?"

"Oh, I get it. Where farmers are concentrated in states or in congressional districts they can elect people who promise to use the government to defend them against their social and economic enemies."

"Now we've got it. That's right," the teacher beamed. "It did take a little time to get us here, but you have it just right, so far as the linkage is concerned between an attentive, or responsive government and a demanding population. There are a few slips, of course. Can you think of what they might be?"

"Well, no. I thought that that's how the system works. I don't know what you mean by slips, even."

"All right. Is there anyone in class here who might be aware of what I'm getting at?"

There seemed little interest among the students in the intricacy that they were being led into, for the moment. Nor did it seem worth the time to draw the point out by extended discussion.

"The issue here turns on a complex relationship," the teacher explained. "The spokesmen of suffering populations, in proposing relief, don't always quite know what kind of policy will produce such relief and they may not agree on a policy. Farmers' spokesmen throughout the late nineteenth and twentieth centuries were in disagreement about the proper remedies for farm economic depressions. The second point is, of course, more serious, from the point of the injured parties, so to speak. They are, after all, not unopposed in the political struggle. The mere appearance of economic ills, even if politically represented, may not cause the right policy to emerge because people and groups in control of the machinery may not be sufficiently interested in it. The farmers' enemies actually had powerful economic and political reasons for refusing to consider what farmers might call a remedy. It took a great many political battles and even some constitutional changes, to accomplish the farmers' purposes."

"For a long time farmers were not properly mobilized for political success at the national level, and even had difficulty making state governments provide remedies for what they thought were unfair railroad rates, improper banking laws governing credit, and so forth. It wasn't really until a determined national farmers' lobby had been put together with support in both major political parties that the national government took on the tasks of trying to solve some of those problems on a national scale. And even then it didn't happen until the Great Depression of the thirties had changed the dominant national opinion about the proper relationship between the economic and the political systems. Federal farm-aid programs then became part of the general growth of governmental intervention."

"But you haven't even said anything about *what* the federal government does for farmers," protested a student, sensing the teacher had come to a stopping point of sorts.

"Quite right," replied the professor, "I haven't. Do you suppose that's because I'm generally longwinded or because of my fascination with the way politics works?"

"Well, I don't know, but I get the feeling that you are more interested in how the political system works than in what it does."

"But," protested the teacher, "isn't the way it works the same thing as what it does?"

"No," replied the student, firmly. "Take me, for instance. I don't care at all how it gets results. I just want to see that it gets them somehow. What happens to the farmers is more important than how the politicians manage to work the system so as to produce something for them. I think that's a much more sensible way of looking at it, don't you?"

"Would you say that this view of yours is generally more appropriate, that, in other words, what government does is more important than in how it can be gotten to take an interest in doing something in the first place?"

"That's right, I do. After all, what really matters to the farmers and to everybody else is results. Isn't that true?"

"Well, of course, there's no denying that the machinery of politics exists to produce results. It's also true that the interest in politics with which we are most familiar is interest in results, in the outcome. So far I am in agreement, and I'm aware also of not having focussed on what it is the government actually does for farmers."

"You're doing it again," protested the student.

"What am I doing again."

"I just asked you to tell us what the government was doing to help farmers with their various problems and you changed the question. I said I don't really care about how things get done, but I'm interested in results."

"Results for the farmers, that is, right?"

"Right."

"You want me to give you a list of things, is that it?"

"Yes, that's right."

"I will, in a moment, as soon as I have made a point about your question which for me is of great consequence."

"Couldn't you satisfy me first by giving me the list?"

"Yes, but I wouldn't consider that I'd done the job I'm here for. Look—my point of resistance is really quite simple but fundamental. Political life does deal in results. One can define politics as 'the art and science of who gets what, when and how.' The point is, there are many different *kinds* of results produced by political action, only some of which come in the form of economic aid to farmers or workers or other people. Other results are exactly what you called 'ways of doing things.' These two aspects of political life are so closely related that it takes great ingenuity to be able to tell them apart, even if one's interest is in the results, as yours seems to be. The ability of the farmers to obtain governmentally sponsored relief from their enemies in the society and the economy depended upon the development of powerful farm organizations, of linkages with political parties, and on their ability to elect a large number of U.S. senators and representatives who were dependent for their political survival upon the support of these organizations and their followers. So, the actual economic benefit was a 'result' of another set of 'results.' There were, in other words, two kinds of important outcomes of farmers' needs which political scientists are bound to pay attention to."

The student, who'd been listening closely to the increasingly warm narrative, responded by saying, "Well, but it's still true that what farmers get out of the government is more important than how they get it, isn't that so?"

"You mean, it's more important to the farmers, don't you?" asked the teacher.

"Yes," replied the student.

"I must confess I don't know of a way to answer the question with a 'yes' or a 'no.' I thought I had demonstrated that there seemed no way of getting what they wanted except after certain other things had happened in the political structure. It seems to me there's no way in which one can explain what farmers, or other people, are able to obtain from government without showing how they got it. And moreover, there's no way of evaluating the significance of what they get without looking at the consequences of getting it for the political system in general. These two results are all the time being produced, don't you see?"

"OK," said the persistent student. "Now can we have the list of what farmers get?"

The class, whose attention had been increasing with the growing passion of the disputants, broke into laughter, the teacher joining in the merriment.

"I count tenacity as a virtue, sir, and you have it in ample supply. It's a long list and I will pick just a few from it. Then you'll know what you want to find out. We'll be square, all around. But the list will include not only 'what farmers get,' but also the political requirements for getting it, in the form of political processes and institutions. Is that all right?"

The student made various signs of intellectual surrender and said, "If that's the only way I can get it, all right."

So the professor began the list:

"Farmers," he said, "have gotten in the past and are getting at the present, the following 'things' among others too numerous to mention:

"Government aid in restricting crop yield for the purpose of price maintenance;

"Government purchases of crops in excess of anticipated yields—or surpluses—to prevent their being marketed to depress prices;

"Governmentally sponsored research into the agricultural sciences for purposes of increasing the yield per acre, of increasing control over quality of foods, of improvements in the animal husbandry and plant quality; of improving land management practices, such as plowing, seeding, irrigation, fertilization, etcetera;

"Government regulation of food imports from abroad—for example, beef from Argentina, sugar from the Caribbean, maintaining production and price levels domestically;

"Governmentally supported electrification programs, farm and home mortgage insurance programs, free public agricultural university and college programs;

"Governmentally regulated access to public grazing lands for nominal fees, and use of irrigation waters and ditches for small fees;

"Publically sponsored. . . ."

"Hold it—I've had enough," called out the student with whom the teacher had disputed over the political meaning of the concept "result."

"Hell," said the teacher, "I've only just started."

"But I want to ask some questions about the things you've just mentioned. Can't I do that?"

"You cannot, no, not now, not until I've finished the list," the teacher insisted firmly. "Because now some of what I call results of another kind which an understanding of the politics of the list just mentioned simply makes imperative, and no less."

"OK, you're the teacher," said the student.

"The other results are:

"The direct election of United States senators;

"The establishment of primary elections, of popular legislative initiatives, of popular referenda of legislative decisions;

"The maintenance of a relatively large administrative apparatus—a bureaucracy at local, state, and federal levels to administer and formulate agricultural activities of government;

"The development of a system of interest groups for each of the many kinds of agricultural interests and the maintenance of powerful leaders for each of them;

"The relatively permanent relationship between agricultural interest groups, the legislative representatives from farm states in the government and the bureaucracies;

"The establishment of congressional committees on agriculture with appropriate subcommittees for each of the major crops and subdivisions of agricultural policy;

"The maintenance of a steady flow of influence in the organizational structures of all national political parties, and all state parties, where pertinent, including the processes of nominating candidates for public office, including local, state, and national legislators, governors and not excluding the candidates for the presidency of the United States. Amen."

"Holy Moses," said a student, "I'm exhausted, just from listening."

"That's a good thing," replied the teacher, "because I'm just about finished with the list. Unless, of course, there are other questions."

He waited a moment. There were none. It was finished.

10

The House I Live In

"Of the three great needs of mankind, food, shelter, and clothing, we have already noted the political aspects of two—food and clothing. But now that we are dressed and have completed our first meal of the day, let's take a look at where we live and the politics of that."

Accustomed to the logic of the progression of the discussions, the students settled back for the questions to begin.

"How many in this class live in single-family homes?" asked the teacher.

Somewhat more than three quarters of the hands rose, and students turned their heads, making their own count.

"And how many in large apartment buildings?"

A few hands showed that time.

"And how many live in other kinds of places?"

"I'm not sure how to answer that," replied a front-row student. "While I'm in college, I live in a high-rise dormitory suite, my home is in an apartment, but my parents also have a summer place in the country that used to be a farmhouse. Which one of these is my home?"

"I suppose," replied the teacher, "we can first establish that with regard to you there's no housing shortage, right?"

"No, not exactly," admitted the student, "but isn't there some legal problem about my residence?"

"Yes, there is. There are certain limitations about the uses of such places as dormitories or hotel or motel rooms or suites as one's legal residence. People who have more than one home usually choose one of

115

them as their prime place of residence, but they're not exempt from paying taxes on the others. However, they may be restricted to voting in only one of them."

"Why," asked the teacher, of no one in particular, "if I'm interested in showing the connection between housing and politics, would I be interested in knowing something about the different kinds of housing the students in this class inhabit?"

"Oh, I know," replied one student quickly. "That must be because you get different kinds of housing in different kinds of places."

"How do you mean that?"

"Well, for instance, there are no apartment houses in the country. Where the farmers live, everybody lives in his own farmhouse, and there are also not many apartment houses in the suburbs, but more than in the country, and in the cities most people live in apartments, but there are no farmhouses, and fewer one-family places. That's right, isn't it?"

"Yes, in a broad sort of way, that's essentially correct, without the necessary refinements. But how is that connected to politics and government, do you suppose? Incidentally, and before we go much further, who are you?"

"Oh, I'm Sandy Eisen. Well, I guess that there would be different kinds of rules about the way people live in these different places."

"Do you mean that the patterns of residence are publicly regulated?"

"Well, yes, aren't there zoning laws and rules like that?"

"Of course, there are—but what's contained in the zoning laws that makes you think that they would have the result of controlling residential patterns?"

"In my village, some builders wanted to tear down some private homes and build high-rise apartments, and the village government wouldn't let them. I never really understood how they could prevent that, but there is a zoning ordinance in town and under that law you can't have multiple dwellings in that part of the village. The builders appealed the decision to the courts, but they couldn't get it changed. That's a way of controlling it, isn't it?"

"Good work, Miss Eisen," responded the teacher. "Zoning laws do seem to have the purpose of maintaining certain kinds of patterns of residence and you gave us one good example."

"Why do you say that they only seem to have that purpose? Isn't it really true that they do have it?"

"Actually, zoning laws do have such purposes, I agree. They separate commercial and industrial users, keep apartment houses from being built in areas of private homes, and so forth, but they can have other purposes which may not be so readily apparent. Miss Eisen, your home is located in a zoned area, isn't it?"

"Yes. My parents were very agitated over the apartment houses and they joined a home-owners' organization that was trying to stop it."

"Do you remember the reasons for their opposition to the apartment houses?"

"Yes, they talked a lot about property values going down, and about school taxes going up because of the many children the apartment dwellers would bring in which would cost money for expanding the school. My mother seemed especially bothered by something the property-owners' association told her. They said that the traffic on our street would increase very greatly because of the two hundred or so people who were going to live in the houses and that it would go on all day and night and would be very noisy, smelly, and unsafe."

"In other words, when the law was challenged, the people who had lived quietly under its protection discovered that it served quite a few purposes, including the protection of their mortgages. That goes quite a bit deeper than the mere maintenance of a residential neighborhood. That's not, after all, a small matter for people who have a very large share of their life's earnings tied up in their homes."

"Can I ask something about that?" inquired Miss Eisen, and continued. "When my parents got involved in that property-owners' association we heard a lot about how people who live in apartments aren't as desirable to have in the community as home owners because they're supposed not to care as much about property values and also that they're younger and move around a lot more, so that the whole town would be less stable than it used to be. It sounded a lot like a kind of prejudice to me. I mean, are all these things true about apartment dwellers?"

"Does it matter?" asked the teacher.

"I don't get it," replied the student. "Of course it matters. How could it not matter?"

"Well, if enough people believe things of that sort, even if they are not true, the effect of their believing it is the same as if it were true, isn't that so?" replied the teacher, somewhat acerbically.

"But that's terrible. You sound so cynical," the shocked student commented.

The now attentive class gave rise to low laughter, to which the teacher responded with wide-eyed wonder.

"Well now, what have we here?" he asked.

"Are you going to answer her?" a backbencher called out, challengingly.

"What do you suggest I say?" replied the amused professor.

"Well, she gave you the answer," the interrupter said.

"Oh?" asked the teacher. "Would you be kind enough to point it out to me?"

"Sure," he said. "When she said that her parents' talk about the people who live in apartments sounded prejudiced to her, she's right. I mean, they're actually prejudiced. They don't know these people personally and they don't know what they might be like. They don't even live in the houses yet, in fact, there aren't even going to be any houses because they're talking as if people were already messing up the village. That's prejudice, so far as I'm concerned."

"You seem very angry about that," said the teacher.

"Sure, I am," shot back the student. "Why not? It's terrible."

"But very prevalent, right?" asked the teacher.

"That's true, but it isn't good," resisted the student.

"Would you say that prejudice has an effect on the way in which laws on zoning get made?"

"It sure looks that way to me, doesn't it to you?"

"I admit there seem to be some signs of it, but I'm not quite sure how it works, exactly. Here are people who believe they are protecting their property and what they call their way of life by means of a law which is usually considered good practice in planning communities. I'm not sure whether the prejudice came first or whether it is a form of rationalization. Having decided that the value of their homes is a vital interest, they are willing to distort the world a certain amount."

"But, as you said a while ago, it doesn't make any difference; the effect is the same. I mean, they could just as well use the law to protect themselves against black people moving into their neighborhood, claiming that it would depreciate property values, couldn't they?"

"Yes, that's true, and we know that zoning laws have been used that way."

"What I want to know is what's so good about protecting mortgages anyway, if the result of it is to create injustices like that."

"Injustices?"

"That's right. When you use a zoning law to keep people who don't have high incomes from moving into a community, you are barring minority group members like blacks who are poor and can't move to expensive houses."

"But why," asked the teacher, "is that injustice any worse than denying the inhabitants of a village the use of a law which defends *their* interests?"

"I don't understand that. You seem to be saying that it's all right to be prejudiced or to discriminate."

"And you seem to be saying that certain kinds of interests are morally more defensible than other kinds and that they are entitled to prevail because of their moral superiority."

"Well, yes, I think that's true. I was saying that. The home owners in that village think the same thing, don't they? I mean, they think their economic interests, or the character of the communities they live in, are more important than the interests of people who might want to live in apartments, or of the kinds of people who can't afford to move in next door to them, isn't that true?"

"I agree," assented the teacher. "Zoning laws are an instance in which economic and social interests and moral values *can* clash. But what does one do when groups of people are aligned in opposition one to another on the bases of what they each consider to be their unassailable right? How does one deal with each of the groups involved and how are the choices made?"

The question had been directed to no one in particular and did not, at first, evoke any response. When put this way it seemed a bit more difficult to grasp than were the obviously prejudicial ingredients in the zoning laws referred to by Miss Eisen. The teacher pressed on.

"I'd like to suggest that the processes of making decisions in government can deal with such problems. In the case of a zoning ordinance, the municipality's governing body will cite some public purpose, such as noise prevention, traffic control, privacy, etcetera, for the adoption of the ordinance. Usually, such laws are the expressions of an active minority sufficiently strong to compel the election of officials favoring their view. When such statutes are challenged in courts, the claims test the appropriateness, or fairness, or reasonableness of the ordinance, and the litigants have to decide whether they want to keep on appealing to higher courts, or whether they want to wage a battle to oust the officials who made the laws in the first instance. All along the line, moral, legal, economic, social rights and interests are placed into competition in various ways. The processes of competition are public and open to almost any number of combatants. It is assumed that, in the competition over policies, some justice is done to all sides. The winners have to justify their position publicly and the losers get a chance to modify public policy by getting a chance to find out whether the law is merely designed to benefit some group or other, or whether it is also fair and tending towards the general good. Principles of public good must be invoked, since public authority is used to enforce the laws. So winners can't hide behind being the numerical majority, and the losers get a chance to appeal to principles other than simple numbers or self-interest."

The student who had pressed the point of the argument about prejudicial character of the zoning law returned to the argument.

"But that's all hogwash. You make it seem as if there were no losers or winners, or as if the difference between losers and winners were not very important. That's wrong. When you're a loser in politics, you're a loser, just like in other things. It makes a lot of difference whether you win or lose. If you lose you can't get a share in the things that other people have because they're in the majority. I mean, if it didn't make any difference, I don't think people would fight in the first place."

"I'm sure that you are right in some of what you say. Losers are indeed losers and the stakes are often very high. That's true. Yet, when the decision as to who wins or loses is made in a way that all acknowledge to be fair rather than foul, the difference between losers and winners is not the same as it would be if the methods of determining winners were immoral or unfair."

"But don't you think that losers generally think the game is rigged?"

"Yes, one could hardly blame them for believing that."

"And, also, don't you think that winners generally think that the rules by which they have won are fair, just because they won?"

"Yes, I agree, but the conclusion surely is that there must be some impartial way to test the fairness of the rules."

"That's right," replied the for-once agreeable student. "But somebody has to decide that, too. And when it gets decided there have to be winners or losers, isn't that true?"

"Yes."

"So, we're back where we started from, aren't we?"

"If you're willing to stop there, perhaps. But what you are suggesting is that there must then be ways for deciding whether the decision about the fairness of the rules was itself a fairly made decision, and *ad infinitum.*"

"I guess that's right."

"But haven't you noticed that somewhere along the line there has been an important change?"

"No, I don't think there has. There'll be winners and losers all the way along the line."

"Agreed, but they're winning and losing over constantly different questions and, if the process is carried far enough, it will be about the essentials of fairly made judgments rather than about whether a zoning law benefits some people or hurts others. In other words, the process tends to change the nature of the conflict between the contestants so that, even though there are winners and losers, the losers can't complain about the fairness of the decision, even though it goes against them and the winners have to hold themselves up to constant examination over the matter of not having gotten anything by foul means. They're winners in a fairly waged contest in which the losers lost fairly."

"You really have to believe that there is such a thing as fairness, though, in order to play the game that way, don't you," asked the student.

"Yes, that is true; at least you have to be able to believe in the possibility of fair judgments," replied the teacher.

"And the people who fight have to be able to agree over what a fair process is, don't they?"

"Yes, they do, and also they must learn something else," replied the teacher.

"And what is that?" asked the student.

"They must learn to bow to the inevitable," the teacher replied.

"But that's the same thing all over again, isn't it?" asked the now perplexed and somewhat irritated student.

"The same thing?" the teacher asked.

"That's right. You first denied it and then you admit it. First you said that there were winners and losers, then you said that losing over a question of what is a fair procedure is not as bad as losing over something you think you have a right to have, such as living someplace. Now you say that you have to learn to bow to the inevitable, in other words, to having lost. So I conclude that one way or another it's all about winners and losers, no matter what the distinctions are between the different kinds of games you can win or lose."

"I cannot completely disagree with your statement," responded the professor.

"But aren't you impressed with the fact that the loser in the first round can go to another arena, challenge the winner to another fight with different rules and perhaps become the winner in the second fight?"

"Yes, that's good because the first loser gets another crack. But the first loser cannot win without exchanging places with the first winner, isn't that right?"

"Yes, that's right. As long as the distinction between the contestants is drawn along the line of winners and losers there will have to be one of one kind and one of the other. As long as the rules of combat are well known, are recognized as fair by all sides, and there is a determination to keep playing the games in such a way as to make the rules fairer, the losers suffer less than they would if mere brute force were at work in distinguishing between them. But, yes, there have to be losers, even then. It is as if society were saying that, in the struggle between winners and losers, it wants to create conditions in which the combat is carried on along lines that are civilized and which represent the interest of society in the general principles of fairness. Another way of seeing it is that the continued keeping open of questions of the fairness of governmental proceedings makes the questions of fairness a prime social value. However, there does come a time when even the rules of fairness are satisfied and there is a winner. But there are then not just *a* winner and *a* loser, because there are not just two parties to a dispute, after all. In the kind of case we spoke of there are *interests in other than the combatants*. The onlookers and the referee who is doing a job of enforcing the rules on behalf of the onlookers are also parties to it. When combat is fairly waged and when rules of fairness are treated with as much seriousness as the question of winning and losing, society has gained, by virtue of being constantly in the process of becoming a fairer place to be in. And so, while I cannot deny, for the fifth time, that there are winners and losers, in political terms I must insist that winning and losing may not be as important as how the game is being played. And, keeping in mind what we are all here for, I'd add for emphasis, that the writing and rewriting of these rules of fairness is also one of the major functions of politics."

The protesting student, needless to say, was not mollified. He persisted in his questions:

"Are you trying to tell us that political systems are fair?" he asked.

"Is that what it sounded like to you?"

"Well, yes, it did. If you say that it is a function of politics to keep the combat fair, as you called it, you are implying that politics tends to be for fairness. Isn't there such a thing as dictatorship? or government by terror? It seems to me that there are even a lot of things about politics that are inherently unfair. I mean, politics makes some things even worse than they would be without it."

"Could you illustrate that idea? Are you arguing that societies without politics are better than those with it?"

"Well," replied the student, "there are some people who think that all forms of political control are forms of oppression, aren't there?"

"Yes, of course there are. But there are others also who argue that social control without politics is too risky and dangerous a way for people to live together. But what can one prove about such arguments, however, by merely saying they exist?"

"I guess we're getting pretty philosophical right about now, don't you think," asked the student.

"Yes, I guess we are," agreed the teacher. "But then, we've been doing that all along, anyway. Being philosophical is, in a way, like talking prose. It's something we do without being aware of it until we become aware of it, and then we continue doing it. Right now I simply have to resist the temptation to go on with that line of reasoning, even though it is a very promising one for people who are interested in the pursuit of political understanding. We must return to our interest in the relationship of housing and politics. So, let's for the present, at least, regard the matter as an unsettled difference between us, and continue our discussion along another line."

The student agreed reluctantly, and the teacher redirected his attention.

"The politics of housing extend quite a distance beyond such matters as laws of zoning, of course," the instructor reopened the discussion. "The community's interests, for example, include the quality of the houses we live in, and almost everywhere there are legal standards of of profit on their investments, charges for premiums, etcetera. Would I be wrong in thinking that the technicalities of the problem are a little heavy going for the purposes of our present discussion?"

"I don't know what you mean," replied Roderick. "It sounds interesting to me."

"I'm pleased," replied the teacher, "but I'm not sure we're getting our major point across about the society's use of political means to protect the homes we live in. Insurance policies are, after all, designed to compensate one for losses. The company's stake in safe homes is, as you say, a result of their desire to keep the payments down. The fire department's interest in that is secondary. It is of general interest to keep fires from happening or from doing damage, because fire is a hazard to all when it is not controlled. That's what justifies fire companies, and not the premiums people pay to insurance companies. At any rate, in my opinion, there are a lot more interesting political aspects of housing than fire protection, important as it is."

"But, couldn't we talk about the insurance business a little more?" insisted Roderick.

"Perhaps a short trip to the library would do as well," replied the teacher, concluding the subject, or so he thought.

"I guess you don't want to talk about it, any more," said Roderick, not without an edge of disappointment.

"Oh, I do, I do," replied the teacher, "but not here and not now. We have some other fish to fry, as the saying goes."

"If you don't want to talk about fire prevention, what do you want to discuss?" asked the student.

"Slums, public housing, and the conflict between rich and poor, and other such assorted trivia," the teacher shot back.

"Oh, well, in that case maybe I'll just go to the library for my insurance information," the student replied.

"I'm sure we'd all be grateful," answered the teacher, and continued by turning to the class. "Is there anyone here who can give us a brief description of a slum?"

There was momentary silence. Students looked at one another, waiting for someone to speak. A stage-whispered conversation between two of the students could be heard:

"Why don't you speak up?" suggested one to the other.

"Do you think I should?" that one asked.

"This is your chance," the first one whispered. "You've been itching to get into an argument, haven't you?"

The class, including the teacher, listened to the exchange. The second student's hand rose quickly.

"I'm Jack Perry," he said, "and I'd be glad to tell you what a slum is like. First of all, it's crowded, with a lot of people. Second, almost everybody living there is poor. Third, where I live at least, everybody is black, like me. Fourth, the places people live in are hard to believe, sometimes. Small rooms, plaster and paint coming off the walls and ceiling, garbage collecting in the hallways, mailboxes without covers, no lightbulbs in the fixtures, toilets in the hallways or out of order, terrible odors of human waste, dirt, food, and other things. Then, there's a lot of crime of all kinds, like assaults, burglaries, knifings, holdups. It feels like the world didn't care what happens to people who live there, or that people were in prison for some sort of crime and they were never going to get out. I personally think that the slums are there because the people in it are black and because they are poor. Those two things make a pretty bad combination in this country. At least if you're white and poor you have a better chance, but if you're black its harder to get off being poor and, even if you're not poor, it's harder finding a place to live in that's not near a slum, at least. So there are even a lot of not-so-poor people who live in the slums because they're black."

"Because they're black?" asked the teacher.

"Damn right," responded Perry. "You know how hard it is for a black family to live where they want to, even if they have the money, or the income, or the credit, or something. I mean, doesn't everybody know that?"

"Well, Mr. Perry, perhaps everybody in this class does know something like it, yes. Yet, there'll be some kind of argument about some of it, won't there? For example, there are slums in which the inhabitants are not black. But there's no disputing the other aspects. The central reason for slums is poverty. Racial hatreds, fears, and prejudices aggravate the slum conditions, and in the United States may even be responsible for them in a secondary way. Poverty among Negroes in the United States is much greater than it is among the whites. That makes black families much more likely slum dwellers than white families, statistically speaking. Yet, the fact is that there is also a lot of good housing being enjoyed by black people."

"Do you deny that slums are a way of keeping black people down?" challenged the student.

"No," agreed the teacher, "I don't deny that. In the case of black people, living in slums is part of a general pattern of social and economic subordination that seems hard to break. White slum dwellers are proportionately fewer and, as you say, have an easier time getting out because the avenues of mobility away from slums and poverty are at least not blocked by racial prejudice."

"When you say it, it sounds so academic, though," replied the student. "It's not that you're wrong, or anything like that, but you talk about it kind of without heat, if you know what I mean."

"I do know what you mean, yes," replied the teacher.
"But you don't care, is that it?"
"Care?"
"Yeah, like give a damn about it?"
"You think that increasing the heat of my description would show that?"
"Sure, what else?"
"Well, would it help us understand things better?"
"Why not? I mean, people in the slums understand, don't they? They know why they're there and why they won't get out. It's because they're black and because they're poor and because nobody gives a damn about them, and because they don't have any power. What else does anybody need to know?"
"Can any of these things be understood better by feeling them more deeply, or by describing them with greater emotional fervor?"
"Sure, I think that. I have the feeling that if people really cared about the injustices and the suffering that goes on there, something would be done about it much more quickly. The slum people don't know about these statistics you're talking about. They *are* the statistics, but a lot of them feel helpless about it. I just don't know how anybody can be so cool about all that."
"I notice," replied the teacher, "that the subject seems to have changed. We were discussing slums, in an attempt to show the political aspect of housing, but we now are getting over to the way the teacher may possibly feel about a subject. I don't mind talking about myself at appropriate times but, for the present, I'd like to bow out of that discussion, if you don't mind, Mr. Perry."
"Well, all right—but don't you think that what I said about the people in the slums knowing all about why they're there is true—that they're black, poor, ignored, and powerless?"
"You have a double question here, Mr. Perry. In my opinion, the reasons you cite for slums are very cogent. What I don't know is whether the people in the slums know the things you attribute to them. Even if I conceded that they must, psychologically, have some of the feelings you attribute to them, I simply don't know the extent or the level of intensity with which they are held, and I don't know how many people really know some of them, in the sense of having information. On the other hand, for our purposes here it really is not so necessary to speculate about that, is it? There is no doubt that the reasons you give are, in fact, among the most prominent ones accounting for slums, though they are not the only ones. So, I will agree with you about the general reasons contributing to the existence of slums and, I share your sense of indignation about the conditions. Now, let me get into the subject a little more

deeply. Your description of the conditions of slum housing was quite vivid and accurate. Have you any ideas about the way in which these terrible conditions can be eradicated?"

"There must be a lot of ways to get rid of slums," replied Perry.

"For example . . . ?"

"Well, you tear all the buildings down and put up decent housing."

"What do you mean by the words 'you could tear the buildings down'? Who could do that?"

"The people who own the buildings could, couldn't they? I mean, they must make a lot of profits on the rents. Why don't they give better housing by building better buildings?"

"And where would the people go who now live in the places you'd tear down?" asked the teacher.

"Well, I don't know," replied Perry, "There must be some places for them to live."

"What apparently happens when you try to clear slums is that the people who are forced to leave look for other run-down neighborhoods in which they can afford to live, with the results that slums are made to spread. And another thing. When the private owners can get buildings evacuated they often replace them with housing in which the original inhabitants of the area cannot afford to live because of the high rents in the new buildings."

"What about public housing?" Perry pressed.

"Public housing?"

"Oh, yes, aren't there a lot of public housing projects in big cities? That looks like a solution to me."

"It is, Mr. Perry. It is a solution of a special kind."

"How do you mean, a special kind? What difference does it make whether the housing is public or private for the people who live in them. At least, they've got a place to live, don't they?"

"Oh, quite so. Of course, that's true. In fact, you might even say that in some ways it is a better solution for poor people at least, because the rentals in public housing are generally less expensive than in equivalent private housing. Moreover, equivalent private housing at the prices charged in public housing is simply not available in a great many critical housing areas."

"Is that what's special about public housing? That it's cheaper?"

"Why do you suppose it can be less expensive? After all, the prices for putting up buildings don't vary all that much, I should imagine. Differences in wages, the costs of materials, and of land, and so forth are probably not the major factors of such differences in rentals."

"Well, maybe they build the public houses in cheaper ways, if you know what I mean. Thinner walls, cheaper pipes, and so forth."

"I'm not expert enough in that part of the problem to be a reliable witness, Mr. Perry. Assuming that there are no such differences, however, we will have to account for great differences in rental by some other money source."

"Do you mean that it's paid for from taxes?"

"I do, at least in part. Taxes and special kinds of subsidies, such as publicly guaranteed bonds at low interest in place of commercial bonds at higher rates, as special devices for purchasing land with public money which is not charged against the cost of building the houses, and various other public subsidies. The methods vary, but the principle is the same. The houses are built and the rents are kept low by means of resorting to public funding charged against the general tax fund collected by state, local, or federal governments in various combinations. In other words, the housing is made possible by resorting to political solutions."

"That must be the reason why there's such a fight every time someone proposes low-cost housing in some area or other," said Mr. Perry.

"How do you mean?" asked the teacher.

"Well, if poor people who want cheap houses can get them from the government, the people who make a profit from private houses would try to prevent that, wouldn't they? After all, it cuts into their business, and it costs tax money."

"That's good, Mr. Perry. The introduction of publicly subsidized housing into a housing market which was essentially free enterprise is sure to stir up opposition from the housing industries. But there are other reasons for opposition to public housing, as well. Some of these have to do with the reasons you mentioned yourself when you accounted for the existence of slums."

"Oh, I get it, sure. If you want to build a public-housing project for poor people in a good neighborhood, people get scared, especially if they're black, for instance, right?"

"Right," agreed the teacher, and continued. "Some of the more common objections to public housing reach very deeply into other aspects of public policy. For example, residents of suburban school districts are known to object to it on the grounds that public housing for the poor would overcrowd their schools with children of families who, because of their residence in subsidized housing, do not contribute to the financing of the schools in the same way that home owners do. They also say that the poor families have more children and are therefore a disproportionate load on their schools, and they add that all of this would tend to make school taxes rise. We know from bitter experience that school taxes are a major point of political controversy in suburban areas."

"Yeah, but I'll bet that the biggest objection is that a lot of the poor are black. They wouldn't get nearly so mad if they weren't afraid of us dark-skinned people."

"Well, I suspect you may have a point there, but...."

"I don't think he has a point there, at all," a voice called out from the side of the classroom.

"I've been listening to the discussion about housing and agree with a lot of it, but I don't think you should get carried away with it. I live in a community not far from here where black home owners are fighting black and white people who want to put up public housing that'll be mostly for black people. They just don't want their schools crowded out by people who won't pay their share of the school taxes, and who would make it necessary to build more schools so that the taxes would rise some more. I have a black friend whose father told me the other day that he was hoping he'd finally gotten away from the ghetto, and now they were putting up another one right next door to him. He's no racist, he just wants his kids to have a chance for a good education without it bankrupting him. He said if it happens, he's going to move out. So I don't think it's just the race thing. Even black people don't like to pick up the tab for poor people, or have them come in and ruin their community that way. That man doesn't object to public housing for the poor, but he just wants to have a chance to live where he wants to without all that next door to him. I don't blame him for that."

"Are you suggesting that the economic or social differences between the well-to-do and the poor are more important than the racial differences between black and white?"

"I don't know about that. There's an awful lot of race conflict going on in this country and black people seem generally very solid on a lot of those things. At least that's the impression you get from newspapers and television. But I know from firsthand experience that the black property owners are just as worried about their taxes going up as the whites, maybe even more so, because they've had a lot harder time getting there than some of the white people did."

"I take it from your comment, Mr. . . . ."

"Schaefer, with an 'a' and an 'e'."

"Thank you. I take it that you find it difficult to sort out the racial aspects of the housing problem from the economic or social ones," responded the teacher.

"That's right. I expected that Negro home owners would feel a little different than whites about things like that because of the sympathy for other black people. I was a little disappointed."

"Would you be disappointed if white home owners resented poor whites moving in?" called Mr. Perry.

"To be honest about it, I guess not. I'd expect that there would be a lot of differences between them. But when you throw in the race problem, I figured that underdogs would have more sympathy towards each other."

"Man, you're really prejudiced," asserted Perry. "Black people just can't do right. First everybody thinks they're less than human and now they think they're superhuman. We're just like everybody else."

The teacher intervened: "I suppose the most difficult part of the problem is that the reactions of blacks and whites are treated almost entirely on the basis of some sort of stereotype. The fact is that the use of the terms black or white may give us very little clue about the way in which given persons who may be described that way will react in a given situation. It's not exactly a prejudice to think that way, but neither is it useful or even clear thinking."

"You mean whites aren't prejudiced against black people?" challenged Perry.

"No, I don't mean that, either. But, despite your generally accurate perception of prejudicial conduct, there are very important differences in the way in which persons in any group will think and act in a particular situation, even when, as in this instance, the subject of race prejudice is involved."

"That's funny. I have a much simpler answer to that story about how black home owners oppose public housing for the poor in their neighborhood. It's just that they're prejudiced against their own kind, and that they're playing the white man's game. What do you think of that, professor?"

"I would like to pursue your line of attack on that, Mr. Perry, but it would take us somewhat away from the main thread of the housing problem, I fear."

"I guess that means you don't think much of that answer of mine, right?"

"Well, let's just say for the present that it seems a little drastic as an analysis, but that it's very time consuming to take apart fairly. I don't want to do you an injustice by simply dismissing it, but we haven't the time to get into it deeply enough right here."

"But don't you think this is more important than public housing?" Perry insisted.

"In a way it really is, Mr. Perry," replied the professor. "The difficulties of thinking clearly about other people or about social problems are visible in all kinds of ways, and especially where deep feelings are aroused that get in the way. There is some sort of lesson here, I'm sure, but it's difficult to state it briefly."

"Well, why don't we get into it, then, instead of talking about housing and politics. I mean, if we could clear that up maybe a lot of political problems could be solved, too."

"That's one thing I'm prepared to agree with you about, and on that ground I would be tempted to go along with your suggestion. But the matter has elements I'm simply not prepared now to cope with, even if I do admit its relevance for political understanding."

"Don't you think that a lot of political conflict is unnecessary and is carried on just because people are so contrary?" pressed the student.

"I agree that contrariness over all kinds of things is part of political conflict, at least," retorted the teacher.

"Well, if you could get people to stop being that way you wouldn't have any conflict, would you?" the insistent student maintained.

"As I said, Mr. Perry, that's more mysterious than you think."

"But why? It looks very simple."

"Yes, so it does," the teacher agreed.

"Well, then?"

"I guess you just won't let go of it, eh?" the wryly amused teacher said, with a thinly veiled sigh.

The class, fascinated by the wrestling match, finally erupted into laughter. Perry and the professor joined in.

"What we have to contend with here is the question of what makes people contrary, as you call them, Mr. Perry. If it is in their nature to be so, it would make sense to look for solutions to political and other problems in getting them to 'think straight.' We'd concentrate on that and, if we succeeded in it, we could live without conflict. But, it might be that their contrariness is located not inside them as persons, but outside, so to speak, in the conditions of society, in which they find themselves. In that case we'd have to look toward bringing social and economic conditions into some kind of harmonious relationship so that conflict is minimized or eliminated. Then we could leave the contrariness alone, because it would take care of itself as social conditions improved."

"That's pretty interesting stuff, professor," admitted Perry.

"Not only interesting," said the teacher, "but very difficult, and very important. Do you agree that it's complicated enough to be left alone for the present? At least, would you agree that it had little directly to do with the housing problem?"

"Hell, no, I don't. I think it has everything to do with it," Perry replied.

"But could you name any kind of problem that exists between people with which it doesn't have to do, however," insisted the professor.

"No, I couldn't, not now," replied the student.

"Well, Mr. Perry, I'll recommend a strong exposure to philosophy for you at an early opportunity. At this point I must retire from the field. Politics is a more complicated enterprise than thinking straight, or the problem of eliminating conflict by eradicating all of the possible causes of it among men. So far we've discovered that political decisions are involved in the eradication, or at least the softening, of some of the effects of slums, and that you can touch the problem by providing better housing at partial public expense under certain conditions. But there are problems connected with providing housing as slum-clearing device. For example, one could argue that the best solution for slums is to provide enough well-paying jobs to eliminate unemployment so that anyone can afford to buy good housing. That would result in good housing being constructed."

"But there'll always be some unemployment, won't there?" suggested a young lady. "I mean there are a lot of reasons people are unemployed, even if jobs for some people are plentiful. Sickness, lack of training, and so on. Our economics professor told us that jobs appear in such a way that it is almost impossible for the people who are looking for them to keep up with them. For example, they can't move around easily, and they don't have the right skills, or they don't have information about work, and lots of other reasons. And there is race prejudice, and some people don't like to work, and in some places the weather is nice, and so on. It really is very complicated."

"I'm impressed by this recitation of technical problems. We should develop some respect for them. However, slum housing is often occupied by people who have jobs at low wages, or at irregular, or seasonal jobs. And, sometimes, the slum is in a community from which people don't want to move because they have all kinds of social, emotional, cultural, religious ties to the area. In the United States, for example, there are the so-called ethnic neighborhoods populated by groups of immigrants or their descendants from the same country, in which the deep roots are hard to sever, even if the housing deteriorates. Ghettos have some of those characteristics sometimes. In addition, there are other factors at work. Some old housing deteriorates because of the way it is used, but in some other cases, very old housing remains good for centuries, if properly maintained. There are many examples of that. And standards of housing at any time are a reflection of the general wealth and of the availability of certain kinds of living space. What seemed adequate for an immigrant family from a foreign country in 1880 or in 1910, is not thought adequate for their great grandchildren, born in this country, accustomed to its standards and able to live well in the 1970s."

The young woman who had displayed her grasp of employment problems returned to the discussion:

"Oh, I'm Holly Barton, incidentally. Well, if it's all that complicated, it seems almost impossible to solve the problem by just providing housing for the poor."

"How's that, Miss Barton?"

"Housing is always deteriorating, the population is constantly growing, unemployment and poverty seem almost insoluble economically. If it keeps up, the government will be the biggest landlord and private enterprise in housing will disappear."

"I'd not be quite as rash as to predict that, Miss Barton. Private investors, such as banks and insurance companies, find housing to be an excellent investment just because of the reasons you have given. So far, at least in the United States, public money has been used to fill the gaps left over by the lack of attractiveness of certain kinds of housing investments—such as low-rent dwellings for the poor. Besides, there are reasons for public intervention in housing that touch on the supply of private money, as well as on the fact that slums represent far more than housing problems for society. The incentive to build housing with public money is, in a sense also an economic one, but one of the public economy, so to say."

"I don't understand that," Miss Barton replied.

"What problems other than bad housing are present in slums that represent a cost factor for the public budget?"

"You mean crime and that sort of thing?"

"Yes . . . and?" asked the teacher, invitingly.

Mr. Perry was back. "Oh, come on now. Let me give you the list, OK? First, there's a lot of crime. That calls for a lot of police and that costs a lot of money. Then, because the fire inspectors usually don't bother to look, there are a lot of fires because of bad electric wiring, gas explosions, kerosene heaters, and things like that. So, double shifts for the firemen and more money. And because the health and housing laws aren't enforced there is a lot of disease among people in the slums. But they don't have much money for doctors, so there have to be health centers and hospitals around, and most of them are run by the city, or the county. And there's more. I think there's a lot of vandalism in places like schools in the slums and the windows keep having to be replaced, and that's expensive. You want more?"

"What's your conclusion, Mr. Perry?" asked the teacher.

"It's only logical, isn't it? Even if it cost money to get rid of the slums you'd probably save a lot in the long run if you spend it on houses in the short run. Besides, I object to people talking about that as if it were a money problem. Deep down, I don't think it is, as I said before. It's rich people trying to hang on to what they have and trying to get more, and poor people not knowing what to do about their troubles."

"But according to your own logic, Mr. Perry, if that were true and the rich people knew what they were doing, they'd help eradicate slums because they're costing them a lot more money than they realize."

"Well, yes, that's true. But it just shows how blind from greed they really are."

"But, how would you explain the fact that there are, as you said a while back, quite a few public-housing projects around and that many more are being built? If the rich were as powerful and greedy as they say they are, and the poor as helpless, how is the money for the public housing units obtained? It surely is no gift of the rich, is it, if you are right."

"Do you mean that it comes from people who make political decisions?" asked Perry.

"Well, doesn't it?"

"Yeah, I guess so. But how can they do that? I mean, they have to be able to tax people, don't they, to get money for that sort of thing?"

"Not only money, Mr. Perry. But they need other things before they can tax people, don't they?"

"I don't get it," said Perry. "That's what it means to be in the government, doesn't it? They can tax."

"Yes, they can, but first they have to 'be in the government,' to use your words. How do they do that?"

"Well, they have to get elected, don't they?"

"Yes, if that's the kind of office they hold. And who elects them?"

"Well, the people are supposed to, but a lot of them don't vote."

"Recall, Mr. Perry, if you please, that we are trying to explain what enables political decision-makers to levy taxes or use the government in other ways for building houses for poor people. Now, how does their having to get elected to public office explain that?"

"If the voters want something, their representatives are supposed to get it for them, aren't they? I mean, that's supposed to be democracy, isn't it?"

"All right, now do you think you can put the rest of that together?" asked the teacher.

"I'm not sure," said Perry.

"Well, try it," urged the teacher.

"You must be driving for a particular thing you want me to say, professor. I'm just not sure."

"Are there any differences in the value of the votes of rich and poor?"

"No, I guess every vote is about the same."

"So that, when poor voters want something they have to be listened to for the same reason and with the same attention as the rich ones?"

"Well, yeah, but still, if that actually happened things would be a lot different than they are, wouldn't they? I mean, there wouldn't be things like slums in the first place, isn't that right?"

"Why not?" asked the teacher.

"Because the political leaders would have had to prevent them to keep the support of the poor voters," said the student.

"But you are assuming, aren't you, that almost all of the poor agree, that most of them vote for representatives, and that these representatives are able to satisfy the demands. And furthermore, representatives of other people, who also vote, such as the rich or the middle classes, are also present when the politicians gather to make laws."

The teacher paused, but did not invite comment. He stood silently for a moment, trying to think of a succinct statement that would focus the issue sharply.

"Our problem is complex but not impossible," he began again. "We can get at it by the observation that in an economic system essentially private, the expression of political demand for housing is, first of all, unlikely to come from the economically well fixed. They can help themselves, after all. For the less well fixed to be able to demand public housing presumes a shortage of suitable housing, at proper prices, but it also presumes that the demand is enforceable. As Mr. Perry suggests, the poor don't vote all that much, so public housing policy is the result of political decisions in which the nonpoor and even the rich, as well as their representatives, provide the resources. Altruism and self-interest seem well mixed in those kinds of decisions. It's pretty upsetting even for rich people to see slums and to observe the life of slum dwellers. Objections to those things come very readily from wealthy or powerful persons."

"Yeah, OK, but why should they care?"

"Must there be a single reason?"

"There's got to be an explanation, doesn't there?"

"But, Mr. Perry, by your own terms you said that poor people don't know what to do about their own troubles. So, if you're right, some people other than poor ones must have had a lot to do with getting public housing, right?"

"Well, OK, I agree—but I think you want me to say that it was the politicians who did it. All right, I'm saying it, but I have a hard time believing it, anyway."

"Actually, Mr. Perry, there is a very ironic way to check that out, you know. The common belief that public housing of the kind we've been building in the U. S. is a major solution to slum problems has to be very closely scrutinized. It is a way of providing better housing at public expense for less money, in place of the terrible housing in slums, but that's not all there's to it."

"I don't get it. What could be better than moving into nice, clean houses, that are cheap and new and in new neighborhoods, instead of what I've been describing here?"

"One set of problems comes from the fact that being able to move into public housing usually depends on the income level of the tenants. Since it's a kind of subsidy, one wants to make sure that only the most deserving people get it. That may have very unhappy results. For example, in one well-known case, the rules of eligibility worked out so that a very high percentage of the tenants were from broken and fatherless families. The effect was that the high concentration of helpless women in the same housing complex began a cycle of crime and degradation which ultimately became so serious that a large number of the tenants had to flee in terror, the buildings began to deteriorate from not having been serviced because the janitors and plumbers and painters refused to work there, the project became a literally uninhabitable slum in a very short time and parts of it were simply boarded up. The point seems to be that the housing project was designed by middle-class people who had a view of the housing problem which was confined to its physical aspects, but ignored completely the nature of social pathologies that beset people in poverty. They strongly believed that the only answer for bad housing was better housing, and, being well intentioned, wanted to do something good for the most helpless of people, who turned out to be mothers with lots of children and no husbands. In doing this, they so concentrated social pathology that the helplessness was increased rather than diminished. Had these helpless people been more thinly scattered among others who were in better shape, there might have been more hope for them. So here we have very ironic proof that public housing was designed by the not so poor for the poor."

Perry returned to the argument. "Do you think," he wanted to know, "that could be changed at all? I mean, the people the worst off do need the most help, don't they?"

"Yes, they do. But the question is what that help consists of. Obviously the housing policy has to be managed with an eye to whether it alone represents such help. Perhaps if the slum erasers and public-housing advocates knew more about what people in slums think they really need, they might be more able to help them, or if the slum dwellers had a way of making it known that new houses have to be made available to all kinds of people, not just the worst off ones, such things would not happen."

"Maybe you could fix up some of the old buildings they live in without making rules about who can live where? In that way there wouldn't be so much control over things."

"Yes, that might be some help. But, at any rate, we can see that even the so-called solutions have serious problems that call out for solutions."

"It sure looks like a never-ending kind of chain. You stop up one hole and make others and then you stop up those and more appear. One damn problem after another. It makes you wish that the whole thing could just be started all over. Maybe we could begin by erasing poverty altogether. Then we wouldn't have such housing problems, would we?" Perry said.

"Perhaps not, but we might have exchanged a manageable problem for an unmanageable one, mightn't we?" asked the instructor.

"What's that?" the student wanted to know.

"How do you go about eliminating poverty?"

"That's quite a problem, isn't it?" the student said thoughtfully.

"That's what I thought you'd have to say," the teacher replied, and continued, "I hereby declare a temporary recess in this meeting of the society for changing the world. We have places to go...."

11

The Joys of Transport

"During the last dialogue we discussed the social policies at work in the maintenance of living quarters for the population," began the teacher, "but it is time that we get out of the house. We have spent altogether too much time there and now we must get to work or, as in our case, to school. How many of you walk to class in the morning?"

Of the thirty-five students, six raised their hands. Of these, four were dormitory residents and two lived only a few blocks away, at home.

"How many travel to school by automobile?"

Of the twenty-nine remaining students, twenty came by car. The longest trip any person took by car to get to school was forty miles one way. The shortest trip was 1½ miles.

Of the nine other students, four came by a bus, and five by a combination of railroad and bus.

"We have in this classroom an interesting mixture of transportation methods. It has a very distinctive flavor. If you were to generalize about the pattern, what do you suppose it would tell you about the students, and the location of the college?"

"I'd say that you would first say that it's primarily a commuters' college," said a student who, after the now established mode of the class, introduced himself as Michael Wilson.

"Good, Mr. Wilson. Do you want to continue?"

"Yes. You can also see that it's not an urban school, because if it were most of the nonresidents would have come by means of a mass-transportation system, like a subway or bus, or even railroads. In addition, you can tell something about the social class of the students. Almost everybody here owns a car. That takes money and that means people are well enough off to buy and maintain one."

"That's not necessarily so," disagreed another student. "I don't have a car but I come with a car pool and pay for my ride. My family can't afford a car for me. We already have one my father uses. Maybe next year I can get one when I get a job to support it."

Wilson stuck to his guns. "All right, but in general we're in a tuition-charging university and that takes money, too, so I'll stick with my middle-class analysis."

The professor intervened. "Are there additions to the transit analysis offered by Mr. Wilson?"

"Yes," replied Wilson, "I'd like to continue."

"Go ahead, please."

"Now you can also show that it is a suburban school because of the balance of the railroad travelers. If it were located nearer the center of the city there'd be more mass-transit travelers but still quite a few motorists. So it's in between."

"All right, Mr. Wilson. Can I ask you some questions?"

"Yes, sir, of course."

"What does your analysis have to do with public policy?"

"I guess by now the smart thing to do in this class is to say quite a lot. So, I'll say quite a lot. But I know you're not going to be satisfied with that so I'll have to actually mention some things."

"Is that so hard to do?"

"I'm sure it'll turn out to be easy. It's just hard to begin. Let's see. I have a driver's license."

"Good shot! How'd you get it?"

"Oh, come on."

"That's what I'm doing."

"All right. I took a test and after flunking it a few times, I passed. And—oh, yes, it was a state government test, and I studied for it in a drivers' education course in school."

"OK, Mr. Wilson. How's your record of violations?"

"I haven't got caught yet."

"Should you have?"

"I'm not saying."

"So, the hundred million and more cars in the country are all supposed to be driven by licensed people. Do these cars themselves have any political significance?"

Wilson continued. "Yes, sure. The gasoline it takes to run them costs as much as it does because about one third of its price is made up of federal, state, and local taxes. That's a lot of money. The government must get tremendous amounts of money from gasoline sales. That's a political matter, isn't it?"

"Yes, it is, and it has a rather special significance. After all, we pay taxes on a lot of things, on a great variety of objects, and by many means. The gasoline is not especially distinguished by that, but we have a case of the uses to which the gasoline tax money is being put, that's particularly interesting, and revealing. What is the money used for?"

"I belong to the AAA," called out a new voice from the middle of the class, "and they send out a newspaper every now and then. I read an article the other day which described the way the gasoline taxes are earmarked for the construction of roads. That way the gasoline taxes pay directly for the streets the cars need. That's fair enough, isn't it?"

"Is it?" asked the teacher. "How do we know that the cost of road construction and maintenance are the same as the income from gasoline taxes?"

"I don't know that," said the student. "The AAA was trying to make sure that the politicians don't use their money to do something else with it, like give it to the farmers, or for welfare. We drivers pay for the roads and in that way we can be sure to get them."

"Are you suggesting that legislatures have the power to impose the taxes, but not the power to decide what shall be done with it?"

"Well, I don't know, but the country needs more roads and that's a fair way to pay for it, it seems to me."

"Does anyone else want to intervene in this very interesting problem?" asked the professor.

"Yes, definitely," said a young man who identified himself as Jeffrey Hitch. "That's just the way a special interest group looks at it. In the first place, roads must cost a lot more money than the gasoline tax produces. I'm not sure of that, but I think it costs about two million dollars to build a mile of four-lane highway now and they're building a lot of roads. In the second place, there's a lot of discussion now that there are altogether too many cars around, and that they cause more harm than good. It would be a lot cheaper to transport people by bus or train than by car, and you wouldn't get nearly so much pollution in the air. I'm taking a course in ecology and we found out that in urban areas more than half of the air pollution comes from gasoline fumes. Who needs more roads in the first place? If you tie up the tax money that way, you just contribute to the stupid problem instead of solving it. And then you have to collect more taxes to clean up the air. That's crazy, even if the government is doing it."

It was an impassioned speech. The teacher urged Mr. Hitch on. "Are you suggesting that government contributes to the pollution problem by building roads which promote automobile travel?"

"That's right. Just because the government does it does not mean it doesn't do anything stupid. During the whole discussion in this class you've treated the government as if it were some sort of inevitable good. I think the transportation mess is an illustration of how terrible things can get with the help of the government."

"Mr. Hitch, aren't there some good things done about transportation by the government, too?"

"Well, they're trying to enforce federal standards of safety in car production, and they made laws about backup lights and now they require antipollution devices on the exhausts, but I think that's much too little and too late. We need a lot more sensible policy."

"Mr. Hitch," asked the teacher, "how can one manage to persuade Americans to buy fewer cars when they have the money to buy them and when owning a car provides them with almost unlimited transportation choices, where mass transit does not?"

"I don't know, but I guess we need to spend money on mass transit so that it's cheaper, faster, and less trouble than it is now."

"How does one get money for mass transit when public funds are used for construction of super highways, encouraging people to use cars more rather than less?"

"They're also spending money on experiments in mass transportation. High speed trains, and public ownership of the Long Island Railroad, and a subway system in the San Francisco Bay area, and in Washington, D.C.," replied Hitch.

"Yes, and the Department of Transportation has just spent millions of dollars on an experimental safety automobile to reduce the accident rate," argued the professor. "Where does all the money come from?"

"The same place as all the other money, taxes."

"How do you suppose it happens that so much of it is spent for purposes that seem quite contrary?"

"Is it the old pressure group game again?" asked the student. "There are a lot of automobile owners around and, like the fellow who spoke up a while ago said, they are organized and have to be listened to."

"Not a bad guess at all. We clearly have a very uneven battle in which the complex of interests identified with automobiles is unusually powerful. They don't only include the drivers, but the whole industrial system connected with cars and with fuel, the highway industries—cement, construction machinery, and the labor forces, etcetera. I would suppose that the combined forces are as compelling as anything we have in politics. They must be nearly irresistible in some kinds of jurisdictions."

"Now I know what it was," called out a former participant in the discussion.

The teacher turned to him, saying, "That's Mr. Miles, right?"

"Right. You remember when we talked about cotton and wool and I said that the pressure groups' way of deciding what's good for the country bothered me?"

"Yes, I recall it distinctly. You said that the process of bargaining between the representatives of different groups left something to be desired, but you didn't know what it was, right?"

"That's right. Now it comes up again with the business about transportation, and I think I can say what I mean. It's that the automobile groups are so powerful as to be irresistible and that the result is that they have their way but it's not good for the country at all. You can even show that it's not good for the automobile owners themselves. There's pollution, high cost of gasoline, very expensive cars, and terrible traffic congestions all over. None of that is a good thing and they all cost a lot of additional money. So what I mean is that the interest of big groups like that, even though it is irresistible, is bad for the country. Maybe it's because they *are* too strong."

"That was well put, Mr. Miles. What kinds of defenses can be built against giving them what they demand, however? There are no laws against their organizing, are there? I suppose you don't think they should be outlawed, do you?"

"No, I don't think so. I guess all the other people would have to find a way of getting together to resist them."

"All the other people? How many Americans have a stake in constantly improving roads and other facilities for automobiles?"

"It must be a lot."

"How many?"

"I don't know."

"I believe it is over one hundred million."

A gasp from the class.

"That's a lot of people who have to be resisted," mused Mr. Miles.

"There are more than that, Mr. Miles. You forget the nondriving children of the families of the drivers and the others whose pleasure and livelihood depends on the drivers. So it is not exactly a question of being able to build up opposition to the automobile complex. It's probably more realistic to ask how many of the drivers would be willing to recognize what burdens they are placing on each other and on the general public and compromise some of their own present advantages for the general good. What do you think the chances are of that?"

"I think you could do that by making car travel more inconvenient. You could tax cars more, raise the parking fees or the insurance rates, or the price of gasoline and oil, or the highway tolls, and use the money to finance buses, trains, and things like that."

"All right, but who has to impose these burdens?"

"Well, the governments. City and state and maybe federal government have to cooperate."

"What chances are there that a major city can increase car taxes?"

"I know New York City tried it, but the car lobby was too strong, I guess."

"Are we saying that political leadership is unable to impose a standard of the common good when the people are not prepared to accept it?"

"I guess so. Maybe we need an automobile dictatorship."

"We?"

"I mean, if they didn't have to worry about getting reelected, they could do it, I bet."

"So you prefer a government that doesn't have to worry about getting reelected, Mr. Miles?" asked the professor, teasingly.

"Well, I don't, actually, and I never said that, but I can't figure out a way around the damned automobile, or the people that own them."

"Is there not a possibility that political leadership can be strong enough to tell people that their heart's desires are creating problems that have to be solved and that the best way of solving them is for people to restrain themselves?"

"I doubt it," replied Miles.

"Even if things got very bad? After all, among the sufferers from the automobile are a lot of drivers and car users. The interurban car commuters swallow a lot of exhaust fumes and, it seems to me, would not resist some kind of transit solution which depended in part on limiting the use of the automobile. Not all owners of cars love them, after all."

"Well, maybe, but if the government had real power, regardless of the political consequences, there'd be less shilly-shally on this."

"But Mr. Miles, how do you know that a government with sufficient power to override the desires of the governed would have the inclination to act properly, or fairly or justly?"

"I don't know it, but short of stopping people from doing what is harmful even against their will, what solutions are there?"

The teacher looked out over the class and asked, "Is there anyone here who is willing to tackle *that* question?"

No one was. It did not surprise the professor. The argument had been put into a form especially resistant to thoughtful response. He took on the problem:

"As you put it, Mr. Miles, one would have to say that something must be made to happen to the wills or the opinions of the governed. They must learn to see themselves in ways other than just automobile clients, by learning about the consequences of automobile congestion to the point where they would be at least willing to permit some people in authority to make some experiments with alternate modes of transportation. The various attempts to use government money for research in mass transit and pollution control, or even alternate kinds of engines for cars, seem to be directed that way. Here the leaders risk little because they are not interfering with anyone's convenience yet, but they are educating people and moving in a direction away from the present structure of costs and advantage. So, they are really not as badly trapped as our previous discussion would make it appear. Enough car owners may become worried enough to enable some politicians to advocate the cause of the train or the subway or some other means without threatening their own political power. Here and there it may be the case that a man may even become popular for his crusade against cars, but that is not likely to be a frequent occurrence at this point."

"Well, I just don't believe it. Most Americans put their own advantage first and they let the devil take the hindmost. We won't get sensible legislation until a lot of people are choking to death on gasoline fumes, I'll bet."

The teacher turned to the class and asked, "How many agree with Mr. Miles?"

Of the thirty-five students, fifteen agreed.

"How many have a more hopeful outlook?"

Twelve thought the teacher was more nearly right.

"And the rest of you?"

"I just don't know," said one of the unregistered ones. "I think it could go either way. If enough young people care about that kind of thing it could change very quickly for the better, I think."

"How so?" the teacher wanted to know.

"Well, I think maybe we're not so committed to the automobile civilization as the older people are, and maybe we'll be more active against pollution."

Mr. Miles was heard to snort loudly.

"Aren't you in agreement, Mr. Miles?"

"I am not. At least there are some people among the older generation who like to walk or ride in trains. Most of my friends would sell their souls for an automobile, and some of them already have. They'll only make it worse."

"Maybe there'll be a technological revolution, Mr. Miles," suggested the professor. "I just hate to see you so pessimistic."

"I don't believe it. If we got electric automobiles, or fumeless exhausts, all that would happen would be that a lot more people would feel justified in having them, because they couldn't be criticized for polluting the air. I think if you did anything to deprive people of cars for any reason whatever the whole civilization would collapse before it changed its ways."

"Collapse?"

"Yes, collapse. If the car owners were inconvenienced beyond the point of tolerance, they'd threaten to overtake the government and establish a new form of government."

"I hesitate asking what you'd call it, Mr. Miles."

"Autocracy, of course."

"Of course," said the teacher, "the very word. And what would that government stand for?"

"No interference with automobiles and their owners. They'd probably pass a constitutional amendment forbidding laws limiting the use and possession of cars."

"Are you always so pessimistic?" asked the teacher.

"That makes no difference, the question is whether I'm right. I think I am. You'll see, just wait."

"You seem to think that automobiles are as vital to their consumers as water was a few discussions back. You will recall that I suggested that water was sufficiently important to be the cause of political philosophy and the basis of governmental authority. I defended that because the relation between water and politics is well established. Whether Mr. Miles is right or not in the end we don't know, but there is no doubt that the automobile complex of interests is very powerful. For one thing, the balance of economic power is now so tilted in the direction of the cars that it is much easier politically to provide for them than for other modes of transportation. For example, bus systems are difficult to maintain economically where few riders make use of them. So, they run on very poor schedules, which makes them next to useless for many people. Public subsidies for bus transportation don't work well when they are in competition with cars because of the tax bite the buses have to take from the public treasury."

"Isn't the same thing true for railroads?" Miles continued. "The more long distance highways you build the tougher you make railroad economics because those highways can be used by trailers which compete over the same territory, and the more you compete with the railroads the harder it is to get good mass-rail transportation, especially for the places where commuters have to go to work every day. So there too the cars are making life tough for people."

"Of course that's true, Mr. Miles. Rail transit appears in serious trouble right now because of the automotive and truck competition. Every mile of public highway contributes more to their difficulty, even though rail transit is more economical than trucks and even though we know that mass transportation for metropolitan areas would be a major way of relieving the congestion of cars and of lowering the general price of transportation."

"Is there any kind of solution here, do you think?"

"I'm not sure. The technicians are playing with combined systems of interurban travel, using cars, buses, and trains and by tieing their routes and their schedules together in such a way as to discourage automotive travel. But mass transit has two major disadvantages over automobiles that are hard to beat."

"Disadvantages?" Miles asked.

"For one, they run on schedules, and the user has to accommodate himself to that. With a car he simply goes whenever he wants to go. Secondly, their travel is, of course, restricted as to direction. The car user can go wherever he pleases, practically. Mass transit users have to change from one mode to another, switching trains or from trains to buses or to subways and buses, and so forth. All the car user needs is a parking place at the end of his journey."

"*All* he needs?" asked Miles indignantly. "The parking lots are making the cities look like hell. I'm sure that property could be used for better purposes than that."

"Yes, that's so, but how are the property owners going to resist cashing in on such a demand for parking space? They'd be fools if they turned down that kind of profit, wouldn't they? There is a third matter of great difficulty here. Because the railroads have found their commuter lines very unprofitable, because their freight can now also be hauled by trucks, railroads have been trying to get rid of commuter lines, to cut their losses. That makes transportation life in metropolitan areas even more difficult."

"But that's not hard, is it? If commuting lines are so important for metropolitan areas, they can do what New York State did, can't they? The state took over the Long Island Railroad and some of the New Haven and Grand Central lines and is operating them as public utilities. At least that way it doesn't make so much difference whether they're bankrupt, just as in the case of subways or, like you said, in the case of the post office. The legislature just makes up the difference. So that's the solution, isn't it? The tax money which would ordinarily be used for building more roads can be gotten for providing more mass transportation, just as they do with subways."

The defender of the automobile revived his interest in the conversation at this point.

"Do you mean you'd be willing to have the money from the gasoline tax used to build more buses and subways and trains? That's not right, is it?"

"I don't see why not," said Miles. "The cars are producing all of those problems, why not let them pay for some of it? In fact, I'd be willing to raise the gasoline tax another dime or so a gallon, to discourage car riding and to make money available for mass transportation. That would be real justice."

"You know you'd have a real fight on your hands in the legislature. If the commuters want mass transportation, let them pay for it, just like the car travelers are paying for theirs."

"That sounds like a good principle," the defender of mass transit argued, "but it really is not, because the use of cars creates the problems to which mass transit is the solution. I think car users can fairly be asked to pay part of the tab for what they are doing to the rest of us."

It was a standoff, at least in terms of rhetoric, so the teacher proceeded to ask some questions from the other side.

"Now we have established that railroads found commuter traffic to be very unprofitable, but the defenders of mass transit say that it is indispensable for solving the car crisis. I take it that means we need publicly owned systems which can be allowed to run at some deficit, doesn't it, Mr. Miles?"

"Well, I don't really know anything about the economics of it at all, but if that's the way to do it, let's do it."

"But don't you recall our discussion of the problems of public enterprises, Mr. Miles? Even the good reasons for having them don't relieve us of the problems they create, partly because they are public enterprises. That is true of mass transit too. For example, the publicly owned mass transit systems are seriously in need of cash for renovation, expansion, modernization, and so on. The fares charged for these mass transit systems are usually highly political and the subject of great controversy, with candidates and parties competing over keeping them low. The great majority of the users are not well-to-do and have an important economic stake in keeping fares low. So, in order for the money to become available, it has to be appropriated by legislatures and raised through taxes. But taxes are imposed on all taxpayers and that creates large opposition among the nonusers of the transit system, many of whom are wealthy, or who live far away, who say, 'Let the users pay.' So the legislators resist the appropriation of money. Instead, they turn to the money market to borrow it. But when the government borrows money, it has to go to people who have it. They lend it out only at an interest rate. That makes the cost of the money much higher and since the income from government bonds is not taxable, the government loses the revenue from that as well. And so, locked in by these barriers on every side, public-transportation systems suffer serious deterioration and breakdowns that are very costly and dangerous for their riders. Not until these breakdowns occur, in other words not until it is much too late, does it become politically possible to raise fares and then it is usually not enough to pay for what needs to be done."

The defender of cars was heard to chortle loudly, and then added, "You see, traveling in cars prevents all that kind of nonsense."

"That is the silliest statement ever made," said Miles in reply. "The fact is that the car created those problems, just as I said, and the car users should be obliged to help pay for them. The management and financing of mass transportation is a lot easier and cheaper and healthier than the pollution and the death and destruction and the money required to keep up those four-wheeled monsters."

The teacher, who sensed that the discussion was developing more heat than light, asked one last question, "Is there anyone among us who would now question that our transportation is a deeply political matter?"

Since there were none, he adjourned the class by saying, "And next we go to school."

"Aren't we there already?" the voice of a mild protester was heard to say as he was rising to leave.

"That's what we'll discover tomorrow," replied the teacher.

12

Schooldays, Schooldays

"And now we're in school," began the teacher. "Row on row, just as you've been sitting since you were five years old. What is the political significance of being here?"

"The question has all kinds of angles," opined one of the students.

"Yes, it has," agreed the teacher, "and that should give you all kinds of opportunities. Who might you be?"

"I'm Harry Stout. What I mean is, that you could look at it in many ways. Right now it means that we have an instructor who's asking us to think about politics while we're in class, and that has some significance. It means that a part of higher education is given over to the study of it."

"Fine," was the professor's response, "but, after all, universities study just about everything else in the world; it would be peculiar if politics were exempt from that, wouldn't it, Mr. Stout?"

"I agree," said the student, "It was just one of the angles. I meant to mention others, too. For example, there are laws in most states requiring attendance at school until age sixteen. That's political, isn't it? I mean, why such a law?"

"Are you asking?"

"No, sir, I was just making a list."

"All right, we'll just let you continue for a while."

"Thank you. And for practically everybody education is not just compulsory but it's also public. Most people in this country don't go to private schools. And public money is used for the purpose of higher education. I think there are now more college students in public universities than in private ones, isn't that true?"

"I hesitate to answer," replied the teacher. "Maybe I'm not being asked. But, yes, Mr. Stout, there are now more college students at publicly owned institutions of higher education than at private ones and, in fact, the numerical gap between the two is growing bigger every year. Some people think that the day of the so-called private university may be past. There is an additional political significance in the public higher-education item you just mentioned. The very fact that the enrollment at universities of any kind is as large as it is, is a political matter. You've given us an interesting list, Mr. Stout. Would anyone else like to add to it?"

A rapidly waving hand begged to be recognized. Its owner identified herself as Joan Turner. "I've just finished a course in the techniques of teaching social studies in the secondary school, and there's a lot more to that. A lot of the content of what students learn in school is political. The curriculum is supposed to teach students to be loyal citizens who believe in our way of life. If you want to be a teacher you have to take certain courses in American history and even this course in political science is required by the State Board of Regents. Our professor told us that in some states there are laws which require every college student in state colleges to take a course in the government of that particular state. Is that true?"

"Yes, quite true," confirmed the teacher. "Moreover, there are some, or at least there were some cases where the State Board of Education determined what kinds of books were to be used in studying the subject."

"Is that right? I mean is that proper? Should the subjects in the school be decided by public officials?"

"In a public institution, how would you have them determined, Miss Turner?"

"Well, couldn't the teachers decide that, or local Boards of Education?"

"Aren't the teachers public officials?"

"Oh, I suppose so, so what's the way out?"

"Why does there have to be a way out? Schools in all states are a function of state government. By law and even by the state constitution, they are financed by state taxes or joint state-local taxes. One of the most important objects of education, and especially public education is political, in the sense that the creation and existence of an informed citizenry can be assured by public education, and in the sense that the money-giving authority can be expected to express an interest in the spreading of feelings of affection and loyalty for the country, its history, and major principles of politics. Political systems have always sought to insure their perpetuation by teaching the young the proper civic virtues. In the modern age, where literacy and political participation are widespread in the population, this has become important in the minds of governmental and political leaders. The official control of the content of learning in the social studies as well as in other fields is practically universal."

"Couldn't it happen that you get only one version of history, for example, or of politics or economics that way?" asked Miss Turner.

"Not only couldn't it, but it has, and does. Don't you think boys and girls should be brought up to love their country and its history and to be taught to assume the obligations of citizenship?"

"Yes, but why shouldn't they be told the truth instead of some propaganda version of it which makes everything American look good and everything else look bad?"

"And everything French, English, German, Nigerian, etcetera? I'll say this for you, Miss Turner. You don't ask trivial questions, do you?"

"Well, it's an important problem."

"So it is," agreed the professor, "so it is. How does one deal with the demand on the part of political authority to produce loyal citizens in schools and with the recognition that not everything, or far from everything, about one's country or system is lovable?"

"I believe that you should always tell the whole truth so far as you know it, regardless," replied Miss Turner, spiritedly.

Loud laughter from several sources in the classroom.

"And what, may I ask, was the comic reaction all about? Yes, weren't you one of the laughers?"

"Yeah, sure I was. I'm Charles Harris. What she said was just silly. The government wouldn't allow books in public schools that they thought were the whole truth. Everybody knows that."

"Does everybody know that?"

"Sure. At least, I know it. Every system tells the truth in such ways that it looks good, especially to the young. In some countries the books change every time the government changes."

"And what happens when the government doesn't change very often, or at all, or only in minor ways?"

"Well, that's because people have been brainwashed into thinking that they live in a great place and can't tell the difference anymore. Or maybe they have nothing to say about it like in some countries."

"So the political system uses education to tell lies or warp the truth in order to help in its own perpetuation?" inquired the professor.

"That's right, they all do."

"Where did you find that out?"

"I've known it for a long time."

"Where did you learn it?"

"I don't remember."

"Could you have gotten an inkling of it in school?"

"I really can't remember. Maybe. That's something most people can figure out for themselves, can't they?"

"Yes, I'd agree that it's possible to distinguish between what one is told in school, and what one experiences and comes to regard as the truth. It's not too difficult to figure that out. But, if it is, all sorts of questions intrude. For example, it must mean that political indoctrination in schools is none too successful. At least, you were able to figure it out, weren't you? What about others?"

"Well, some people swallow everything teachers tell them."

"That must mean that part of the secret must lie in who you let into teaching, right?"

"Right. Some of what they say is just crazy."

"Are you surprised that teachers are required to pass through certain kinds of examinations?"

"Surprised, no. But I wonder how some of these people ever pass them."

"Do you mean that they don't know enough?"

"Yes, and also because of the political attitudes they have. They just can't accept that there's anything wrong with the country."

"Are you sure of that, as a fact? Did all of your teachers agree about public policy? Were they equally defensive about the country and its history?"

"No, I can't say that. One of the teachers understood the problem, I think. He really encouraged criticism, but he always made us back up what we said in the classroom with facts."

"Did he get fired for it?"

"Oh, no, but a lot of people didn't like him."

"How did he feel about the others?"

"Oh, he didn't care, as long as they let him teach."

"Did they?"

"Yes, but sometimes he had a rough time."

"Did he recite the pledge of allegiance?"

"Sure."

"Was there a flag in the corner of the room?"

"Yes."

"Did you open assemblies with the singing of the national anthem."

"Yes."

"Look," argued the teacher, "the treatment of historical truth by public authorities, including educational ones, is a very important problem, and universal in scope. At this point, I need merely to establish that the political system is bound to have an extremely high interest in the schools. Some political systems prescribe what is taught in great minutiae and permit only politically reliable persons to teach the young. They manufacture convenient versions of history from time to time. Others are much more casual, open, and free about it. It does seem inconceivable to me that there should be any system of government which provides the schools and then not care about their political uses. But schools also teach that political criticism is an accepted form of behavior, and in institutions of higher education, even that is developed into a fine art. Quite a few political philosophers have argued that without some mode of civic education, political systems are doomed to fail. May I add a point of opinion, here? In view of the facts just presented to us by Mr. Harris, I'm of the opinion that he learned to be critical without becoming disloyal in the schoolroom. The teacher who demanded that criticism have a factual basis did it in the context of a patriotic setting and promoted political loyalty and political criticism. They are not, after all, the worst enemies in the world, are they?"

Mr. Harris persisted. "Well, I'm not sure. I have the impression that the school system is really overdoing the loyalty bit."

"What impression do you think people have who think that the schools don't go far enough in inculcating respect for authority and affection for our way of life?" asked the teacher.

"I guess they think the opposite."

"Who do you suppose is right, Mr. Harris?"

"I am, I'm sure."

"Don't the others also think they are right?"

"Naturally."

"Well then, who is correct, you or they?"

"Professor, I've noticed that you always do that when we get to that kind of question."

"What do I do when we get to what kind of question?"

"Whenever we get to some issue where there is a right and a wrong you never say who's right or wrong, or you almost never agree with one side or another. You just say that there are two sides or several points of view or something like that. I think you know the answer and I also think you have an opinion of your own on it. You just don't want to take sides, or something. It's very annoying."

"What does being annoyed do to your ability to learn about things, Mr. Harris?"

"I get frustrated and mad."

"What are you likely to do when you get frustrated? Will you stop to learn?"

"Right now, you're just doing to me what you did before. I know I'm right in thinking that schools are too hung up on the loyalty bit, and a lot of people think so. Do you deny that?"

"No," said the professor, "I don't deny that many people think so, on the condition that you won't deny that there are a lot of people who think the exact opposite. In fact, there is some evidence to indicate that the others, those who disagree with you, are in the majority."

"I don't care about that. They're wrong."

"If there are very many of them, and very few of you, who is more likely to have his way, Mr. Harris, you or they?"

"Well, I think they've been having their way all along, anyway."

"But, as I just told you, they are saying that a lot of our trouble in the country with young people is the fault of insufficiently strong inculcation of respect for authority and of loyalty to the country."

"But you know that's a crazy way of reasoning."

"I know no such thing. I'm satisfied with showing you that the schools' concern with political loyalty reflect deep-seated feelings among the population and its leaders that it is one of their purposes."

"There! You did it again," responded Harris, with anger. "You said that you're satisfied in showing what's going on, but you won't take a position on whether it is right. That's as bad as saying that whatever is going on is right, even if you know it's wrong."

"But, supposing that you don't know whether it's wrong?"

"Do you mean you think it's right?"

"And, supposing you don't know it to be right, either?"

"That's absurd," said Harris.

"What's absurd?" asked the teacher.

"That something isn't either right or wrong."

"Is it?"

"Sure, it is. Everybody knows that."

"Impossible. I'm part of everybody and I don't know it."

"You're just saying that to tease me."

"Now I'm being called a liar," protested the teacher, arms akimbo. "My task here is to probe beyond the simple levels of belief in right or wrong, so that we can understand the effects of people thinking that one thing or another is right or wrong in the political system. Regardless of who's right or wrong, public schools in a democratic political system are inevitably the focus of intense conflict over the political uses of the institution. The only way to end that conflict is to establish beyond all dispute the precise relationship between school and society and to maintain that relationship in the face of all possible disagreement over who's 'right' or 'wrong.' Should either antagonists ever get complete control over that question without being subject to disagreement or protest, something very important will have changed in the political system itself, and not just in the schools."

"You're overlooking the fact that the political loyalists have control of the educational system anyway, even though there is criticism. It doesn't make any difference."

"I suppose one of the differences between us, Mr. Harris, is that your language is fairly sweeping. I agree that political authority and educational control are closely linked in many instances. But the people in educational institutions, including those in this very classroom, are able to exercise political criticisms even with the help of the very authorities you seem to be decrying. I agree that there are limits beyond which, even in a liberal setting, students and teachers may not be permitted to go. But, in light of recent events all over the world, I wonder what the limits are? It is the subject of important controversy wherever controversy is the traditional habit of the political culture. But even where there is not supposed to be any controversy over such questions, it exists anyway, even in unorthodox and dangerous ways. The portrait of totalitarian society as it is supposed to exist differs sharply with what really happens. Moreover, and here is a terribly important addition, schools are neither the only source of information about a society nor the only source of attitudes toward it, even though teachers, principals, and students, to say nothing of other people, like to think of them as all powerful and irresistible.

"Well," the teacher interrupted himself, "that was a long speech. We must move on. Are there any further questions about education and politics?"

There was another question. Miss Cohen asked it.

"Don't you think that despite what you said, that governments use schools to perpetuate the power structure too, and not just their own existence?"

"How are you using the term 'power structure' here?" asked the teacher.

"Well, I mean that the way things are arranged, the sons and daughters of the rich and the upper classes get a much better education than the poor kids do, and in that way they can stay on top of things."

"All right, but you might have added something to that by pointing to the special cases of the education of black youngsters and of American Indians. In these cases there was, for a long time, an apparently deliberate policy of providing only the most marginal kinds of learning and many people agree that we're still a long way from providing them a good education. Yes, in a general sort of way I would not disagree with what you have said, even though it lacks certain detail and does not account for the exceptions to the rule which, in the United States, and other places, has been remarkably great. Even higher education of good quality is now accessible to nearly all who can absorb it and this was accomplished by political means. And further, the redress of educational wrongs against Negroes and Indians, to the extent it is being accomplished, is also finally passing through the political process. The struggle over the extent to which the educational system should be egalitarian, like the political system, is a political question. A bright son or daughter of poor parents can and does get a far better education than an unintelligent child of the rich. That's because he knows how to make use of it. It has to do with more than politics, but politics makes it possible by providing the means for it."

"But isn't it true that the people who really run things in this country are well educated, and come mostly from middle- and upper-class homes?"

"I'm uncomfortable about the phrase, Miss Cohen. By and large, greater political influence is in the hands of middle-class persons, but the question about who 'runs things' is ambiguous. Some 'things' are run by people whose education has played only a marginal role in their lives. They inherited their places or their properties, or their attitudes and aptitudes. In other things, such as the scientific establishment, or perhaps even education, leadership is far more widely dispersed. The social origins of college faculty are now very diverse, mostly because of public policies in education in the years since 1945. In other words, political power has tended to produce some changes in the rulers of this country by making education more widely accessible. At any rate, even if what you said were true, it certainly would not refute the intimate connection between education and politics, would it?"

"But some kinds of educational institutions give you a better break in life by the kinds of contacts you make!" resisted the student.

"I think it is widely believed to be the case, but I'm not too sure it's true. The best colleges value intelligence, discipline, creativeness, and hard work most highly and they are populated by outstanding students and by leading scholars and teachers. At their best, educational institutions are not at all like political systems. In a democracy, there is stress on equality, especially in politics, but in a university the central values are intellectual excellence and not everybody is created equal in that, so there is a good deal of tension between the two. You can and do get great intellects from all parts of the social system."

Again the professor interrupted himself. "It seems to me that my responses on the subject of education are a good deal more extended than they were on other subjects in our discussion. That's probably because of what I do and where we are. Were I a water engineer, I could probably not stop talking about water, either. It's a professional hazard. Miss Cohen has directed our attention to a fundamental problem in society which joins education and politics where they both live, so to speak. Since ancient times the question has been considered whether ruling over men is not the kind of work which calls for special kinds of knowledge and which only a few specially gifted persons may acquire. Once having gotten it, and being revealed as possessing the knowledge of ruling, such men, it was proposed, should be given full authority to rule over others because, after all, the others do not know about ruling, even as they don't know about medicine or music or astronomy. This is the Platonic argument and it is fundamentally antidemocratic, and very tempting, especially for those who have studied politics and other similar subjects. To the extent that universities promote excellence and intellectual gifts, they do not exactly jibe with egalitarian political ideas and practices. For Plato, the problem of government was, in the last analysis, exactly the same as the problem of education, differing in no regard from it. Most modern analysts believe the matter is a bit more complicated than that, to say the least."

Miss Cohen came back to say, "Well, don't you think that we'd have a better political system if it were run by the best people with the best minds?"

"Better for whom?" retorted the professor, with a smile.

"He won't say yes or no to anything like that, so why do you ask him? You heard what he did to me when I asked about the loyalty thing in the public schools." The interlocutor was Mr. Harris, who had never been satisfied.

Miss Cohen, surprised at the interruption, fell silent momentarily, but recovered her spirit to ask, "I meant better for everybody, of course. Isn't it logical that better educated people would make better decisions?"

"Perhaps it is logical, but I'm inclined to doubt it, anyway," responded the teacher. "But I don't think it matters whether it's logical. For purposes of political understanding what matters most is whether it accords with the experience of mankind as we understand it."

"I'm not sure what you're driving at," replied the student.

"It's a very difficult point, in the first instance, and an extremely old controversy which seems, in the nature of things, not capable of settlement. It depends almost entirely on what you think politics is all about, you see. If you think it's a matter of applying superior wisdom to the problems of society, you'll come to one set of conclusions about it, and if you think that everybody, regardless of educational attainments, knows his own problems best and must be consulted about them, you'll come to another one."

"Well, what do you believe, sir?" asked the student guilelessly.

"Ha—there she goes again," called Harris. "I told you he won't say. That's the game here, don't you see? So why do you keep on asking him those questions?"

"To an extent, Miss Cohen, Mr. Harris is right. You'll have to figure out my own position from evidence other than my direct replies. I'm trying to get you to examine all manner of argument seriously, and I'm trying to follow that rule. So, let's get back to the problem. You were saying . . . ?"

"If you think that being better educated doesn't make that much difference in making better decisions, what's the sense of educating so many people so well?"

"You are persisting in your definition of politics as a matter of making wise choices by learned people. I suggested before, as you know, that's not the only definition. But, if you're asking whether I think that uneducated people can make wise choices, or that educated people can make bad ones, I would agree to both possibilities."

"But you didn't answer *my* question. Why do we educate so many people, if it makes no political difference?"

"Well, Miss Cohen, the demand for widespread education is not necessarily a political kind of demand. It might have to do with certain kinds of social changes, or with the increase of abundance in society, or with greater need for literacy or technical expertise, and not only with politics. But in some ways it *does* make a political difference whether many people are well educated. In some special way it makes a political system possible. That showed up during our discussion on teaching loyalty, didn't it?"

"I understand your problem, I think," continued the teacher. "The point I was working on was this: politics is a means by which a great variety of purposes may be accomplished. In our case, the distribution of educational benefits is a direct outcome of politics. Through political means the laws were passed requiring attendance in school and through political means the money is appropriated for paying for all of the things that make it possible to have so many people in schools for so many years. Politics are used to determine the rough outlines of the curricula and a thousand other minutiae of the educational processes. *But*, political processes serve as methods by which to accomplish purposes that are, in their origin, hardly political at all. Doing calculus, reading Latin, or running the mile in less than four minutes are all things you can learn in school, as are computer mechanics, poetry, history, woodturning, archeology, and zoology. These are not, in *themselves*, political. But they may be obtained by political means and they may have political consequences. Now, are we a little closer to understanding?"

"I think so," the student agreed, hesitatingly. "In other words, it *may* make a political difference for so many people to be educated, even if that wasn't the intent?"

"I'll accept that formulation for the present, if you'll add one more point."

"What is that?"

"Different kinds of political systems, so-called, tend to favor the kinds of educational systems most conducive to their own perpetuation."

"Well, I guess that changes it some, because it makes it look as if education *is* politically motivated," replied the student.

"At least," said the teacher, "it shows that political calculations are not omitted from the reasons for building educational institutions and programs."

"OK," Miss Cohen said cheerfully. "I've got some answers, anyway."

"Fine. Now may we turn our attention elsewhere? Some educational problems have specific characteristics of great importance to the nature of political authority. Can any of you mention a problem of that nature?"

There was a silence, which the teacher broke by saying:

"All right, then, let's take a poll. I'm going to ask each of you to name three of the most significant educational problems with national political implications. I'll start in the rear of the class, and I'll put each of the lists you give me on the blackboard. In that way we'll get a kind of inventory which we can then discuss. You may want to justify your choices briefly. Be quick about it, because we haven't got much time."

Just as he prepared to write the first items on the blackboard, the proceeding was interrupted by Mr. Perry, who had waged a lively contest in the discussion of housing.

"Professor, don't you think that's a big waste of time?" he said. "I mean, you're going to have to write thirty-five lists of three items each. Your arm'll get so tired and it's going to be very repetitious. All the lists are going to be the same, aren't they?"

"Well, I'm prepared to go ahead with it," replied the professor, "but I am interested in your reasons."

"It's easy. The most important educational problem connected to politics is the school segregation business, don't you think so?"

"Actually, I was trying to find out whether the class thinks so, Mr. Perry."

"Well then, why not ask?"

"Wasn't I asking?"

"No, I mean, why not ask them how many of them think that's true about school segregation? Wouldn't that be a good idea?"

"Yes, I think so. It would be quicker, too, of course. So, let's see. How many of you in this classroom believe that the problem of racial segregation and integration is the most important political problem in education in the United States."

There rose a solid wall of hands. Everybody's arm was raised high. For the sake of form, the teacher asked: "And who disagrees?"

There were no takers.

And then he asked, "And who abstains?"

None did. And so it was settled.

"I told you it was simple," said Perry, triumphantly.

"So you did, and I thank you. Now then, what makes this educational problem political?"

Hands were everywhere. The teacher picked on one.

"Well," its owner replied, "that's not hard. It's political for a lot of reasons. First, the schools are public. That makes the controversy political. Next, people who wanted to end racial segregation had to go to the court and get a case decided in their favor, and that's political because the courts are a part of the government. And also it's political because the rules of segregating students were laws made by governments. Golly, when you think of it there's very little about it that isn't political. You could even say that the reason for segregating Negroes was political, in the first place. Couldn't you?"

"Well, how would you do that?" prompted the teacher.

"It was part of a whole trend of whites coming back to power after the defeat and military occupation of the South following the Civil War."

"And we have already spoken of that in connection with the politics of cotton, haven't we? Now, what do you suppose we can learn from the fact that the process of segregation was carried out by political means and that desegregation, or the attempt to reverse the policy, uses the same techniques of political action?"

"I don't know what you're driving at," responded the student.

"All right. Let's break it down into the components. Why do you suppose the legislators who wanted to segregate students by race bothered to make laws about it? Wasn't there another way of doing it?"

"But how can you do it otherwise?" the puzzled student asked.

"One might have attempted to let people do what they please about racial contacts, and encourage both groups to keep away from each other by means of social pressure or custom, or economic power, or some such method."

"But then there might have been less segregation," the student concluded.

"Are you suggesting it wouldn't have worked out?" the teacher urged.

"I don't know. I always thought they used the law so that they could punish black people who didn't want to be segregated, and white people who wanted to help the blacks."

"Punish them?"

"Yes, you know, accuse them of breaking the law and bring them to trial and send them to jail."

"But weren't black people already being punished in a way by whites without benefit of the law during those years?"

"You mean the Klan and all of that?"

"Yes, I do."

"But the Klan couldn't put people in jail. I mean, the white segregationists were after legal power. That way nobody could resist."

"I see," said the teacher, slowly. "Is that, do you suppose, in the nature of political authority—that resistance is illegal?"

"Sure. Isn't that the whole thing?"

"At least, it's a very important part of it, yes. Now let us look again. Are the reasons that the opponents of segregation are using political means to bring it to an end the same reasons as those used by the segregationists to bring it about?"

"Do you mean that the integrationists also want to use the law so that the violators can be punished for breaking it?"

"Yes, I do mean that."

"Well, yes, I guess so. Yes, that's right. That's just how it is."

"Fine," the teacher beamed. "Now what does that tell you about politics?"

"The same thing I was told by the segregationist use of the law. It's a way of using power that's impossible to resist, except if you are willing to be punished for it."

The teacher permitted a small dramatic pause to develop.

A voice from the middle of the class was heard to say, "Yes, but the integrationist had no choice. When segregation was legal the only way to end it was by getting the law changed, wasn't it?"

"The only way?"

"What else could they do?"

"What do you think?"

"I really don't know."

"What have people done in other circumstances when they've found the laws unbearable?"

"Sometimes they have revolutions."

"Yes, sometimes they do. Is *that* political?"

"What kind of question is that?" the irritated student replied.

"I beg your pardon?" the teacher inquired.

"I'm sorry, I don't mean to be fresh or anything like that but, of course revolutions are political. Everybody knows that. What else could they be?"

"Are you asking me a serious question?" the professor inquired.

"Yes, I am."

"Revolutions can span the entire gamut of human experience. There are esthetic revolutions, intellectual ones, social revolutions, and other kinds as well. It depends in part on how careful one is in the use of language. Some people use words very loosely and that makes for a certain amount of mischief. But, to return to our subject, do you suppose that the school segregation problem had the ingredients of a political revolution?"

"I really don't know," replied the student. "Weren't there some other things that could have been done?"

"For example," challenged the teacher.

"Well, they could have disobeyed the law and refused to go to school or send their children as long as they were segregated."

"Yes, that was certainly an alternative."

Perry spoke up quickly. "That's a silly way of acting. It would just play into the racists' hands. Black kids wouldn't have gotten any education at all in that case. They probably wouldn't even have bothered to punish them."

"And so, what else was there to be done?" the teacher pressed, looking for another participant.

A student who had participated prominently in an earlier discussion returned to say, "You remember when somebody here said that when people elect the representatives who make the laws they have to give them what the voters want or else they don't get reelected?"

"Yes, I recall that very distinctly. Do you suppose there is a point to be made about segregated education here?"

"Yes, don't you think so? The state legislators who made segregation laws could be persuaded to change them, couldn't they? That would have been a good strategy, wouldn't it? That way there wouldn't have to be revolution or civil disobedience."

The laughter which followed this point was not general, but quite audible and widely shared. The teacher's mien remained serious as he returned to the student who had just provoked it. "What do you think of the reaction to your analysis?" he asked.

"I don't see what's so funny, actually," the surprised student replied.

"Can't you think of any reason why that strategy couldn't work in the states where racial segregation was most serious?"

"But all through the whole discussions we have been having here you and some of the students in the class have talked about how the government has to respond to voters."

"Yes, we did say that, and we'll take none of it back. But which voters were you talking about?"

"Well, you know, the people who elect state legislators."

"But who is that?"

"Well, the people who vote."

"All right—but who does the voting?"

The student's face registered consternation. There was some point of fact which escaped him for the moment.

The teacher came to his help. "In your opinion, was the influence of black voters sufficiently strong to protect their interests in preventing a segregated-school system from being established during the 1880s and 1890s and after in the southern states where most of the Negroes lived?"

Among the poorly suppressed snickers of the class, the student saw the light. "Sure, I got it. Of course, how could I have been so stupid?" he smilingly confessed.

But the teacher did not let him off, and demanded, "What have you got?"

"There were state laws and customs that kept black people from voting; I knew that all along, but I couldn't put it together properly. That's it then. The vote. They didn't have the vote."

"All right then. Without a vote there's not enough influence and therefore legislative influence is a poor method. So, we have dismissed revolution, we've dismissed civil disobedience, and now we discover that the ordinary linkage between people and their government can't be worked because of the effective denial of the vote to enough blacks to make a political difference. Now what?"

Before the student could reply, another participant moved in. He announced himself as Bob Freeberg.

"Look, why take so long with this business? Everybody knows by now that school desegregation was accomplished by the Supreme Court. So the strategy they could use and did use was to bring a lawsuit against the government for violating the constitution. They did that, and it worked."

"I'm going to be a little contrary, Mr. Freeberg. When did they do that?"

"Oh, you remember, don't you? Back in the fifties."

"The fifties?"

"Yes, don't you remember that decision?"

"Yes, I do. I thought you might have been talking about a lawsuit in the United States Supreme Court of 1896 or so."

"1896?" the student said.

"Yes, the opponents of racial segregation laws didn't wait around until after World War II to challenge those laws in court. They pursued a strategy available for almost everybody who can't use other avenues of redress. They took the State of Louisiana to court and claimed that its laws violated the Fourteenth Amendment of the Constitution, because they denied them the equal protection of the laws. And, of course, they got their decision."

"What decision was that?" asked Freeberg.

"It was the decision of the Court that segregation was not a denial of the equal protection of the laws as long as the facilities for both races were equal."

"In other words, they lost."

"That's right, they did."

"So what good was the strategy?" asked Freeberg.

"The strategy was first rate, because it was, in fact, the only one available which, if used and if it were decided in their favor, would work. But it failed because of the Court's decision, and not because of its inherent character as a strategy."

"That's really a very fine point, isn't it?"

"We'll see, Mr. Freeberg, we'll see. Did you think it was a bad strategy when you reminded me that it had been used in the 1950s?"

"No, but it worked then, didn't it?"

"Yes, in a way it did, but it was the same strategy, wasn't it?"

"But it was good only because it worked."

"I will simply disagree and say that a strategy is good when it takes into consideration all of the elements necessary to lead to a desirable result. It is tested not only by its outcome, but by its ingenuity and the intelligence of its design. The strategy in both cases was the same. In 1896 it didn't work and in 1954 and 1955 it did." The teacher had made the point with force and a somewhat elevated tone of voice, pounding his left fist into the open palm of his right hand.

"But it didn't work at all. Freeberg is wrong *and* you're wrong, too, professor."

The disputant was John Mason, who had reminded the class early in the discussions about the prime purpose of government in the maintenance of order.

"It's true that the Supreme Court decided that segregation was a violation of the Fourteenth Amendment, but after that it took a long time and caused a lot of trouble to enforce the decision. Everybody knows it's really not finished with public school segregation, but the decision was made long ago."

"I don't think you've demonstrated that I was wrong, Mr. Mason. I will grant you that the decision was not as effective as it was expected to be. But it did come out right, from the point of view of the people who brought the suit, didn't it?"

"Yes," the reluctant student agreed, "they got the right decision, but it didn't do them as much good as they had hoped."

"Are you suggesting that it would have been better not to bring the suits from which the decision came?"

"No, I don't think that's what I'm driving at. It's just that the decision caused a lot of uproar and it took a lot of political authority to back up."

"How do you mean that?"

"Didn't a lot of southern states resist by passing laws repudiating the decision?"

"Yes, some did, or at least they tried."

"And didn't the President have to get into it? I mean, he even had to send parts of the army into Little Rock to put down the governor and help nine kids go to high school."

"Yes and, in fact, presidential power had to be used again in Alabama and in Mississippi to back up court orders for school integration. What are you driving at, Mr. Mason?"

"It seems to me that even the legal power of the government wasn't enough to integrate the schools."

"It wasn't?" asked the astonished teacher.

"Well, that's not exactly what I meant. I meant that even the legal power of the government can't make things happen immediately after the law has been changed. People just don't seem to obey of their own accord. I think they should, of course, but some laws make them do things they really hate and when that happens, laws are hard to enforce, aren't they?"

"Yes, undoubtedly they are," agreed the teacher. "Are you suggesting that the difference between what government demands and what it is able to obtain is often very large?"

"Isn't it easier to obey a law you agree with?" Mason continued.

"Yes, but it must be obeyed anyway, mustn't it?" replied the teacher. "Don't you recall the early part of this discussion about schools and politics in which it was suggested that the segregationists and the integrationists were both following courses of action which would result in using the instrumentalities of government to enforce their own wishes, to protect what each of them regarded as their proper interest in society against the other?"

"Sure I do; it was just a few minutes ago."

"Does it seem to you that, in a very special way, they were therefore in agreement with one another, even though they wanted diametrically different kinds of things?"

"In agreement? How is that possible? You just said they wanted diametrically different things."

"Yes, but by the methods they adopted to obtain them they conceded that these things were obtainable with any degree of security only by means of employing the unique characteristics of political authority."

"Well, I guess I'd have to agree, but it seems like a paradox," the student consented.

"Perhaps," said the teacher, "a paradox is merely the unusual placement of things whose true relationships are often misunderstood."

"It sounds very pretty," said the student, "but I don't know what it means."

"You mustn't be too demanding, Mr. Mason. Let us merely suppose that, for the time being, we're done with school and politics."

And that's what they did.

13

"... By the Sweat of Thy Brow..."

When the class had reassembled the teacher introduced the new dialogue to the waiting class, which had, up to that time, no inkling of its contents. "During our last discussion," he began, "we examined the political implications of the very place in which we are now engaged in the pursuit of political understanding. We have to take another step now. I'm sure you realize that only a portion of the population of your age group is either privileged or interested enough to attend school. The rest of mankind are out in what is sometimes called the real world, working at some sort of gainful employment which seems to be a precondition of life for most, if not all of us. It doesn't take a lot of imagination to see that such a universal phenomenon as the need to work must have fairly deep political implications and we turn next to some of these problems. That may be a bit more difficult for us to do because of the fact that most of you, if not all of you, have had relatively little experience with the world of work, since, even at your age, you're still going to school for your own as well as society's good, presumably."

The teacher's introductory statement was interrupted, somewhat rudely, by an ill-concealed, and resentful grunt, followed by the comment, "I'm working right now."

Turning in the direction of the speaker, the teacher invited him to make his contribution public. "What do you work at?"

"I'm a bartender down the street; don't you remember me?"

The burst of laughter from the class was full and genuine. The surprised instructor confessed, "No, I don't."

"Well," the relenting student admitted, "I've never actually seen you there but I've heard you come there now and then."

"Oh, yes," agreed the teacher, "I do. Office space being what it is, one must hold conferences with one's students somewhere, right?"

"And it's a real nice place," the bartender said.

"Have you been working there long?" asked the teacher.

"No, I started this semester. I had a job before this one, but I needed one closer to school so I wouldn't have to travel so far."

"Do you suppose, Mr. ...."

"Ryan."

"Do you suppose, Mr. Ryan, that your work is related to politics and government?"

"Oh, yes in lots of ways. Some of them have already been discussed in the classroom, but yes there are a lot of things political about it. Well, for one thing, bars have to be closed on election days and on primary days too."

"Why?" asked the teacher.

"I heard that in the old days political bosses used to give out drinks right next to the polls and influence a lot of votes that way. Also, a man who has been in the business a long time told me that in some places a long time ago, they put the voting booths right in the barroom and they would set 'em up as the voters came in. But that was before the women got the vote. So now it's all messed up and everybody goes to the polls stone cold sober."

The amusement of the teacher was, in large part, shared by the students, and the professor was tempted to pursue the line, but there were other things to be done.

"Are you aware of any public controls on the bartending trade, Mr. Ryan?"

"Public controls? What do you mean?"

"Do you have to be licensed to be a bartender?"

"No, I don't have a license. My boss does, though."

"Your boss? Is that a license for tending bar or for maintaining a place of public accommodation?"

"I guess it's a license for having a liquor-serving business."

"What do you suppose justifies such a license?"

"I guess it's a way for government to keep control over a business activity. I think you have to keep certain hours, and you used to have to serve food, and keep the place clean, and I think also that if you had a criminal record you were not allowed to own that kind of business. I'm not sure why."

"Good," the teacher said. "There's a public interest in the supervision of certain kinds of establishments. In the case of bars, it probably was established very early in history. Protection of the safety of places of public accommodations. Do you know of any other kind of work which cannot be done except through governmentally granted permission?"

"I guess you have to have a license to be a barber."

"Right. What else? Why don't you try to enumerate a few activities like that, Mr. Ryan?"

"Oh, all right. Let's see. Doctors, nurses, teachers, lawyers, plumbers, electricians, certified public accountants, taxi drivers, airline pilots, ship's captains, ah—I guess I'm running out."

"What do you think is the general purpose of public control over the people who do work of that kind?"

"Well, I think it's fairly obvious. All of those people have important responsibilities to do a certain kind of work. Somebody has to make sure they know what they're doing and that they keep doing it well. So, they have to be educated or trained in a certain way and have to pass tests. In some cases they have to be tested every few years. Isn't that true with doctors?"

"I think people are talking about it, but it has not been accomplished yet. Why would people want to have doctors periodically tested?"

"Well, it would be a way of making sure they're keeping up with advances in medicine."

"Right, it would."

"Mr. Ryan, how far do you suppose one could carry this business of public supervision of trades and professions?"

"I don't quite get your question. What do you mean how far? Do you mean how many kinds of people could be included, or something like that?"

"Yes, or how many different kinds of occupations could be included?"

"That's hard to say. I guess everybody who has some kind of responsibility that has to do with health, or professional competence like accountants, or people who have to be trustworthy, like lawyers, could be included."

"Do you suppose political loyalty is one of the things that testing of that kind seeks to insure?"

"Political loyalty?"

"Yes, don't you think that it has anything to do with occupational tests?"

"I thought it was only to make sure that people knew what they were doing and that they were trustworthy that you had licenses and controls like that."

"Yes, it is, but did you know that teachers are commonly being asked to affirm their support of the state and federal constitutions, and, until recently, many of them were also required to swear that they were not inclined towards political subversion? Or, take the case of soldiers of all kinds. Wouldn't you want to make sure that they are politically reliable as well as competent? Or, what about all the many hundreds of thousands of public servants? As you know, most public bureaucracies are based on the principle of the division of labor and vocational or professional competence. Almost the only way to become a civil servant is to pass some sort of test of competence, and, of course of political reliability."

"You know, I never thought of it this way. That must mean that there are just millions and millions of people who have to have some sort of license to practice their work, or who have to pass some sort of test before they can get a job. I just never thought of it that way."

"On the other hand, there are many others who don't, aren't there?" the teacher asked and continued, "the world of business, advertising, of buying and selling and trading and building has a lot of nontested, nonlicensed people in it, doesn't it? There doesn't seem to be a lot of public interest in those kinds of occupations. That's even true of certain so-called skilled trades which are not governmentally regulated, for the most part."

The class was very attentive. Hands were everywhere. The teacher recognized the owner of one of them:

"Is there a question?"

"No, but I have a comment. A lot of the jobs you mentioned may not require any licenses, but even private employers give tests. I wanted to be a clerk in a department store and they gave me a whole battery of psychological tests and aptitude tests and interviews. It was just a job behind the counter selling handbags and they did that to me. I felt I was being screened for the CIA. So there must be a lot of employers doing that. That adds a lot of people, because I think if you don't do well on one of those tests they don't take you in quite a few jobs. That's almost as important as being tested by the government, isn't it?"

"Why do you suppose they gave you those tests?"

"The personnel manager said that they have to make sure that their people don't hurt their customers' feelings and are well mannered and so forth. I think that's very funny. Some of the people who were working there would make you crawl up a wall. It must be that somebody in a testing service sold them a bill of goods about what they can find out with tests like that."

"In other words," the teacher said, "we have a case of a widespread application of an idea that competence and faithfulness in doing one's work can be assured or promoted by the giving of tests which measure it, and the idea is applied not only to the protection of the public interests by governmental agencies, but is also prevalent in private businesses in which some sort of competence is also valued."

"How about school?" someone wanted to know.

"School?" the teacher asked.

"Well you can't get into certain colleges without some good academic averages which you earn course by course in high school, and you can't get into graduate school or professional school without having an outstanding record in college, and in college you can't get a degree with honors without doing well. That adds a lot of people to the tested population, doesn't it?"

"If you think of going to school as an occupational category—and I see no reason why one shouldn't—it adds about forty-five or so million people in the United States and seven million of them in college alone."

"Yeah—and now they even want to license the automobile mechanics," someone called out.

The laughter was general.

Taking advantage of the temporary interruption, the teacher decided to shift the topic elsewhere, and returned to his friend, the bartender:

"Would you tell us, Mr. Ryan, what wages you are earning now?"

"When you're a student like I am," Ryan replied, "they don't give much better than the minimum. It's not really skilled work, you know, and there are a lot of us looking for work. So I get the minimum."

"The minimum?" the teacher asked. "Do you mean the minimum you're willing to take or something else?"

"No, not that. I mean the legal minimum. There's a law, you know, saying that people must be paid a certain minimum wage. And in jobs like mine, that's what we get. I think that I come under the state law."

"Do you suppose you would have to work for less money if that minimum-wage law were not in effect?"

"I guess so. Wasn't that the idea of passing the law in the first place?"

"Yes, it was," the teacher replied. "But wages paid to people differ on the basis of a lot of considerations. Minimum-wage laws have an effect on only a small portion of the working population. I thought part-time bartenders might work for high wages so that the laws have less impact."

"I know that the regular bartenders make a lot more money than the minimum," the student responded and continued, "that's because they have a strong labor union. But they don't let part-timers in. They hardly even let you work. We have to pay a fee to the union. I guess that's the way they protect themselves against nonunion men taking over their work."

"Are you saying that the unionized bartenders have wages that result from their contracts with the employers?"

"Yes, isn't that how it works? You join a union and the wages are set in a contract. That's the idea of having a union isn't it?"

"Yes, it is the idea, or at least a part of it. What prevents the employers from hiring people who want to work at wages different from the union contracts?" the teacher asked.

"Isn't that illegal?" asked Ryan. "I thought that when you have a union contract, the employer isn't allowed to hire labor at different prices. I mean why have a contract?"

"All right, that's true. In that case, why would an employer be willing to sign such a contract if he can get workers to perform the job for less money than the union members?"

"But he doesn't have choice, does he? I thought the law said that employers have to bargain collectively when their employees vote to join a labor union. Doesn't the law say so?"

"Yes, it does provide that, broadly speaking, give or take a few details. Now Mr. Ryan, you've pointed out that your work is touched by public law at two important places, so far as your wages are concerned. Your own wage is set legally and your fellow employees are unionized under the provisions of the law compelling a certain kind of bargaining process between workers and employers. Politically speaking, what's the significance of laws such as these?"

"Do you mean why there are laws like that? Well, I don't know, of course, but I guess they were passed to protect the interests of people who have to work for a living."

"Assuming that you're right, why do you suppose that their interests, as you call them, *need* the protection of the law?"

"We found out in these discussions that almost everybody can get their interests protected by the government. Why shouldn't people who work for a living get it too?" the student asked.

"I'm not inquiring about the morals of it, Mr. Ryan. You will recall that, when we discussed other interests which have succeeded in obtaining the protection of government that they were able to do so on the basis of some politically enforceable demand, rather than on the basis of justice, alone. That was true, if you recall, of the various forms of agricultural policies, of the tariff, of doctors, as well as of other policies and groups. Do you know how long the relationships between employers and employees have been regulated by protective legislation of that kind, Mr. Ryan?"

"I'm sorry, I don't know that."

The teacher, blaming himself somewhat for the unduly academic character of his question, treated it as a rhetorical one and said, "I guess it's time for another little lecture: In the United States, at least, wage laws date back to the Great Depression of the early 1930s. National legislation came into force in 1937. Before that, several states had experimented with wage regulation for women along with other kinds of labor laws. The adoption of such laws came as a result of long conflict, and, naturally, employers and employees were arrayed against each other. During the same period major changes came also in the laws governing the relationship between workers and employers over the question of unionization. Up until the 1930s it had been generally assumed that labor unions were illegal in the sense that they were considered to have no legally protectable right to require an employer to make a contract over wages and working conditions with his workers who belonged to a union, nor that he could be prevented from hiring whomever he wanted to in his place of employment. In fact, there was a period when the union organizations were treated as unlawful conspiracies and strikes were also illegal in the sense that they could not be used to infringe upon or interrupt the business against which they were organized. Until the law changed it, employers could not be barred from firing or discriminating against workers who were trying to organize unions. In other words, neither the ability to organize unions nor the power to require employers to honor them as bargaining agents were legally protected. Aren't there any students in this classroom who are employed at a job protected by a union agreement?"

No hands were raised.

"Look around the classroom," instructed the teacher. "There's something important here isn't there? I wonder what it means?"

"I guess it has to do with the fact that we're full time students," one member of the class offered. "Everybody here who has a job at all, does part-time work, and around here the unions don't protect that kind of work."

"All right," the teacher agreed, "let's assume that's true now. It raises at least two other questions, doesn't it? The first one is this: How many of you in this class are engaged in gainful employment, as it is sometimes called?" To the teacher's surprise, almost two-thirds of the students' hands rose.

"I'm impressed," he said. "For purposes of discussing the politics of work, at least, it's a lucky thing that so many of you have at least some experience with certain aspects of it. But what do you suppose it means that so many of you are working at jobs in the first place?"

The wry amusement was written on the students' faces in plain terms, and one of them put it into words:

"That's simple, isn't it?" he opined. "It means we're none of us rich enough to go to school without earning some money. Tuition costs a lot and if you want to have a car to get around in, or if you don't constantly want to ask your parents for money, you have to get it somewhere. So, we work."

The nods of agreement were universal. "Do you suppose that economic problems of that sort are serious enough to keep people from becoming college students in the first place?" the teacher asked.

"Well," the first student replied, "a lot of people have to study at night so they can hold a job in the daytime. I read somewhere that in this country there are almost as many people studying in the evening in colleges as in the daytime. That must mean something like that, mustn't it?"

"Yes," the teacher agreed. "The major distinction seems to be economic in the cases you mention, even though there are many other reasons for going to night school. Now let me get to another question. How true is it, do you suppose, that in the world outside these university walls a major line of distinction between the population is the difference in their capacities to sustain themselves without working for wages or salaries? In other words, is the population of this and other countries mainly divided between people who must work for wages and salaries and those who don't need to?"

"Can I answer that?" asked a student in the front row. "I'm Jack Miller. Sure I think that's true. If I had enough money I wouldn't work and neither would anybody else, I'm sure. That's just plain common sense. If we didn't have to work we wouldn't."

"Who is this 'we' you're talking about?"

"The human race. Nobody would do any real work, if they didn't have to. I'm convinced of it. The smart ones fix it so that they don't have to do anything for themselves but they let the others do it for them."

"Surely there are at least some people who work for pleasure or for a sense of creativeness, or for altruistic reasons, don't you think?" the teacher asked.

"I'm afraid I don't, professor," the student replied. "There are all kinds of jobs. Some are well paid and some not, some are pleasant and others are not, but when you boil it down it's the same business. Even the best-paid jobs and the most pleasant ones, are still jobs. You have to do something to get money to live with."

"So, in your opinion, mankind is divided into those who have to work because they have no alternative and those who know how to manage to get by without having to do so, and, according to you, that amounts to having a choice or not having it."

"That's right."

"Unfortunately, Mr. Miller, we don't have the time to explore some of the interesting implications of your statement, but for the purposes of this classroom, we can at least accept your fundamental observation: in modern societies, overwhelming proportions of the adult populations have, as their only means of sustenance, some sort of salaried employment in an enterprise owned or managed by other people or in publicly owned or operated ones. That is a major social fact of the modern age. It accounts for the major social conflicts in most of these societies, and goes a long way towards explaining how economic and social interests are defined, organized and translated into political needs."

Miller, the advocate of nonworking responded, saying, "But that's how it's always been, hasn't it? I don't see what's so special about it in modern society. Our sociology professor argued the other day that the division of labor is really *the* major social problem. He said that the human race can't live without people working to produce things we need and want and that every society has to find ways of dividing the work somehow. So, there's nothing special about this society doing it too, is there?"

"No, Mr. Miller," the professor agreed, "there's nothing special about this society having a division of labor, but the division itself is rather unique and differs from those before the industrial revolution. Before the nineteenth century the proportion of manpower required to produce food was everywhere so great that only a small proportion of people could be spared for doing other things besides food production. The division of labor in agriculture makes for social organization very different from the industrial societies, even though each of them can be arranged in different ways. When techonology enables people to leave the land they congregate in large centers of population called cities which spread as the proportion of the industrial population increases. And, as they increase, their dependence on jobs with incomes increases, as does also their dependence on the social organizations which produce these jobs and which protect their interests in them. That whole pattern produces social conflict unknown in agricultural, rural or as some people have called it, traditional societies."

"I didn't understand all of that," the student replied. "What's it got to do with unions and with minimum wages, for instance?"

"How do you suppose labor unions got started, Mr. Miller, and why?"

"I thought it began during the middle ages, when the tradesmen had organizations to protect the prices of their labor against competition. They called them guilds, didn't they?"

"Yes, there are some historians who trace the beginning of unionism as far back as that. Most modern explanations don't bother with that, of course, since they are concerned with relatively recent events. But the idea of unionism is certainly not a very far cry from the fundamental principle of the guilds, even though guilds were concerned with more than the price of labor and had functions labor unions rarely engage in. Most of the explanations I know agree that modern unionism is a result of the fact that increasing numbers of individual workers saw themselves at a disadvantage in negotiating over satisfactory wages and working conditions with their employers. Those people were very powerful, comparatively speaking, and employed increasingly large numbers of people under the then-existing laws, had practically complete control over the conditions under which work was carried on, including the wage. If you wanted to find a single term for those reasons, I think one could use 'powerlessness' with telling effect. It was to try to correct social and economic powerlessness that labor unions were organized. So the question we have to ask is what kind of power workers might have in a union which they don't have without it?"

"All I can think of is that they can go on strike," Miller replied.

"What does that mean, in the relationship between the employer and workers?" asked the teacher.

"I guess he either has to shut down his plant or his shop or look for other workers."

"All other things being equal, those are the major choices he has, that's right. But, in many cases things were sometimes so balanced that employers had weapons of a kind that wouldn't make that necessary. You must all have seen movies or read novels about the mining towns in which some of these conflicts took place. Many of these showed how the employers' power extended far beyond the factory or plant or shop or mine. In the so-called company towns, bankers and other businessmen, including grocers and others, were economically beholden to the main employer. Often, the employer might be the main owner of residential housing occupied by the workers. Or, as was sometimes the case, local government officials were politically dependent on one or more of the big employers in towns and did their bidding."

"A lot of those movies show violence," the student said. "Was there a lot of that when unions organized?"

"Yes, there was, quite a bit. Some historians have kept track of the casualties, almost as if they were studying a kind of war. In fact the term 'industrial warfare' was very often applied to the struggle between employers and employees."

"That must have been the unions' doing, right? If the employers had all of the economic and political power you say they did, and if the law was on their side, the unions must have started the violence."

From the rear of the class came an objection. "I don't know a lot about it," a protesting student called out, "but there are a lot of stories that show everybody used violence and what's more they still do. You can read about it almost every day in the papers, isn't that right, professor?"

"Yes, there appears to be violence still in the constant friction between employers and workers, even if they are unionized. As in the other cases of violence in the society, the sources are not too easily pinned down. We know that both sides, so to speak, used violence. Fights would often break out between the striking workers and others who had been brought in to operate the plant or mine during the strike. Or, the local or state police, called in to protect the property of the owners would get involved in it. Quite often workers and their leaders felt that they not only had to fight the employers, but the police as well, because it was they who protected them by letting nonstrikers enter the factories. Occasionally unions and employers would resort to the hiring of professional gangsters or strong men. The struggle to unionize was a very bitter one, and, of course it's not over by any means."

"Don't you think that the workers were justified in trying to equal things out between themselves and their bosses? I mean if you say that things were as bad as they were for them, they had to find some way of protecting themselves, don't you think?"

"I suppose it depends on what you mean by the word justify. There's little doubt that large numbers of workers were helpless. The law was on the employers' side, economic power was almost completely located there, and political power was very often allied with it. Besides that, working people themselves were actually very divided on the merits of organizing, with many of them feeling that it was somehow wrong to force one's employer that way and with others feeling that they had less need for unions. The grievances of workers were, of course very deep. Certain industries, such as mining or steel-making were particularly harsh in their working conditions. So, yes, one could say that the justifications were thought to be very deep. Some of the leaders of unionism became great heroes for their followers because of their physical courage, their organizing skills, and their moral leadership. The controversies ran very deep and came to divide almost the whole of society, eventually, in a durable and deep way."

"In short, your answer to my question was yes, isn't that right?" the student persisted.

"Yes, looking back at that history, it is very difficult not to feel sympathetic to the workers, especially in view of how, subsequently, the relationships seem to have changed in the workers' direction. But we should try to see that the employers felt equally justified in taking the positions and in pursuing the tactics they did. It was true, after all, that, in terms of the law as it was then understood, their right to their property was clear and undisputed, and the workers' attempts at interfering with it was, legally speaking, wrong. So far as the intervention of local and state police is concerned, the cases were not always clear. If the employers had legal rights to be protected, governments were, of course, bound to come to their aid for that reason alone. What else do legal rights amount to, after all, but an expectation that their violation will be stopped by constituted authority? But there were, of course, many cases of illegal or brutal uses of the police power. The whole thing looks different when it's considered from that angle. Naturally, owners of factories would associate their legal rights with moral propriety. In that they were and are no different from others in society. You will recall that the same tendency appears among the combatants in the race problem, as well. I'm sure we'd find it a general condition of political life, and perhaps even mankind."

"But," the student persisted, "they finally did get what they wanted, didn't they? I mean the right to organize unions *was* made legal, and strikes were allowed, and the law requires collective bargaining. So you'd have to say that the struggle was won and that it was worth it, showing that violence is a successful method of changing things in society."

"Well, Mr. . . ."

"Porter. I'm Bill Porter. My father is a shop steward in a local union and we talk a lot about that. I'm sure he'll be interested in what you have to say about it."

"You've made several observations, Mr. Porter. Perhaps we can take them one by one. First, as to the effectiveness of violence. One would have to agree that violence is an effective and oft-used tool of social relations. But it doesn't only make for change; it can also be used to prevent it, and, of course it is very costly and dangerous and not very predictable or controllable. Still, all kinds of people resort to it from time to time. On the other hand, it is also one of society's main purposes, and especially that of government, to prevent it, suppress it, or to control its effects in some way."

"But you said yourself a while ago," Porter shot back, "that the police used to help employers in labor disputes. That doesn't look like they were trying to prevent violence. Besides, there's the whole business about government using violence in the first place. I mean don't governments have more guns and soldiers and policemen and other kinds of stuff than anybody else in the society? It seems to me that they have a hell of a nerve saying they exist to prevent it when they use it more than anybody else."

"Your comments are timely, Mr. Porter. It's true that one of the characteristics of government is that it is able to use violence to a greater degree than anyone else in society, and it has always been painfully obvious that this fact is *one* of the major problems of politics. Your comments present no real difficulty logically. One effective way of preventing violence is the superior ability to inflict it. That much is true for practically all government. So their claim that it is a major purpose of government to prevent it is still a good one. Our problems derive from the fact that governmental violence is often used to favor some in society over others, or it is used simply for the purpose of maintaining particular regimes against the will of the governed. But that's one of the great paradoxes of power, and as long as government exists among men, we'll just have to put up with that as best we can."

"You sound like you're saying that the only organization in the society justified in using violence is the government. Are you saying that?"

"Well, yes, I was saying something like it, of course. The very word 'justify' requires careful attention, however, as I suggested before. It is usually assumed that, legally at least, there is no justification for violence as long as legitimate governments exist. But such a definition is very narrow and it probably can't be made to stick, if only because there's no end to the kinds of justifications people seem to be able and willing to use on behalf of violent means of one sort or another. You will notice, Mr. Porter, that one of the major reasons for the changes in the public law about the relationship between employers and employees was a growing consensus in the country that the methods in use before the 1930s or so were just too costly and disruptive. It wasn't only that the country had come to take a different view of how wages and hours and working conditions should be determined, but also that the means used for settling them had become too costly. The justification was, in part, that regularized procedures, the details of which were carefully provided for in the law, were to be substituted for the methods of industrial warfare, including the violence which had been so widespread since the end of the Civil War. You have here, in part, a case of the government imposing its superior will on unwilling combatants."

"Well, anyway, I think that they were justified in raising hell. It got them a lot of protection didn't it?"

"Yes, it is true that the present labor law provides a good deal of protection to organized workers—and to nonorganized ones as well. But the workers are not the only beneficiaries, you will note, of that law. The frequent and violent interruption of economic activity by strikes, lockouts, and other such tactics, is socially very expensive.

"During the period of the late 1920s and 1930s, and even afterward, the general business of society was frequently interrupted by nationwide strikes in vital industries, such as transportation, communication, steel production, and others. Those strikes were very obviously regarded as something more than just a struggle between unions and employers. They showed that there might be a possibility that there is a limit beyond which the combatants would not be allowed to fight it out by paralyzing the economy. So the law was altered to place certain limits on nationwide strikes.

"Society benefits from a low level of combat, or from having the struggle between social classes carried on in civilized, nonviolent ways. Workers benefit from not having to be out of work or walking picket lines, or getting their heads bashed in and employers benefit from the increased security in the conduct of business. So, the benefits are fairly great, all around, aren't they?"

"That's right," Porter agreed, "but that only shows that I'm right. If the new labor laws do all of that, and if the old laws only satisfied the interests of one side then I think it was worth it to upset things to the point where there were just no alternatives to making new laws. I'm still right, I think."

"That's a very solid response, Mr. Porter. But, think a while longer, if you please. Why do you suppose it was the case that nineteenth-century labor law appears to us to have been so one-sided in its distribution of social protection? Do you think there was something inherently unjust about the content of the law at that time, that it was, in other words 'rigged' against workers and for the owners of property?"

"Well, yes, it seems that way, from the way it worked, doesn't it?"

"But do you suppose it got that way by some deliberate design whose intention it was to benefit one group in society to the detriment of another group, in such a way that the second group had no recourse?"

"Well, I don't really know that, of course, but that's how it seemed to work out, didn't it?"

"Yes, I agreed to that assumption a while ago, but perhaps the explanation of its origin is not the same as the observation of its consequences, Mr. Porter."

"I don't get that, professor."

"Look at it this way, Mr. Porter: What kinds of conditions would have had to prevail in society in, say, 1880 or so for the laws on the relationships of workers and their employers, or workers and their economic stake in society, to be of the same general content as they are now, about ninety years after that time?"

"I'm still not sure what you're driving at," Porter replied.

"I'll put it very simply. Before 1840 or so, society simply had no experience with the new conflict between employers and employees, which developed during the industrial revolution. The laws' values reflected the social conditions of an earlier time and could not have contained provisions for the problems to come. You see, I'm describing circumstances of a very dramatic kind, which may be thought of as the birth of a new age, in which gigantic social forces which never existed before were coming into being. It took some time for society to accommodate these social forces. The conflict between labor and capital, as it is sometimes called, has been called the birth pangs of that new age. For that reason the laws about those relationships have all got to be new and the politics of it were new as well."

"All right, but what has this to do with who's right and who's wrong or with justice?"

"I suppose," replied the teacher, "that depends on what you think is going on in society. As we discovered, the people we were talking about were of the opinion that they were right, and had justice on their side. A more dispassionate analysis may, perhaps, suggest that their discussion about justice was really a part of a larger combat in which ideas figured but were only a part of the struggle. The stakes of that struggle were obviously very great. They involved, first of all, the price of labor, which is one of the most important factors of the production of goods. Another way of saying that is that it was all about profits. Part of it was about economic power, since it dealt with the question of who had the capacity to decide on the level of wages to be paid and on determining the level of profits or the outputs of production. In another sense it was a struggle over political power, because its outcome could decide whether the government would favor the interests of the owners or of the workers. The struggle over getting the government on one's side was in some ways the most important one, because government is the most irresistible of social agencies. Whoever gets it on his side has a powerful ally."

The class seemed somewhat subdued by the list of serious consequences and no student could be immediately found to respond to them. Finally, a somewhat hesitant hand arose and its owner asked for the floor.

"You know," he said, "that sounds a lot like you were calling the conflict between workers and employers a kind of class struggle. Isn't that a Marxist theory?"

"Well," the teacher agreed, "I wasn't actually saying so, but I'm impressed that it should be suggested to you. What do you know about Marxist theories of politics, and do you think they might be pertinent here?"

"Well, I'm not sure," the student replied. "I never got that very straight. But didn't Marx say that political power is always on the side of the owners?"

"Yes, he did."

"And didn't he say that the conflict between workers and owners is a struggle between classes?"

"Yes, he did."

"Didn't you also say that the fight over unionization was a kind of class struggle?"

"Well, I hinted at it at least, yes. Are you suggesting that because Marx said so, one ought not to say that there are classes in society?"

"No, but I was never really clear what that was supposed to mean."

"Well, you're in good company, Mr. . . . ."

"Oh, yes. I'm Pointer."

"Well Mr. Pointer, the Marxian concept of class is not an easy one, nor is the concept of class struggle. In short, Marx argued that all of politics is a product of the owning class's needs to keep the nonowners in check and contributing their labor to the owners partly by force of law. He saw politics simply as the superstructure of economic power, and argued that only by depriving the owners of ownership could political power be destroyed, and only by the abolition of private property could classes in society be prevented from forming. That would, in turn, make political power obsolete. Hence, the secret for the abolition of political power was thought to lie in the abolition of private property which gave rise to it. Now what do you think this has to do with what I said?"

"Well, the fights between employers and employees look a lot like the kind of thing Marx was describing, don't they?"

"Yes, of course they do, and . . . ?"

"Isn't it true that when the government protected the employers, they were really helping them to exploit workers and keeping them defenseless?"

"It sure appeared like that to a lot of people, especially the workers, yes."

"Well, doesn't that make Marx right?" Pointer pressed.

"If government acted that way and only that way, and if political power were used for those purposes primarily or exclusively, it would appear to be very nearly the case, yes," the teacher responded.

"But isn't that true? I mean you yourself said that workers were helpless because they were powerless."

"Yes, I said that they were, but do they continue to be so? Remember what the argument made by Mr. Porter was all about a few minutes ago. He tried to show that workers are not powerless and that they are able to get political power to protect their interests, at least in part, didn't he?"

"So what does that show?" Pointer asked.

"Don't you think it shows that the relationship between workers and employers may be remedied by political means because, through politics, governments must respond to the needs of the governed?"

"Yes, but how can the government be made to respond if it defends the interest of the employers in their property?" the student inquired.

"Do you think that depends on how the government is constituted?" the teacher asked.

"What do you mean by that?"

Some impatient whispers were heard in the classroom, and one student called out impatiently, "The vote, the vote, right, professor?"

"Well, Mr. Pointer, what about it?" encouraged the instructor.

"Oh, you mean that political power has to satisfy the electorate so that they don't defeat the government at election time!"

"Well, don't you think it's a reasonable theory?"

"I guess so, but for some reason it doesn't seem a good enough answer."

"And why not?"

"Well, just look at it. I mean there are still a lot of poor people around and people who earn very little, and in that way the government doesn't seem all that responsive, does it?"

"And you might add also that there's still a lot of difference in the power in society between workers and employers and other rich people, mightn't you?"

"Oh yes, you could add that too."

"But, on the other hand you would also have to admit that government in democratic, industrialized countries acts as a prime redistributor of considerable wealth, wouldn't you?"

"How do you mean?"

Another student, ostensibly impatient and dissatisfied with Pointer's responses joined in. "My God, Pointer haven't you even heard of government taxing people by taking money from the wealthy to give it to the poor?"

"Sure I have, but I really don't see much evidence of it," Pointer responded.

The interruptor appealed to the teacher. "Isn't that what you meant, professor? I thought everybody knew about that. Boy, you should hear my father complain some time. He says every time he turns around there's some other form to fill out for the government and some other tax bill to pay just so the government can please the poor and keep the workers happy."

"What does your father do?" asked the teacher.

"Oh, all sorts of things. He has different kinds of plants that make things and he's always tangled up with some sort of bureaucracy, as he calls it."

"Do you recall any of his specific complaints?"

"Well, let's see. Oh yes, there's a lot of safety inspection of machinery going on, and of course the social security taxes. He has to contribute half of the payments for each employee's retirement fund, and for unemployment insurance, and then of course there's the minimum-wage law. He says that some of the labor that has to be done in his shops isn't worth the minimum wage, but he has to pay it any way. And of course he has several union shops, and he says that's really a bother. He thinks a lot of the men wouldn't join a union if the law didn't require him to bargain collectively with a union chosen by the majority of the men in the shop. Of course he thinks the government favors the unions because he thinks that that's how the politicians keep peace."

"A nice list. Who are you?" asked the teacher.

"I'm Jerry Kaiser."

"Now Mr. Kaiser weren't you the fellow who, a few minutes ago, interrupted our friend Pointer here?"

"Yes, I was. I could see your point coming a mile away but I didn't want to interrupt any earlier."

"But you had a point about the political power of the working people, as distinguished from their economic helplessness, didn't you? Do you want to make it again?"

"Well it's obvious, isn't it? What workers can't get from their own employers directly, they may be able to get from the whole class of employers by making the government get it for them. I mean all of the things my father complains about are really taken from him. At least that's what he says. But it's true, you know. He keeps talking about how nice it would have been if he were living in the age of the robber barons. Then he wouldn't have to worry so much about government and its concern for social welfare, and he could just keep piling up the wealth. We have a lot of arguments about it. I keep telling him that he's wrong, and that it's a much better society when working people have protection. I keep egging him on by saying that they're going to get more and more as time goes by and the rich will have less and less."

"Are you confident that's true?" the teacher asked.

"No, I don't really know, but isn't it true that political leaders have to be sure to provide some degree of increasing economic security, even if for no other reason than to try to stay in power?"

"Can I ask you a difficult question, Mr. Kaiser?" the instructor wanted to know.

"Why not?" the student replied.

"Do you suppose politicians would go as far as to eliminate private property as an economic principle altogether with the promise that if that were done the wealth could be equally shared, the differences in economic and social power be eliminated, and with it also the need for political power?"

"Oh you mean would they do it whole hog according to Karl Marx?"

"Right. What do you think?"

"In this country?" Kaiser wanted to know.

"You pick it," the teacher suggested.

Kaiser waited, ruminating about an answer. Hesitatingly, he began. "I guess you warned me," he said, thinking hard. He sat bolt upright then and called out "Hey, there are a lot of places where they did that, aren't there?"

"What did they do, Mr. Kaiser?"

"Abolish private property as a principle so that the wealth could be shared."

"What about the disappearance of differences in social power, economic inequality, and political power?"

"I guess that's a little different. But most of the communist countries and socialist countries claim they're working on it, don't they?"

"Now, a while ago you weren't sure whether the rich in this country would be getting less and less and the working people more and more. What about your guess about the disappearance of political authority in socialist or communist economies or countries?"

"I don't know. A lot of them seem to be dictatorships, aren't they?"

"Well, are they?"

"Yes, sure. Russia, Poland, China, Cuba, and so on. They're all dictatorships and some of them have been pretty bad."

"Are you sure that has anything to do with being socialist or communist, though? A lot of these countries were no different politically than they are now even before they became what is called socialist."

"Well, professor, aren't there any democratic countries that are socialist or communist? That would prove it."

"What would it prove?"

"Well, it would prove whether political leaders eliminated private property to satisfy a working population's demands."

"But why wouldn't that be proven by a dictatorship?" the teacher wanted to know.

"Because you never really know whether dictatorships are popularly supported, isn't that true?"

"In a general way, yes, but it's complicated by the fact that on occasion great popularity attaches to dictatorial regimes, in a kind of voluntary totalitarianism. But, Mr. Kaiser, we have a much more serious problem than that on our hands."

"What is that?"

"The problem of defining what a democracy is, of course," the teacher replied.

"I don't get it," replied Kaiser.

"Are you aware that, according to socialist doctrine, political democracy in the context of the private ownership of the means of production is regarded as logical and historical nonsense?"

"What?" the student exclaimed. "How come? I always thought that democracy meant government of the people, and that we had to have representative government because there were too many people to decide things with everybody's actual participation. Isn't that right?"

"Yes, we regard that explanation as fairly correct. But Marxists will tell you that as long as economic and social differences exist among people, political power will always be in the hands of the economic ruling classes. So far as they're concerned, democracy means first and foremost, what they call economic democracy. After that is accomplished, they claim, political rule can be eliminated and true self-rule be established."

"Boy is that ever ingenious," Kaiser said admiringly.

"Why so?"

"Well, it could be used as a justification for perpetual dictatorship, couldn't it?"

"How?"

"I mean how does it get decided whether there is economic democracy? It's a tight system. It makes it seem as if dictatorship were needed to establish economic democracy first, and it leaves it up to the dictators to decide whether the time has come for self-government."

"On the other hand, Mr. Kaiser, Marxists will say that bourgeois, or capitalist democracy is merely a sham designed to give the impression that the people have political power by voting, but in protecting the institution of private property absolutely it keeps owners in economic and social control of the supposedly democratic system."

"Fantastic," responded Kaiser. The class was amused.

"I wonder how much of the truth is contained in these theoretical defenses of different social and economic and political systems?" the teacher mused. "After all, they are only theories. I'm sure that the so-called real world will differ quite considerably from what the theories claim or from how they define reality."

From somewhere in the classroom a quiet voice was heard to say, "Oh, oh, I can hear one of those little lectures coming on."

The teacher turned towards the sound of the voice and said, "Well, miss, why don't you solve that problem by asking me what in the world I mean by such mysterious remarks?"

The young lady obliged. "All right, I'm Carole Jasper, sir. What do you mean by these mysterious remarks?"

"What mysterious remarks?"

"The ones you just made about reality and all that."

"Oh, yes. Well, students of society know that, as a general rule, the actual condition of social relations are very difficult to identify and that they correspond only in part with the claims made by the ideas with which they are defended or justified. So with the difference between various definitions of democracy and the actual conditions existing in the political systems which are called by that name. That is also true of the descriptions these theories make of themselves and of other systems. For example, we know that a major source of social, economic, and political conflict in all modern societies is the result of the conflicting claims of the rich and the poor, of the powerful and the powerless. We also know that this conflict has taken many different forms in different cultures and countries, and has given rise to an interesting variety of theories and political and social movements. But the actual state of affairs about the way that conflict is managed will vary greatly and we should be attentive to the variations.

"For example, Mr. Kaiser's father complains of the complexity and cost of social services that government must provide at public expense, and partly at his expense, to satisfy the political claims of the less affluent, which they have the power to enforce at the polls. But, the non-affluent are not at all agreed about what they want, and large proportions of them don't even participate in any political activity, including the vote, with which to back up their demands with political power.

"For another example, socialist political parties have had political power in many countries, but in some they have not eliminated or altered fundamentally the institution of private property, and have stayed away from other vital relationships of social and economic power. And, moreover, they have in some cases governed for a few years, only to be defeated at the polls by the very people whom they were claiming to represent in the struggle over the goods of the world.

"For another example, the ideas of Marxist socialism are in several important countries being implanted in society by narrowly based dictatorships which don't look in the least as if they were about to disappear, and therefore contradict the Marxist idea that the disappearance of propertied classes would also make ruling classes disappear."

"I was right, wasn't I?" said Carole Jasper.

"What were you right about?"

"That I felt another one of those little lectures coming on." Laughter from the class.

"So you were, but you talk about them as if they were a disease. Is that how you feel about them?"

"Oh, no. They're very interesting."

"That's kind of you. Now what did I say?"

"Well you said that politics is a very complicated business and that things are rarely what they seem."

"Miss Jasper, I couldn't want for better students, could I?"

"Thank you."

"Miss Jasper, does it seem odd to you that the subject of socialism has arisen in our discussions several times and for various reasons?"

"Well, no, I don't think so. I mean it's important, isn't it?"

"What do you think makes it important?"

"Well, I guess because there are a lot of people interested in it, aren't there?"

"Yes, that's one reason. But remember the present context. We were talking, as you remember, about the fact that mankind, in order to feed, clothe, and house itself, must work."

"But we were also talking about the fact that there is a lot of conflict between rich and poor, weren't we?" the student replied.

"Yes?"

"And that there are many people who think that there ought to be no difference between them; that the poor are just being exploited for the benefit of the wealthy."

"And so?"

"As I understood it, socialism promises to do away with that by abolishing private control over property. So that's what makes it important to talk about that. Is that the answer you wanted?"

"Is it an answer that makes sense to you, Miss Jasper?"

"I guess so, unless there's more to it, of course. Is there?"

"What do you think?"

"I'm not sure. I think there must be more because you keep on asking me about it. Is that right?"

"Good guessing. Now what more might there be to it?"

"Well, I just don't know."

"Are the ideas connected with socialism very influential in the world today?"

"Do you mean whether a lot of people believe in it?"

"Yes."

"Well, a lot of countries are run along socialist ideas, aren't they? Is that what you mean?"

"Could you name some of these countries?"

"Oh yes. Well, there's Russia, China, and the countries in Eastern Europe, I guess. Is that enough?"

"It certainly accounts for a large part of the world population doesn't it? You might also include England, Germany, France, Sweden, India, and others such as Cuba and Chile where the principles of socialism have been important aspects of governmental policy, and where large segments of the economies are socialized."

"So you're saying that socialist ideas are important because of the many countries in which they have been applied, is that it?" the student asked.

"Yes, that is certainly one very important reason, as we said, but there is, perhaps an even more important one than that," the teacher pressed.

"Well, I just can't figure what that might be."

"What makes the reference to the ideas and practices of socialism important, as much and more than the reasons already provided, is not only the currency of the ideas and of the controversies around them in present-day politics. Those facts alone are possibly of passing importance as the world goes. In my view what's important is that we extract some meaning beyond contemporary politics. So, I'd suggest that the discussion we have just been having shows that political systems are used for the management of great conflicts between contending groups and ideas in society; that the tasks assigned to those systems reflect the character of the conflict in the society in which the political system works; that because societies change, and to the degree they change, political systems and their tasks change, too; that among the most powerful of these social forces, if not, perhaps the single most powerful of them, is what is called economics or the production and distribution of goods and services, or, in even shorter terms, the organization and management of work."

The teacher paused for a while, sensing receptiveness for his sweeping conclusions. He continued.

"When mankind was condemned to labor in the sweat of its brow, it was, in a sense, also assigned the task of trying to solve the many deep and lasting conflicts associated with that necessity. And that's the political significance of work."

The teacher paused again and said, "According to the story of the creation of the earth, God rested after he saw that what he had wrought was good. Unless there's somebody here who will say that we haven't been doing a good job, I propose that we act in a godly way by contemplating our work and resting."

No one responded, and they rested.

14

Arrivals

"We've gone from a peaceful sleep and moved through the routine of our daily lives until we came to school and work, and all the while I've asked you to consider the impact of political relationships upon the activities that brought you from one place to another. Now we're here and we've touched on some of the more fundamental problems of politics and education, and the train of thought with which I opened the course is about complete. Only a few questions need yet to be posed before we can leave the subject. The next question is this: Now that there is no longer any possibility of denying the intimacy of the contact you've had with politics today, this very day only, how long in your lifetimes has the relationship existed?" The professorially composed inquiry had been stated slowly and had produced the desired effect of thoughtfulness on the class. There was a moment's silence.

"I've got it," said one student finally. "It's the birth certificate. Right after you're born they take your footprints and you're registered with the government, and then you exist as a person."

"That's strong language, Miss er . . . ?"

"Stowe, Deborah Stowe. Well, but it's true. If you haven't got your birth certificate you just don't exist. Anyway, you have to have some proof that you're you."

"All right, Miss Stowe, let's not debate the fine points of it, and agree that you're right about the birth certificate, but are you so right about it being the first governmental intervention in your life."

"Do you mean to tell me that they get to you even earlier?"

"I certainly do mean to, but I'd rather have someone else do the telling, if you don't mind. I'll save myself for arguing with whatever people say."

"Well, I don't know. That's pretty early in your life. I think they do it a day or two after you're born. What could be earlier than that?"

"Were you born at home, Miss Stowe?"

"No, in the hospital. My mother says it was touch and go with me for a while before I was born so they decided to go to the hospital for it."

"Was it a nice place, the hospital?"

"Oh, yes, it's kind of small, though. It only has about a hundred beds or so. It's in this small place in Pennsylvania."

"I see. Is it a proprietary hospital? Did the doctors who practice in it own it, or was it owned by somebody else?"

"Gosh, I don't even know that. Why, does it make a difference?"

"Well, I thought you might know. Do you know the doctor's name who attended your mother?"

"Oh, yes, and we still go to him. The whole family does."

"Does anything begin to ring a bell at this point, Miss Stowe? Do you recall our discussion about medicine and some of its political ingredients?"

"You mean the thing about socialized medicine and all that?"

"Yes, that's right."

"Well, no, not directly."

"All right. Now, when you visit that doctor nowadays, do you ever look around at the office walls while you wait for your appointment, or while your blood pressure is being taken?"

"Oh, yes. I know where he went to college and medical school and where he interned, and all that."

"Among the framed diplomas on the wall, isn't there one with a fancy kind of letterhead in official looking script saying, 'The Commonwealth of Pennsylvania' and showing that the man has a license to practice medicine?"

"Is that what you mean?"

"Yes, that's what I mean. How long before you were born did he attend your parents?"

"Oh, I think he knew them even before they got married. He's a local boy who came back home to practice. I think he went to school with one of my uncles."

"Good. Now we have established that your doctor was publicly licensed to practice and the hospital was, of course, inspected and approved before it could open. So that we have to conclude that the government had some intimate kinds of contact with your life even before you were conceived, certainly before you were born, right?"

"That's right, I guess so."

"Since we're talking about prenatal care, are there any other possibilities that occur to anyone at this point?"

"Here, right here, I've got one."

"Yes, and your name?"

"Sorry, I forgot. I'm William Bolt. Sure, it's obvious now, after all that medical talk. If they had had liberal kinds of abortion laws in her state she might never have been born."

"Who, me?" retorted Miss Stowe, angrily. "That's not a nice thing to say. How do you know a thing like that?"

Bill Bolt, a little more worldly wise than the rest of the students, to judge from his age and his comments, apologized and added, "I really didn't mean anything by it, and I'm sorry. But there are laws about abortions in all of the states and that's not all. There are laws about sexual behavior for everybody, including married people, and about the distribution of information about birth control devices. The Supreme Court of the United States had to get into the business about a Connecticut law, I think it was, which a doctor violated by giving advice about family planning to some of his patients who asked for it."

"We thank you, Mr. Bolt. You've got it right. The laws about sexual behavior demonstrate beyond all doubt that government and politics are used for the purpose of making rules about the most intimate details of our lives, including our very existence or the conditions under which we are allowed to live. In addition to your help so far, Mr. Bolt, would you be willing to answer a few intimate questions for the edification of the class?"

"Oh yes, I'd be happy to do that, if you think I can be of help," the student replied.

"Would I be stepping on any toes if I asked whether you were born to married parents?"

"Well, let's put it this way: My mother would be very offended if you asked her, and I would resent it if we were just strangers meeting in a barroom but, since we're just in an academic situation, I'm pleased to tell you that my parents were married when I was born."

The students relished the elaborateness of his communication, as did the teacher.

"All right then. Now what do you think the political aspects of marriage are?"

"The political aspects? Well, marriage is a legalized relationship, and that means that it's not a private matter in the sense that it's just between two people. A whole set of laws control a whole lot of things about it. For example, you have to have a license to marry and you can get that only if you're old enough—so the age is controlled. In most places you have to have a blood test for it, so that the license is used to make sure that married people don't have venereal disease that could be communicated to the spouse or to their children."

"You're doing very well. You didn't learn all that in your childhood, did you?"

"Oh no, I'm a married man, actually, so I know some of that. Let's see. Well, I guess a lot of the marriage laws are actually economic, aren't they? A wife is legally entitled to a man's support. And the law also stipulates how the wealth of married people is shared, and in the case of death, or of divorce and so on, and it also states how the money is handed over to the heirs, the children, and who is entitled to it if there's no will. That's quite a bit, isn't it? It shows what an important institution it really is, and how the authority of the government stands behind it and makes sure it works in the public interest."

"But of course you have only scratched the surface, haven't you, Mr. Bolt? You have omitted the law governing children in the marriage, children born out of wedlock, or of adoption. What about those?"

Before Bolt could reply, another student, a woman of mature years who had contributed previously, but without giving her name, spoke up. "May I talk about that? I've done some social work over the years in juvenile courts and I have some experience in it."

The teacher invited her in with a wave of his hand.

"I guess the law tries to safeguard the interest of the child, in keeping with the proper role of parents. Parents are permitted to punish their children, but the laws against abuse are there to stay their hand. In addition, there are the laws governing incest and other sexual violations of children by parents or with their help. I'm sure many here would be very surprised to hear how often those kinds of rules are violated and brought to the courts or the police. I could go on talking for hours. But there is some sort of principle you're trying to extract here, isn't there? I mean that's what this class was about, wasn't it?"

"Yes, there is, Miss . . ."

"Oh, I'm Mrs. Peterson."

"All right, Mrs. Peterson. Yes, there must be some kind of principle here. What do you suppose it is?"

"Well, of course children are defenseless. If parents don't protect them they can't fend for themselves. So I guess one principle is that public authority is used to come to the help of the weak."

"That's really very good, Mrs. Peterson. You sound as if there might be more."

"Well, of course children grow up and become adults, and if they're not raised right and educated properly and don't have the right feelings of respect for themselves and for others and for the society, they become a real problem. You know juvenile delinquents are thought of as future criminals. I guess the principle here is that society is trying to protect itself against crime."

"All right, that was very instructive. Thank you. I'd like to get to another matter. Mr. Bolt referred to the law of property in marriage a while back. Is that more important than the time we gave it? I seem to recall that there are some historians who have treated marriage as a way of protecting and preserving property. How does that work?"

Bolt was back again. "That depends on the inheritance laws, doesn't it? In a lot of places, property is in the husband's name and in some states both partners share equally in the total amount they own, regardless of who bought it into the marriage. I recently heard that in some states a wife can't have a joint bank account with someone else, like her son or daughter or a brother or sister without the husband having some claim on the money, should the wife die. It looks like the government is trying to use its authority to preserve property by making marriage a more profitable deal for a lot of people. You can also tell that from the income tax laws which give married heads of households a break. What about marriages of royalty and people like that, though? Property used to pass through the male line and some of that property consisted of whole duchies and even countries, at least in theory. They had to look for marriages that would enable them to hang on to this or that kingdom and so on. Well, I guess that's pretty important, when the only way to become king is to have the right kind of parents, isn't it?"

"If marriage is a way of acquiring and preserving property, what does that say about the way the law looks at the institution, though?"

"Well, you could look at it both ways. You could say that society looks on marriage as a stabilizing force and uses property to strengthen it; or you could say that, marriage being as stable a relationship as it is, you can entrust property to it, to insure the property's safety."

"That was a very elegant formulation, Mr. Bolt. Was marriage regarded as a virtually unbreakable relationship under the law in Western society at any time?"

"Oh sure, in fact there are some countries where it is still true. I guess until recently you couldn't get a divorce in Italy. And even where you can get it, the laws usually say something about the way property is divided."

"So you'd say that the laws of divorce also indicate society's interest in using public authority to discourage the disruption of marriages."

"Yes, that's right, but that's more complicated, isn't it? I mean you have to make sure that the children's interests are protected, don't you? So there might be quite a few reasons for that."

"All right, then," the teacher interrupted, "No matter how we examine it, political power has been applied to the most intimate details of our lives long before we're even conceived, and is at work in protecting us and the whole machinery of social institutions that are needed to bring us safely into the world."

"I was going to say that's pretty terrible," contributed a slightly hesitant student, "But I think I know what you'd do if I said that."

"What would I do?" asked the professor.

"Well, you'd probably ask me why and I'd say that the government shouldn't have the right to interfere in such things because they're private, and then you'd say that there were a lot of people who thought the government isn't going nearly far enough in butting in and that there are more of them than of us, and so on, just like you did with Harris over there when he talked about schools and political loyalty. So I won't say it. But I resent it."

"What do you resent, Mr. . . . ah . . . ?"

"Leffer, George Leffer. Well, I resent your always pointing out that there are other points of view."

"Should I say that you and I agree and that we are obviously right, and let it go at that?"

"It would be a lot easier on me, I can tell you that."

"All right, I understand, but how are we going to learn about this business? Are you sure that you're not resenting the people who insist on there being such laws?"

"Oh, sure, I resent them, but at least I can understand that people have different opinions about it. But honestly, don't you think it would be better for people if they didn't have to worry about laws about sexual conduct and birth control and other things that really have nothing to do with society, but only with themselves?"

"I don't honestly know that. I have nothing to compare it with in the past or in other societies. I don't know for a fact that people would be better off, whatever that means, without such restrictions. So far as I know, no society has ever failed to attempt to exercise control of sexual behavior—even though they have never completely succeeded at it. I don't know on what historical or behavioral grounds one could argue for their abolition."

"But it's an invasion of freedom of the individual," urged Leffer.

"I understand the logic of that," responded the teacher, "but is it a plausible position? Can one deny society's right to impose sanctions against some actions on the mere grounds that they invade freedom? The ten commandments invade freedom, but they also define it, at least in this sense, and they impose obligations. If people would obey the injunction 'Thou shalt not kill,' no one's life would be subject to a violent end at the hands of other persons and he would, by that token, be free from being killed."

"But that's not how it is with sex laws. It's purely individual."

"Does sexual conduct have no consequences which the society is bound to try to prevent?" asked the teacher.

"Do you think that's why they have these laws?"

"I'm not sure that it is the whole reason, of course. But many of the laws are grounded on the need to protect some people against other people, especially helpless ones, such as infants, or minors, or women, against being raped or injured. The sexual urge is, after all, one of the sources of behavior which society is likely to classify as criminal when it becomes dangerous to others."

"But, if you can interfere in sex is there anything that politics can be kept out of?"

"If there is, I don't know of it," said the teacher, slowly and emphatically.

"What do you think of the laws on censorship about sexual matters, Mr. Leffer?" he continued, after a moment.

"I'm against all of them."

"All of them?"

"Yes, they really don't appeal to me. I see no reason for preventing people from seeing anything they want to, or reading it, and so forth."

"You're not impressed with the view that children and minors have to be protected against being sexually corrupted or exploited before they are mature enough to handle sexual matters for themselves?"

"No, I'm not."

"Is anybody here in favor of censorship for any reason whatsoever?"

In the front row of the class, the hand of a woman considerably older than the rest of the students, rose slowly. "I'm Mrs. Ambler," she said, slowly, "and I just hate to see the teacher being made to hold up all the arguments in favor of government control in this classroom. I think some of you," and here she turned to the class in general, "really don't believe all that about how bad government is. Anyway, I can see the intellectual position against censorship and I support it. I don't think it's a good thing for anybody to have the power to decide what other people should not read, or see. But there are some reasons why I favor such laws, even though I have reservations about them. When you weigh one thing against another, it is a lot worse to have sexually corrupted children than it is to have governments with the power to keep sexually depraving things away from them."

Hands were up all over the class. Great agitation. Mrs. Ambler had hit a nerve.

"Who's first now?" asked the teacher. "Yes, in the second row, third man from the wall."

"I'm Martin Regan. I don't go for that at all. The lady thinks that sex is sinful and corrupting. I know they used to believe that in the old days, but nobody believes that any more. The government couldn't even enforce censorship if it tried."

"Are you certain, Mr. Regan, that the belief in the sinfulness of sex or, at least in its capacity for corruption, is so completely different now from what it was in the past?" asked the teacher.

Mrs. Ambler interrupted with, "Wait until you have children, young man, and then see how you feel about it."

Regan came back, "I hope my kids won't have to be protected against that kind of stuff. A lot of countries are giving up all kinds of censorship laws and I don't think they are going to go to hell or get corrupted all of a sudden."

"Does that mean, Mr. Regan, that you are opposed to all public regulation or control of sexual conduct, or the consequences of it?"

"I'm not too sure," the student answered, "but a lot of these laws sure seem antiquated."

"Perhaps they are, but aren't they connected to a deeply located set of ethical precepts about the potential harm that may arise from sexual conduct?"

"Yes, I realize that, but aren't they just customs?"

"Just customs?"

"Yes, I mean, there are a lot of differences in sexual customs of different cultures, aren't there?"

"Of course there are, yes."

"So why should the laws enforce any one set of customs over another?"

"But isn't it the case that laws are used to enforce or back up whatever the customs teach as valuable?"

"Oh, I see what you're driving at. You're saying that the laws about sex can only forbid what the customs already disapprove of?"

"Actually, Mr. Regan, the relationship is a good deal more complex than that, I'm sure, but there are certain connections, wouldn't you agree?"

"How do you mean?"

"I'd imagine that it would be very difficult to enforce laws on sexual conduct which clashed with deeply ingrained customs, wouldn't it?"

"I think I understand that, yes."

"Can you think of examples of attempts to do such things anyway?" the teacher asked.

"I'm not sure. I was just talking about censorship laws before. I think that's a case, isn't it?"

"It may well be such a case, but I'm not sure about it. Censorship represents a much more complex set of problems that those of limits on sexual conduct. I was hoping that you'd bring out the specially interesting case of population control."

"Population control? What's that got to do with it?"
"Are you aware of the problem of overpopulation?"
"Oh, yes, we hear a lot about it."
"Well, what are some of the things you hear about it?"
"That in some countries the population is growing too fast, and that the world population is going to be too big to be supported with the food and the space we have on earth."
"That's correct. Now how did such a state of affairs come about?"
"Well, that's not hard to see, is it," Regan replied. "People all over the world are having too many children."
"What do you suppose the reason for that might be?" the teacher asked.

Laughter from the class.

"A while ago you argued that government had no business in matters of sex because it's private. Do you suppose that overpopulation is a private problem?"
"I guess I don't," the student agreed.
"Why isn't it?" the teacher pressed.
"If there are too many people, there might be hunger or disease or poverty, or not enough space, and so on."
"And those are not private matters?"
"Right."
"Now we have a problem, don't we?" the teacher inquired, and stated it.

"What is a proper dividing line between private sexual conduct and the public nature of its consequences? Other people, whole societies and, as you pointed out, the entire world population have a stake in the outcome. If government may not interfere because of its private character, it is left helpless in the matter, isn't it?"

Mrs. Ambler returned to the discussion. "Aren't there some ways that overpopulation can be solved without interfering in private sexual relations?"

"How does that solve our problem of finding a proper line of division between private behavior and public consequences, Mrs. Ambler?"

"Maybe you don't even have to worry about that. For instance, if people in a particular country think they have a population problem there may be ways for the government to control population that don't require it to interfere with sex at all."

"How could that be managed?" the teacher asked.

"I think in Japan and in some other places they offered cost-free surgery for people who didn't want to have children. And they provided cost-free abortions. In that way they left it up to everybody's own discretion, but they held out certain rewards. You could do other things like that. For example, you could tax people with larger families or take their tax exemptions away from them. In other words, you could make it attractive to have few children or none by offering rewards for small families. In that way you wouldn't have to interfere directly, so to speak, with sexual relations."

"Some countries tried some of these methods, but found that the sexual customs were very resistant, even to rewards."

"Well, yes, I heard about that. Couldn't you do a lot by educating people, though? A lot of families seem to have children because they are too ignorant of how to prevent them, and some people whose works I have read tell how in some places in underdeveloped countries people are too poor, actually, to buy contraceptive devices."

"What's to be done about that?"

"You could use tax money to distribute birth control information and even the devices, in those cases, couldn't you?"

"Yes, you could and, in fact, that's being done in many places. We don't quite know what the effects of these policies will be, of course, since they have all been introduced only in recent times. Let's assume, however, that they don't work at all, and that it turns out that the present set of awards don't work. What then?"

Mrs. Ambler suggested, "In that case you could raise the awards. You could actually support small families or people without children and put greater burdens on the large families. I guess you could even get the idea going that having children is unpatriotic or something."

"In other words, you're suggesting that indirect controls of one sort or another, including education, subsidies, special training, be used in order to avoid the governmental intrusion on the private personal life of the people."

"Yes, actually, I can't imagine that anything else would work, anyhow. I mean, you'd have to have an awful lot of government interference to control that sort of thing directly, wouldn't you?"

"I'd agree, of course," the teacher assented. "Aren't there other possibilities still? Several religions we are familiar with advocate sexual continence, or abstention, as the surest way of preventing unwanted or socially undesirable births. Do you think that a religious ethic of sexual continence may be developed as the best of all controls? If people could be persuaded to abstain, or to postpone their marriages beyond an age of high fertility, the body politic wouldn't even have to get involved, you see, and a good deal of conflict over that kind of policy could be spared."

Mrs. Ambler smiled, and answered, "Of course, that would be very nice if it could be done. But it's like some other things we discussed here. If enough people restrained themselves there are a whole lot of problems mankind wouldn't have."

"You're suggesting, of course, that such hopes are forlorn and that other means should be found."

"Oh, yes, I am. It might be nice to get that kind of behavior, but I doubt if it would work, especially with something like sex. It's almost unnatural to ask people not to engage in it for the sake of saving mankind from starvation."

"And so, the political system gets called upon to make up the difference between the lack of individual restraints and the needs for the survival of the human race. That's quite a burden for politics to carry, don't you think?"

"Yes, but it's no worse than making war or a lot of other things we ask from politics, is it?" she concluded.

There was agreement from the teacher. Nor did the rest of the class disagree. When the teacher suggested that the connection between politics and birth had been well demonstrated, they did not protest.

15

Departures

"After looking at some implications of governmental involvement of our entry into the world," began the teacher, "we're prepared to ask the logical next question: At what point in life can we say that government as an institution and politics as a process ceases to be of consequence for us?"

"They have to quit when you're dead, don't they?" asked an unidentified voice from the class.

The students, who had by now become a working intellectual enterprise, chimed in with general laughter, from which there came another anonymous voice, calling, "I'm betting five bucks the professor can top that." More laughter, joined in by the teacher, who invited, "Place your bets now, before the dice start rolling, place your bets, bets anybody?" Nobody did.

"We can expedite the discussion a little by listing a number of items which will quickly establish that the government is not through with us when we die. We have to be certified as dead by an authorized person. If we die of causes other than natural, the government will look at the remains carefully for clues about the cause of death, and will pursue the agent of our demise with alacrity whether the destroyer be a person or some strange disease. I don't suppose there is much need to debate the justifiability of those particular aspects of our departure, is there? If not, we can go on to others from which other lessons may be learned."

No one disputed the list and the teacher was about to proceed, when the next interruption occurred.

"Wait a minute," called another anonymous voice. "Aren't we gonna get buried?"

The laughter of youth at the distant enemy death was loud and gay.

"Your enthusiasm for funerals overwhelms me," said the teacher, "and I don't want to dampen your spirits by refusing you the pleasure. So, let's get buried. Do any of the happy mourners here know the political relevance of burying?"

"My family's graves are in a churchyard in New England," observed one student, "and I don't think it has anything to do with government. At least, I never thought it did."

"Is it a very old churchyard?" asked the professor.

"Yes, there are some headstones in it with middle eighteenth-century dates on them."

"Chances are that it was not the object of public law when it was begun, but that it was closely regulated by church law. The question of who had the right to be buried there and so on were commonly dealt with by congregations. Usually, these were restricted to parish members, but in Europe, strangers who die within the parish are commonly thought to have a right to burial in the churchyard, too."

"A right?"

"Yes, a right. It means that the church wardens or the minister or priest may not refuse to bury a stranger without running afoul of the public law."

"Does that mean that anybody can claim burial in a churchyard?"

"I believe that he has to have died within the parish and that he must not have been executed for a crime. I don't know whether he needs to be a member of the faith or sect which maintains the yard. I am aware that European churchyards or burial grounds have sections set aside for unknown persons, and that must be a response to that legal requirement."

"Why do you suppose that laws were passed about the strangers?"

"I'm not familiar with the reason, but I suppose it was a religious matter."

Another student, interrupting, "I thought that you buy a place to get buried in. My parents just recently signed a contract for a lot in a cemetery."

"In the United States and elsewhere, large numbers of people are interred that way. The cemetery is maintained by an ordinary business enterprise, operating under the laws like other businesses. The plot is brought as a simple business transaction. There are even nonprofit burial societies based on religious affiliations or national descent, or even political and geographic origin."

"So why does the government get involved?"

"Well, Mr. . . . ?"

"Daniels, Ed Daniels."

"What kinds of things do you have to have to get into the cemetery business Mr. Daniels?"

"Oh, land and gravediggers, and funeral parlors and embalmers, coffins, hearses, things like that."

"I see. Now what might any of them have to do with government control?"

"You mean the land?"

"Yes, you might start with that. Are cemeteries located in the heart of business districts?"

"No, I've never seen one like that. But maybe there are some, in older cities. Most of them in this area are on the outskirts of town or what used to be the outskirts. In some places, the city has grown around them, sort of."

"Good. Now who regulates their location, do you suppose?"

"Oh, you mean it's like a zoning law or something?"

"Or something, yes."

"How deep into the ground are people buried, in this part of the country, anyway, Mr. Daniels?"

"I don't know. I hear people talk about six feet under."

"Is that just a custom, do you suppose?"

"I don't know."

"Neither do I, exactly. But let us suppose that you had a large cemetery, the water from which drained into a nearby creek which was part of the water supply of the town?"

"You wouldn't want that, of course," said Mr. Daniels.

"And, do you suppose that a public interest attaches to that?"

"Without question."

"You're very cooperative, sir."

"It's not so hard."

"What about the profession of undertaker or embalmer, does that seem to you to be a matter of public concern?"

"Yes, I thought it was one of the licensed professions we talked about when we discussed work. Don't you have to have a license to practice it?"

"Yes, one does need such a license, and the professional schools are supervised by state education departments. However, do you have any information about the political power of undertakers to influence the general conduct of their occupation?"

"Political power?" asked the student. "No, I never heard of that. What do they need political power for?"

"Supposing, Mr. Daniels, a family should choose to have a deceased person cremated as a matter of principle as well as a way of not spending money on burial costs. Would they be allowed to do it?"

"Allowed? Why not? Cremation's not illegal, is it? That would be absurd."

"No, it's not illegal, but in many places there is a requirement in the law stating that the body must be placed in a casket before it is committed to the flames."

There was a slight gasp from some members of the class. Daniels, the current discussant, said, in a surprised tone of voice, "Whatever for? I thought caskets cost hundreds of dollars. Why spend all that money?"

"Undertakers will tell you, I think, that it preserves the dignity of the occasion and spares the family pain and suffering. Political analysts may tell you that the reason is, more likely, that the combined economic interests in burials, which are very well organized into groups and lobbies, are extremely influential with the appropriate legislative committees in the state legislatures, and that they can be so successful because of the general lack of organized opposition from the public. After all, the dead don't object, and it is very difficult to get the living to organize in opposition to such laws. Death is fearsome and private."

"But why don't the political parties resist, then?"

"That's hard to account for, but I think it has to do with the same reasons. There's very little political benefit in doing that. As an issue it probably has no appeal at all. Can you imagine a candidate running on an antiundertaker platform like that?"

"Well, I don't know, but it seems very unfair that a group like that would be able to use the government to take money out of people's pockets, so to speak, doesn't it?"

"No doubt it does seem like that, yes. But, of course, you will remember that such arrangements are quite commonly made on behalf of other groups. Remember farmers, and workers, and subsidized industries, and so on."

"But at least in those other cases you could argue that there is some public interest there, such as the economy, or the price of labor, or something like that, even the national defense. But what's involved here, I'd like to know?"

"Funeral directors will tell you that everybody is entitled to a decent burial—and the law states that—and that one of the elements of decency is being buried in a box of some sort. Incidentally, you knew of course that if the family should choose to watch the cremation, they may do so through a small aperture provided for the purpose. Now would you say that the family's feelings would be protected better when the body is in a box than in a simple shroud or cloth cover?"

"Actually," said Daniels, "the whole subject is sort of gruesome. But I think they should leave that whole thing up to the family."

"There is some kind of public interest, then, if only protection against gruesomeness, isn't there? At least undertaker and casketmaker lobbies are relying on some sort of sense of common decency in the population, upon which they can build a claim before the legislature, and in that they are not too different from other organized groups who use government to protect their interests. In addition, there are certain technical kinds of questions in the handling of the dead for preservation and for shipment that are carefully regulated, and we could discuss the fine line between questions of esthetics and public safety on the one hand, and the tendency of the funerary professions to maximize their profits on the other, for a time. But I think the subject has been sufficiently exposed for now. There are other political lessons to be learned from death. We must turn to those now."

The teacher paused briefly, waiting for other questions. None came and he plunged ahead to the next argument on death.

"Let me shift the focus of the discussion *very* sharply, if you don't mind. It's easy to show that the common interest in the burial business is an important component of it, and that health regulations, the licensing of embalmers, and public supervision of other aspects such as the size, location, and general appearance of cemeteries are of common interest justifying the use of governmental authority. It is also very important that burial is regarded almost everywhere as having religious significance. It is therefore involved in the extremely complicated relationship between church and state as we commonly describe it in this culture. The focus I wanted to provide was another one, however.

"One of the most famous of all speeches of Western culture begins by pointing out that the state, (what we call the political system) had decreed that men who have acquitted themselves bravely in battle be buried in a public tomb and with a public funeral. The funeral oration of Pericles speaks of the importance of the state's concern for those who die in battle and so forth. Does this have relevance for us?"

"A lot of people have gotten killed in battle or in wars," said a young girl in the third row, soberly.

"War is a political problem?"

"Of course," she answered.

"Does our 'state' own cemeteries, and do we, also, bury our battle dead in public tombs with public burials?"

"Well, there's Arlington National Cemetery, and I think there are other places where veterans can be buried, if they and their families prefer, at no cost, I think."

"Miss . . . ?"

"Schacter, Wendy Schacter."

"All right, Miss Schacter, what do you suppose is the significance of public burial places with honor for those who died in battle?"

"Well, when you die in a war, you've died for the country."

"Is that because only countries conduct wars?"

"Yes, of course."

"Don't people die at each other's hands without it being connected with politics?"

"Oh, yes, lots of people do, but that's different."

"How is it different?"

"Because the government compels you to go to war, so there is a duty connected with it."

"Many soldiers killed in wars were volunteers, and many men volunteer for dangerous missions, even among draftees," the teacher replied. "What makes them do that?"

"They must be people who are brave, and I've read some things about people believing in the glory of it."

"The glory?"

"Yes, it means something like honor, or heroism."

"What do you suppose makes a soldier's death honorable or glorious?"

"I never understood it too clearly," answered Miss Schacter, "but I think it has to do with dying for other people or for a belief in something, some idea or something like that, or from a sense of duty."

"Do you think of this as an interesting problem, Miss Schacter? Are we likely to understand something about politics by talking about it?"

"It's sort of gory, I guess, and gruesome. My father was in the second World War and he talked a lot about it. He was a marine and he saw some terrible things, but he was always very proud, as if he had performed a great service to the country."

"As if . . . do you mean he didn't?"

"Well, I don't really know. I think wars are terrible, don't you think so?"

"For once I'll commit myself. Yes, I think they are terrible, too. But apparently they continue to be fought. That means they must be of some use to the people who fight them, doesn't it?"

"But that's like saying that killing is right, isn't it?"

"Right?"

"Yes, you know, acceptable, and I don't think it is."

"How do you suppose fighting wars is related to the existence of countries or nations or political systems, Miss Schacter?"

"I don't know, exactly. It sometimes looks as if living in a nation and having to fight for it are almost the same thing. I mean, there have been so many wars and so much killing over what kind of countries there should be, and where the borders should be located, and who should run things; it's really frightening to think about. One teacher told us that he thinks there isn't a single country in the whole world that was ever established without a lot of fighting and killing. That's why he's against nationalism."

"Nationalism?" asked the teacher.

"Yes, the idea of people being separated into different countries and having to fight each other."

"Is that nationalism?"

"Well, it looks that way to me."

"Do you suppose the killing would stop if we had no nations in the world?"

"I don't know, but we should try, shouldn't we?"

"We?"

"Yes. Everybody in the world should want peace."

"Well, isn't there peace within most countries, at least?"

"Yes, mostly, but even in the United States there was a Civil War, and other countries had them at one time too; like Spain, and Russia, and Germany, and England."

"Do you suppose that soldiers who died in these civil wars, as you called them, thought about dying gloriously, too?"

"Oh, sure, we read a lot of novels about that. You know *The Red Badge of Courage*, and others like that."

"So, glory is not reserved for the nation alone, is it, but may be gained by sacrificing yourself for a much smaller group of people."

"Well," replied Miss Schacter, thoughtfully, "I guess if somebody sacrifices himself for any group of people he belongs to, he deserves to be honored because he puts the survival of others ahead of himself. That kind of unselfishness is really very remarkable."

The teacher had become very thoughtful, along with the students who were listening. He asked very seriously, "You suppose then that the group for which the sacrifice is made has some sense of obligation towards this act?"

"Yes, if they really believe that the sacrifice has been worth it. I mean, if they believe in the nation or in the tribe or maybe even if it's a city in the middle ages, they would just have to honor it."

"But how does one do that? Before you answer, you might consider that not every act of defending groups or nations results in the death or injury for the defender. Most people involved in such activities survive. How does one honor that kind of service?"

"My father got quite a few medals. He really treasures them."

"Treasures them?"

"Yes, he keeps them in a little velvet-lined box. They are very pretty."

"Are there many kinds of medals?"

"I understand what you mean, professor, we don't have to go through the discussion. Honoring dead people is not enough, because others also made sacrifices, and you don't have to die for the country to defend it and deserve honors. Maybe it's enough to be willing to defend it."

"Does it seems to you, Miss Schacter, that the need for men to give up their lives, or to offer them on behalf of a nation, or of any group which thinks itself in danger, is putting a low value on life?"

"No, I don't think so. It depends on the country, I think. I can imagine that one would be ready to defend some kinds of countries much more willingly than others."

"Yes, but can you imagine any kind of country nobody would be ready to die for?"

"I just don't know. There are some terrible countries."

"Yes, but there seem to be people who're defending them, aren't there?"

"Yes, but also a lot of people who're not."

"But that's true even in countries which most inhabitants love and esteem."

"So, what does the question mean?" asked the puzzled student.

The teacher replied, "Could it be that without some number of people who are either selfless enough, or foolish enough to defend the country against others, one could not organize people in territories large enough to call themselves countries at all? Isn't selfless loyalty a precondition for any kind of human association?"

"Well," replied Miss Schacter, "if nobody were willing to die, maybe there would be no wars any more and nobody would have to die."

"Nobody would have to die?"

"That's right."

"But, Miss Schacter, aren't we all going to die?"

"Yes, but we shouldn't need to be sacrificed for others like that."

"Shouldn't need to be?"

"That's right."

"Do you mean there shouldn't be any danger, or that there should be no love for others, or loyalty?" asked the teacher.

"What's love got to do with it?"

"Wouldn't you be willing to die to save your child from death or injury?"

"I think so, . . . yes."

"Why?"

"Well, I don't know. I would want it to live."

"Even more than you want to live?"

"But you just said we're not going to live forever, anyway."

"So I did. Isn't it true?"

"Yes, it is."

"So, what does it mean to make the choice to die in order to enable your child or another member of your family to continue to live?"

"Well, it's a way of showing love and a way of continuing life."

"Have you ever been to a place where a military man or many of them were buried?"

"Yes."

"Just a minute," interrupted another student, loudly. "Professor, do you mean to say that it's a necessary thing for people to be willing to die so that other people or even nations can live?"

"I didn't actually say that, Mr. . . . ?"

"Pastor, Tom Pastor."

"No, I didn't say that, but I indicated that many men and women have made the choice for those reasons, and that at certain points it may be required."

"But that's putting the group or the family or the nation ahead of the individual."

"In some ways, Mr. Pastor, it is, that's right."

"Isn't that objectionable, morally?"

"Why?"

"What right does any group have to require that one person must die in order to perpetuate itself?"

"I wasn't talking about anybody requiring it only, but also of people offering it willingly when they are confronted with what looks to them like a clear choice, and doing it out of love, as a gift, or as a duty."

"That still puts the life of the group before that of the people composing it," insisted the student.

"That's right but, in part, it's a voluntary act."

"I see," said the student.

"Should we insist that a person must preserve himself at all costs, even that of watching other members of his family die?"

"If you put it that way, I'm not sure."

"I'll put it very simply, Mr. Pastor, and it was the question I was about to put to Miss Schacter when I asked if she'd ever been to a military memorial. Has nobody ever died for you?"

"I don't know."

"Has anybody in your childhood ever given you the idea that some people really did die for you?"

"Oh, yes. I get that from reading history books, and so forth."

"Do you believe that the members of your family would die to preserve your life?"

"Yes, I do."

"Are you able to put people into a scale of closeness towards you in terms of their willingness to sacrifice their lives for you?"

"Yes, but it's hard beyond the family."

"Hard?"

"Yes."

"Suppose the country were attacked. Would you feel yourself to be in danger along with millions of other people?"

"Of course."

"Of course? Why of course?"

"That's what an attack on the country means, doesn't it?"

"What does it mean?"

"That everybody in it is in danger."

"Everybody in it? How many of these do you know to speak to?"

"Just a few."

"A thousand?"

"Maybe."

"And the others?"

"Well, I don't know them, but it's their country, too."

"Are you saying that you are counting on them to believe and act in a certain way towards it?"

"Yes, that's right. If they don't defend it, I might be in the same kind of trouble they would be in if I didn't care about it."

"But, supposing you found out that in fact they didn't care, or that they weren't willing to help defend it, what then?"

"Well, it might depend on the circumstances. If there were a real and immediate danger of being taken over it would, of course, be very serious."

"For you?"

"Yes, and for others, and for the country as a whole."

"What could be done?"

"I guess sometimes nothing at all. Some countries have been conquered with the help of people who were supposedly loyal. Then it's just too late, I guess."

"Suppose you are in a situation where you have already been taken over. What should one's attitude be in that kind of situation?"

"Well, you're supposed to want to fight back, of course, but I guess a lot of people would not and would try to save themselves first. I'm not sure I could blame them for that, but I don't think it's admirable. I admire the underground in France during the German occupation a lot more than the collaborators, and that would be the same for me in any situation like that."

"Now, Mr. Pastor, how does the situation differ when there is no danger or little danger?"

"Oh, I guess there's little to worry about. I mean, if there is no threat to the country you really don't have to worry about how many people would be loyal if there were a threat."

"I see. Why are school children being asked to recite the Pledge of Allegiance to the flag every day? Doesn't it seem silly to have them recite it? After all, how much help could they be if things really got bad? Children are pretty helpless anyway in war, aren't they. So, why not dispense with it?"

Mr. Pastor gave it some thought. "I guess it's training, for later. How do we know they would be loyal in a crisis if they hadn't learned it when they were young?"

"Good! How does that answer the question about the relationship between loyalty and the condition of safety for a country?"

"Well, I suppose it means that if you're trying to have a country, you have always got to take some kinds of steps to create feelings of love for it among the people, even if there is no trouble. If you wait until trouble happens, you just might not have enough people to defend the country."

"Very good. In asking children to develop feelings of affection for their country one is getting them ready for possible acts of self-sacrifice on its behalf, or at least for loyal support in times of trouble."

"If you put it that way," mused the student, "one could interpret that kind of training as the creation of cannon-fodder for future wars, couldn't one? I mean, that's what being a soldier is all about, isn't it—loyalty and obedience and sacrifice? The motto of the West Point Military Academy is 'Duty, Honor, Country,' isn't it?"

"Yes, that's sensible, but is being a citizen so different from being a soldier? In modern life, vast numbers of civilians are being called on to be soldiers, and many more are exposed to the ravages of war and conquest, aren't they?"

"That's true," agreed Pastor. "Are you suggesting that the relations between modern nations are such that there is always a kind of war going on, you know, that all over the place political systems are training their people to be loyal against the possibility of danger from without? That comes back to the same thing Wendy Schacter said a while ago. If none of the countries did that maybe there wouldn't even be that kind of condition to worry about."

"Are you saying that patriotism is a kind of self-fulfilling prophecy when it comes to war?"

"Something like that, yes."

"And if that's the case," suggested the professor, "and if we are against war, we must, of course, find a way to persuade nations not to make their citizens so patriotic any more, mustn't we?"

"That'll never work," called out a new participant.

"Why won't it work, Mr. . . . ?"

"George Morgan."

"Mr. Morgan, why won't it work?"

"Well, the first country that tries it will get swallowed up by the one next to it with a disciplined population."

"And in that way the countries would get bigger and bigger and soon there would be only one country left in the world, right?" asked the teacher.

"It sounds a little ridiculous, when you say it that way," replied Morgan, "but maybe that would be the sequence, yes."

"I completely disagree with that," another student asserted. "I'm Cilford Wilder. That makes no sense at all. If people stopped caring for their country, they would care only for themselves and their families and maybe their religious group or their race, or their own province or state or city, and there would have to be very serious conflicts between the people in all of these different groups, and instead of their being no war anymore there would be complete chaos all the time, because loyalties would intensify on these small levels. Nationalism, and I learned that in a course last year, doesn't make things worse, so far as danger of war is concerned, at all. It has made them a lot better in the last few hundred years. There used to be constant fighting all the time between all kinds of people for all kinds of silly reasons. At least now we have peace within the nations, and in fact, we have peace between whole groups of nations for long periods of time. Maybe we could find a way to get people to be patriotic about the whole world, but we'd better not destroy their feelings for their countries first, because then we'd never make it to world peace."

Wilder, who had, surprisingly, waited his turn until this moment in the discussion, ceased and leaned back in his chair, awaiting the response of the class and the teacher.

"I'm very impressed by your position, Mr. Wilder. You're saying the opposite of what Miss Schacter and Mr. Pastor were suggesting. Loyalty and patriotism are not matters of death, but of life, also."

"That's putting it very strongly," said Wilder, "but, like it."

"We can be satisfied," concluded the teacher, "that the connection between life and death and politics have now been well established. I thank you all. Let the discussion end here. It is a fitting point for it."

16

From Here to Eternity?

"We are about to end our introduction to the work of this course," the teacher began, "and it has to be a special kind of ending. Our discussions have taken us from the peace of a night's sleep into school and work, and from the pains of birth to the problems of dying. Those are long intervals and they represent great contrasts. The conclusion of this beginning should be so framed as to enable us to speculate about the topics of our conversations and to open wide the possibilities of learning more about them. There is much to be learned, even though we have made a good beginning. Our task is to consider whether we can see what we have discovered by looking at those familiar things."

Before the question could be properly put, the hand of Mike Gillis shot up quickly and its owner insisted, "Before we get into that, I have a question."

"Yes?" the professor invited.

"This whole thing has been very interesting and all that, and I've learned a lot from it, but it was very different from what I expected."

"What did you expect?"

"I thought we would be talking about the big political problems we have in the world and in this country now and how to solve them. I mean, there's war, and pollution, and poverty, and the generation gap. Those things worry a lot of people, including me, and I figured that this course would tell us how to find solutions to problems of that sort, so that we can make the world a better place."

The teacher's glance about the classroom revealed considerable assent in the form of nods and smiles of approval.

The student, warming to his subject, continued, "I mean, some of these problems are so serious that we have to find solutions to them or we may not even be around much longer as a species. Aren't we going to discuss them at all?"

"Of course," responded the teacher, "this society, and indeed the whole human race, has major problems of special seriousness. Do you think it would have been more instructive to define what these problems are and to develop solutions for them?"

"Yes. Shouldn't a course in political science tell us how things got the way they are now and how we can go about changing them for the better?"

"Well, Mr. Gillis, what do you suppose these fifteen discussions we have had here were actually about?"

"I thought that they were all about showing us how much of our daily life depends on politics and government."

"Yes, that *was* one of the main reasons for going about our business the way we did. But there are other things one might observe about these discussions, aren't there? For example, didn't each of them also talk about particular social problems and the attempts of various people to solve them by making them political?"

"Sure, but most of the problems we talked about aren't so serious any more, are they? With the help of government they've actually been solved. I thought we would be talking about things that are problems *now* so we can solve *them*, too."

"I see," responded the professor. "You've handed us no small task here, Mr. Gillis, and I hope we'll be equal to it. May I ask you which of the fifteen dialogues were especially good examples of problems solved by the intervention of politics? Let me help by listing them in order of their appearance."

With that, the teacher turned to the blackboard and quickly wrote out the list of fifteen subjects that formed the heart of the preceding dialogues:

Public Safety	*Commercial Regulation*	*Electric Power*
International Trade	*Sewage and Sanitation*	*Water Supply*
Medicine and Health	*Fiber for Clothing*	*Food*
Housing	*Transportation*	*Education*
Birth	*Death*	

The list complete, the teacher turned to the class. While he was writing, the students murmured, whispered, conversed, and noised about the classroom.

"You were saying, Mr. Gillis, that we have been talking about problems which were essentially solved. Would you care to take your pick?"

The student and the entire class, including the teacher, scanned the list thoughtfully for a period, trying to recall the substance of the discussions about each item on it. Finally, Gillis responded.

"Come to think of it, none of them have actually been solved, have they?" He seemed somewhat disappointed, and the teacher came to his aid, saying:

"That is an important statement, especially in view of your earlier opinion. Would you care to elaborate on it?"

"Well, there's still hunger, and sickness, and problems about sanitation, even though politics and government are used to deal with these things. I mean, they are still a lot of trouble. For instance—water. That's pretty serious, despite the fact that it's practically entirely a governmental matter."

Contented, the teacher asked the natural question: "Well, Mr. Gillis, if these things were problems before government ever got to them, and they are problems afterward, what has been gained by making them political? Is the imputation that nothing much has changed?"

"Can I get into this?" interjected another student. It was John Mason. "I don't completely agree with what you and Gillis just said, and before you go on, I want to say that you're probably wrong."

"All right, Mr. Mason," the teacher invited, "Let's hear your side of it."

"As I see it, your position has to be modified. I agree that almost all of the problems we talked about haven't been solved. I mean, they haven't disappeared. Despite having police forces, there's still crime, and despite the public water supply, there's still pollution and scarcity, and so on. I know that, but I would still say that the introduction of government to these problems can be called a solution."

"That does sound contrary to me, I must say," the teacher teased, with a slight smile. "If the problems remain despite the uses of government, in what way can they be said to have been solved?"

"Well, in the first place, I didn't say that *the* problems remained. The problems that remain are not the same problems which existed when government first got into them. I would say that the problems that remain are the problems of the solutions, but that sounds hopeless."

"The problems of the solutions?" asked the teacher, but with ill-concealed pleasure. It was an ingenious formulation, he knew, and he wanted to give it all the play he could for the benefit of the class. "Mr. Mason, please replay that for us, would you?"

"All right," the patient student explained. "When you have a police force to prevent disorder and crime and to find and accuse criminals, that's supposed to be a solution for these problems. But everybody knows it isn't. Riots continue, crime doesn't end, life is not completely safe, and property is destroyed. But, there *is* a police force and they *can* act for the whole community to put a stop to some of it and to try to catch people after crimes are committed. That's a lot better than having to do without cops."

"I see," said the teacher. "In your opinion, then, a solution of sorts has been accomplished when a problem can be dealt with, even though it can't be solved."

"Yes, that's right. And the more we talk about it, the more I'm convinced I'm right. Having a police force is a solution to the problem of not being able to deal with crime and riots and things like that."

"Fine, Mr. Mason, now what did you mean by saying that the remaining problems were problems of the solutions?"

"Why, it's simple, isn't it? The reasons police forces aren't effective in eradicating crime or riots or keeping order may be because there aren't enough police, or because they're not well enough trained, or because some of them are corrupt, or because there are just too many rotten or angry people around for policemen to cope with. Those are the problems of the solution."

The class was very impressed with Mason, as they well should have been. Not the least among those was the teacher, who had some trouble keeping from deluging the student with praise.

"That was really very well put, Mr. Mason. We're in your debt. What do you think of that, Mr. Gillis? Are you impressed, too?"

"Well, sort of, I guess, but it's not very satisfactory. I mean, it sounds so hopeless, doesn't it? It makes it look as if any kind of solution we try is going to produce other kinds of problems. I wonder whether it's worth the bother. Considering what it costs to run government, it doesn't make it look as if it does nearly enough good. If that's true of the problems we have right now, maybe we'd all be better off if we just let things drift until they go away by themselves," the student concluded, despondently.

"Do you suppose that the serious matters with which our dialogues were concerned could have been ignored by the people who had to suffer their consequences?" the teacher asked.

"No, I really don't think so, but maybe it would have been worth the experiment," Gillis replied, somewhat lackadaisically.

"The what?" asked the teacher.

"The experiment. You know, maybe they wouldn't have tried to solve some of those problems if they had known that the solutions don't work the way they expected them to."

"Let me propose an experiment, since you are so minded, Mr. Gillis.

Would it be a good idea to dismiss all of the policemen? Since the problems they were set up to solve are still here, perhaps we should reduce the force for suppressing crime and disorder to find out whether they're really necessary. What do you say, will you join me in advocating it?"

"I wouldn't dare," Gillis shot back. "That's much too dangerous for everybody. Nobody would be safe. No, I wouldn't do it that way."

"Well, how would you do it?"

"I talked to a friend of mine the other day and he thinks that we have to change our whole way of bringing up children to believe more in law and order and in authority. He said that way they'd be less tempted to break the laws when they grow up and we wouldn't have so much crime and could do with less policemen."

"What do you think of that solution?"

"It sounds nice, but how could you do it; wouldn't it take a long time to find out if it worked?"

"Is that how you answered your friend?"

"No, I don't remember what I said to him. We got to talking about something else."

"Do you recall our discussion about education and the community's stake in it?" the teacher asked.

"Yes, but I don't remember that we talked about educating children to obey laws."

"Sure we did," a voice called out from the back of the class. "I remember that. That guy over there complained about how the whole school was hipped on the loyalty thing and on teaching you to love your country and so forth."

"Well," the teacher agreed, "It wasn't exactly to the point but it was pretty close. It's interesting, isn't it, that another possible solution that government can apply to the so-called law and order problem is education."

"Well, I don't believe schools can do that. I mean, people would violate the law no matter what they're taught in school. I really don't think that criminals connect breaking the law to learning American history and saying the Pledge of Allegiance, or loving one's country, and all that. They do it because they're mad, or greedy, or sick, or just because it's a good way of getting away with something, or maybe their parents didn't bring them up right."

The speaker expressed himself in sardonic tones. "I don't think you could stop crime no matter how well you taught children to believe in their country, even if there were no poverty, or if all of the so-called crime-producing reasons were to disappear tomorrow. There's a lot of crime even when the police are very powerful and the government can do anything it wants to people. It's just human nature, that's all. There's no solution for that. The only thing is, you have to keep trying because some people might be educated right and some people might be kept from stealing or killing because they're afraid of the police, or some people because they're afraid of God. So you can't give up, but I just don't think that it will disappear, no matter what you try. It's human nature. I'm sure of it."

The teacher heard the student out and replied in measured tones:

"Discussions of this sort often turn to that famous problem of the nature of human nature. I must say I regret that we can't spend much time on it. I gather you're pretty convinced, and I must say that many people now and in the past have similar beliefs. Of course, you know that there are people, quite a few of them, at that, who will argue that crime is a part of the conflict between social and economic classes in society and that, when one eradicates that conflict, crime will also disappear."

"Well, I don't believe that at all. People are people and some of them are just that way," the student answered.

"Yet, you don't seem especially hopeless about it, do you?" the teacher asked.

"No, but I'm sure that's how it is. You have to keep trying because maybe if you stopped trying things might be worse, that's all. I don't think a lot of things about politics are nearly as complicated as a lot of you are making out, you know. As I said, it's human nature and you have to keep trying."

"Do you suppose that your argument explains anything about politics?" the teacher asked.

"Well, I don't know. A lot of the time we were talking about problems that people use government for solving. I figure that mostly people want to be safe and they're willing to let somebody protect them against other people and that's how it works. As long as the protection is there, you can have some kind of government. When they can't give it any more people get it someplace else, and that becomes the government. They get protection wherever they can. That's how I've got it figured."

"But don't you think that's a pretty simple argument?" the teacher asked. "All kinds of governments promise protection against all kinds of things, but some governments are so powerful there's no way of protecting yourself against them. Don't we have experience with that in the world?"

"Well, yes, that's true. Some of the people who promise to protect others are really very dangerous themselves. I know that, but that's how it is, you know. The world isn't all full of the milk of human kindness, whatever that may be. Sometimes people *aren't* safe, even against their own government. I figure you just have to be lucky to live in a place where that doesn't happen too much, and if you're not lucky you just have to get out, or you have to try to change it or if you can't do that, you have to make the best of it."

"But, wouldn't you rather be safe *and* have a say in what government can do?"

"Oh, yes, I would, but I figure I'm just lucky if I do. If I can do something about it, fine; if not, fine, as long as I'm safe and don't get hurt. Also, I don't go for a lot of what's been said here because most everybody here thinks that you can solve all kinds of social evils if you can only get the government into it. In my own mind it doesn't take a lot of brains to figure out that there are some things that government makes a lot worse than they really are. You know, ambitious people know that they can become famous and powerful by promising all kinds of heaven on earth and they promise it, even if they can't deliver. I'm very suspicious of the lot of them. They don't even know if they can deliver on their promises and a lot of them really don't care. They just want to see their names in the history books, or to have their friends and relatives boast about them. Some of them are just greedy, and are looking for a buck. Meanwhile, they get a lot of innocent people to believe in them, even if they can't do anything for them or even if they don't intend to."

"But, don't you think that we have demonstrated here that political methods have, in fact, worked to a remarkable degree? Aren't you impressed at all by the fact that there *are* political systems in the first place and that they endure? Do you suppose that they would even exist if they didn't do enough good for enough people?"

"I never thought much about that. Are you saying that people who promise other people protection really have to deliver it?"

"Yes, I am," the teacher replied. "It seems to me at the very least that there has to be enough satisfaction with the rulers to enable them to rule, isn't that right?"

"At the same time," the student replied quickly, "there's an awful lot of dissatisfaction with them everywhere, even when they're elected, like in a democracy."

"But don't you think that there is a lot of difference between being dissatisfied with rulers and being willing to be ruled? Don't enough people understand that the willingness to be ruled gives authority to the rulers with which they can do things *nobody* can do for himself? In other words, isn't there some sort of exchange involved? You give up part of your power over yourself and in return you permit other people to apply power to social problems you care about."

"I'm sure I don't understand all of that," the student replied.

"I'm suggesting that political life which is, after all, the ability to gather a certain kind of authority over people for certain purposes, is directly based on commonly shared needs and, for that reason alone these needs must be satisfied to a considerable degree in order to make politics work at all."

"Does that mean that when the government takes tax money it has to use it to make people happy?"

There was laughter from the class.

The smiling teacher retorted, "If I recall correctly, happiness is included in the list of basic rights which the writers of the American Declaration of Independence claimed for all mankind and which, according to them, it was the purpose of governments to secure. Don't you remember the phrase? Let me see. It goes: 'We hold these Truths to be self-evident, that all Men are created equal and are endowed by their Creator with certain unalienable Rights, that among these are Life, Liberty and the Pursuit of Happiness—that to secure these Rights, Governments are instituted among men, deriving their just powers from the Consent of the Governed.'"

"Oh, yes," the student replied, "I remember that. But you don't think that mankind's happy, do you, because of government? It looks to me as if they were more *unhappy* because of it."

"It might be a good thing if you looked at it from the perspective of mankind's long experience, rather than at present-day impressions or feelings. I'd suggest that this experience indicates at least two very contrary impulses. One of them is to find a way of applying social power to the solution of shared problems, and the other one to resist the application of that power. Some of our happiness appears to come from knowing how to employ means for helping ourselves, and some of it from our ability to escape the consequences of our own solutions."

"But governments do a lot of dangerous things, don't they, even if they say they're instituted to secure rights?" offered another student.

"Yes," the teacher agreed, and added, "but they also do try to secure those rights."

"That's a pretty hard choice to have to live with, isn't it? I mean it sounds as if you were saying that you can have political power only if you're willing to put up with the danger."

"It sounds that way, doesn't it?" the teacher agreed.

"Do you think that's fair?"

"How do you mean?" the teacher asked.

"Well, I don't see what difference the whole experience of mankind makes. It sounds like you could excuse almost anything the government did with its power. I mean, if people resisted, the government could always say that they represent the will of the people or that resistance is illegal and they could get away with anything that way, couldn't they?"

"Not only that, Miss...."

"Harley, Jane Harley."

"Not only that, Miss Harley, but that's what all governments *do* in fact claim, and they do, in fact 'get away' with an awful lot because, just as you say, they are irresistible. On the other hand, it wouldn't do to say that any particular government is eternal. After all, there's a very brisk turnover among governments. For one set of reasons or another they are found wanting. They might be too powerful or too weak, too ineffectual or too threatening, too old fashioned or too revolutionary. The range of reasons for doing away with them seems inexhaustible. Revolution is not a rarity, and most governments spend a lot of time securing themselves against this. So their irresistibility is limited, at least from the perspective of history."

Miss Harley, thoughtful at the teacher's extended reply, argued stoutly, "But if you live in a system that's oppressive and which can't be overthrown, because you're weak, that doesn't make a lot of difference, does it? I mean, the person in a dictatorship can't take comfort from history. He has to worry about surviving, doesn't he, and it's very dangerous to try to overthrow them because they have all that machinery on their side."

"Yes, it is cold comfort to know that governments can go only so far before they endanger their own existence, while you're rotting in some prison, or concentration camp. Individuals and groups out of favor are especially weak and defenseless. I regret to say that the only comfort is that there are a good many political systems where the extremes of such risks don't have to be run. The arts of politics have taught us how to build responsive and responsible ways of governing, in which men may be required to obey the rulers, but in which the laws are fair, the rulers freely chosen, and political opposition is a lawful activity in which one may engage with relatively few risks."

"Oh, yes, I know that," Miss Harley persisted, "but they do some awful things too, don't they?"

"Oh?" the teacher inquired.

"Yes, even when there's political freedom, supposedly, there can be a lot of abuses. Look at the whole race question in this country. Isn't that an example?"

"Of course it is," the teacher replied, "it's plainly true that a good many of these abuses are broadly supported by the politically effective population."

"So, in other words, not even democracy is a guarantee against injustices like that," insisted the student.

"Yes, I agree. But our question is more difficult than that," the teacher pointed out. "It's this: would life without political power or government be more or less fair or just than it is *with* it? Have you an opinion about that?"

"Well, I don't know. I guess that when I see an injustice done by a government I feel we'd be better off without political power."

"But aside from recognizing individual acts of political injustice, how do you think the entire concept of justice would manage to survive? Don't *all* governments seek to embody or aspire to some sense of it, at least, and wouldn't it be much more difficult to enforce a standard of justice without sufficient power to do so? Isn't *that* really the dilemma?"

"I'm not sure what you mean now. Don't *you* think you could have any justice without political power?"

"That is a very difficult matter which has plagued philosophers for ages, and will continue to do so, I'm sure. Much depends on what one means by justice or just action, of course. But it appears true that a *sense* of justice, at least, pervades the societies of all men, and that government or politics is called upon to vindicate or enforce a society's particular views of it in one way or another. It *is* hard to accept the notion that some of the worst political tyrannies act like that, but one has to be impressed with the fact that, even though they are powerful enough not to have to bother with it, they all try to *appear* to be just in one way or another. The dilemma is sharp: to believe in justice, whatever it means, seems to require that one must find a means of insuring its survival or presence among men, and since some men do not agree to act justly, they must be made to do so. That cannot be done without proper authority, which cannot be employed without a degree of involuntary force, which *may* be unjust in the nature of it. So, what is needed for justice is a sense of what is right *and* the means to enforce it. But, Miss Harley, your question puts me at the great disadvantage of having the sinking feeling of not being able to deal with it well in this short time remaining to us. It has always been asserted that power among men is necessary and it has always been challenged, and the debate has almost always turned on the meaning of justice. That's the best I can do for now. Politics *is* an enterprise in pursuit of justice and one of the most important of such enterprises."

The long answer had to be interrupted. There were other things yet to be done.

"I'd like to return to Mr. Mason's formulation," the teacher began again. "You will recall that he said the existence of police forces are a solution to the problems of public safety, but never a completely adequate one. We can also say that the invention of politics or government is the general, all-purpose solution for the management of social problems that require authority, and that the problems of politics are the problems of that solution which also don't just disappear, but only become more manageable. What do you think of that, Mr. Mason?"

"Well, to tell the truth, I like it fine, even if I do say so myself," replied Mason, proudly.

"It wouldn't have anything to do with the fact that you said it, would it?" the teacher suggested.

"Yes, it might, but it is good, just the same, isn't it?"

"It is, yes, that's why I went to the authority on the subject."

"What more can I say, except that I agree?" the student replied.

"Well, you might say, for example, that the formulation leaves us with a lot of serious problems to talk about. You might say that the problems of the solution are great in number and magnitude, or you might say that it's misleading because it hides a lot that shouldn't be hidden, or that we really haven't gone very far down the road to understanding politics by just defining it in a clever way."

"If I were smart or if I'd studied a lot of politics I might be able to say that, yes, but as it happens, I didn't think of any of them. But I'm willing to learn," Mason replied.

"All right, but a good deal of politics does remain hidden from us, partly because we've gone about our business here by indirection. We have managed to reveal that politics involves power and authority, that it is about striving for justice, that it is animated by shared social purposes, that it deals with the management of conflict among men and with designs for freedom as well as schemes for oppression. When we did those things we displayed many of the characteristics of political life and, for that reason, we should be satisfied. And yet, I cannot help expressing the sense that we have not yet grasped many other aspects which, were they known to us, would satisfy to a greater degree. Do you suppose that I am asking for too much here?"

"Well, I don't know. I feel pretty ignorant about that but didn't you say a while ago that the end of this discussion had to be some sort of beginning? We could just let it go at that and let this *be* the beginning, couldn't we?"

"Yes, that is a good way of putting it," the teacher said. "We really *could* let this be the beginning, couldn't we? Now that we know what we have had to do with government and politics before coming to class, we may well be ready to take a much closer look at it. And so, at least for now, the class is dismissed."

As the students filed out of the room, the teacher emptied his dusty pockets of the chalk they contained, and joined them in departing.

Bibliography

Further Steps toward the Acquisition of Political Knowledge

Books that seek to impart knowledge ought, at some point, to say where the knowledge they lay claim to comes from. If they are books such as this one which try to raise questions, open doors, and point to the possibilities of discovering as yet unfamiliar social and intellectual territories, they ought also to furnish some guides for further exploration.

The spheres of knowledge touched upon in this first book about politics and government are, at one and the same time, familiarly close and remotely strange in their connections and consequences. My intention has been to cause the reader to look deeply into his immediate and everyday experiences and to reflect about the myriad ways that they are connected to the life of politics across great distances of time and space. If I have succeeded in this, the book now must meet that further obligation of providing its readers with guidance to further knowledge. As usual, this takes the form of bibliographies, but a reservation must be entered in this case.

Our subject is vast in scope and significance and no bibliography that can be contained in a single book would suffice, even for any one of the sixteen dialogues. Neither would any cursory listing of the most outstanding of the many good textbooks be enough, nor monographs, government reports, budgets, newspaper accounts, records of conversations or histories.

The appended list of reading has been compiled to show, firstly, the variety of sources from which political knowledge can be obtained. Secondly, it reveals the continuously controversial character of political processes and of the information about them. Thirdly, it is intended to show that the study of politics has engaged the best and the worst minds of the civilization of man, and that it is a worthy undertaking.

Thus, in the absence of completeness, variety has been aimed at, controversiality has been taken to be the natural state of knowledge and belief, and temporal, spatial, and moral depth has been intended.

Equipped with these good intentions of the author, the further acquisition of political knowledge must be the reader's.

1. MY HOME IS MY CASTLE

Adams, Thomas F. *Law Enforcement: An Introduction to the Police Role in the Community.* Englewood Cliffs, N.J.: Prentice-Hall, 1968.

Clark, Ramsey. *Crime in America.* New York: Simon & Schuster, 1970.

Davidson, Bill R. *To Keep and Bear Arms.* New Rochelle, N.Y.: Arlington House, 1969.

Glueck, Sheldon and Eleanor. *Juvenile Delinquents Grow Up.* New York: The Commonwealth Fund; London: H. Milford, Oxford University Press, 1940.

Harris, Richard. *Justice.* New York: E. P. Dutton, 1970.

———. *The Fear of Crime.* New York: Praeger, 1969.

Leites, Nathan, and Wolf, Charles, Jr. *Rebellion and Authority.* Chicago: Markham Publishing Co., 1970.

Lipsky, Michael, comp. *Law and Order, Police Encounters.* Chicago: Aldine Publishing Co., 1970.

Newton, George D. *Firearms and Violence in American Life.* Staff report submitted to the National Commission on Causes and Prevention of Violence. Washington: U.S. Government Printing Office, 1969.

Parker, Herbert L. *The Limits of the Criminal Sanction.* Stanford, Calif.: Stanford University Press, 1968.

Rubinstein, Richard E. *Rebels in Eden: Mass Political Violence in the United States.* Boston: Little, Brown, 1970.

Summers, Marvin R., and Barth, Thomas E., eds. *Law and Order in a Democratic Society.* Columbus, Ohio: Charles E. Merrill Publishing Co., 1970.

Vollmer, August. *The Police and Modern Society.* College Park, Md.: McGrath Publishing Co., 1969.

Williams, David G. T. *Keeping the Peace: The Police and Public Order.* London: Hutchinson, 1967.

2. THE PILLOW

Campbell, Angus, Converse, Philip E., Miller, Warren E., and Stokes, Donald E. *The American Voter.* New York: John Wiley, 1960.

———. *Elections and the Political Order.* New York: John Wiley, 1960.

Duverger, Maurice. *Political Parties.* New York: John Wiley, 1963.

Epstein, Leo. *Political Parties in Western Democracies.* New York: Praeger, 1967.

Gross, Bertram M. *The Legislative Struggle.* New York: McGraw-Hill, 1953.

Herring, Pendleton. *The Politics of Democracy.* New York: Holt, Rinehart and Winston, 1940.

Key, V. O. *Politics, Parties and Pressure Groups.* New York: T. Y. Crowell, 1965.

———. *Public Opinion and American Democracy.* New York: Alfred A. Knopf, 1961.
Lindblom, Charles E. *The Intelligence of Democracy: Decision-Making through Mutual Adjustment.* New York: The Free Press, 1965.
Milbrath, Lester W. *Political Participation.* Chicago: Rand McNally & Company, 1965.
Phelps, Edmund S., ed. *Private Wants and Public Needs.* New York: W. W. Norton & Co., 1962.
Rossiter, Clinton. *Parties and Politics in America.* New York: New American Library, 1967.
Schattschneider, E. E. *The Semi-Sovereign People.* New York: Holt, Rinehart and Winston, 1960.
Tullock, Gordon. *Private Wants and Public Means.* New York: Basic Books, 1970.
Wilcox, Clair. *Public Policy Towards Business*, 3d ed. Homewood, Ill.: R. D. Irwin, 1966.

3. POWER FOR THE PEOPLE

Firth, Robert E. *Public Power in Nebraska.* Lincoln: University of Nebraska Press, 1962.
Haskins and Sells. *Revolving Funds and Business Enterprises of the Government.* A report with recommendations, prepared for the Commission on Organization of the Executive Branch of the Government. Westport, Conn.: Greenwood Press, 1970.
Held, Virginia. *The Public Interest and Individual Interests.* New York: Basic Books, 1970.
Hobday, Victor C. *Sparks of the Grassroots: Municipal Distribution of TVA Electricity in Tennessee.* Knoxville: University of Tennessee Press, 1969.
Hunt, Edward Eyre. *The Power Industry and the Public Interest.* New York: The Twentieth Century Fund, 1944.
Ransmeier, Joseph Sirera. *The Tennessee Valley Authority.* Nashville: The Vanderbilt University Press, 1942.
Schumpeter, J. A. *Capitalism, Socialism and Democracy.* London: G. Allen & Unwin, 1965.
Steiner, George. *Government's Role in Economic Life.* New York: McGraw-Hill, 1953.
Tennessee Valley Authority. *Annual Reports, 1934–1967.* New York: Arno Press, A Publication and Library Service of *The New York Times,* 1969.
———. *Annual Reports 1967– .* Washington, D.C.: U.S. Government Printing Office.
———. *Municipal and Cooperative Distributors of TVA Power.* Washington, D.C.: U.S. Government Printing Office.
United States. Library of Congress, Environmental Policy Division. *The Economy, Energy, and the Environment,* a background study prepared for the use of the Joint Economic Committee, Congress of the United States, Sept. 1, 1970. Washington, D.C.: U.S. Government Printing Office, 1970.

———, Federal Power Commission. *National Power Survey.* Washington, D.C.: U.S. Government Printing Office, 1964.

———, Federal Power Commission. *Northeast Power Failure, Nov. 9 and 10, 1965: A Report to the President.* Washington, D.C.: U.S. Government Printing Office, 1965.

———, Office of Science and Technology, Energy Policy Staff. *Electric Power and the Environment.* Washington, D.C.: U.S. Government Printing Office, 1970.

Vennard, Edwin. *The Electric Power Business.* New York: McGraw-Hill, 1970.

Wildavsky, Aaron. *Dixon-Yates: A Study in Power Politics.* New Haven: Yale University Press, 1962.

4. THE ALARM CLOCK

Ashley, Percy W. Llewellyn. *Modern Tariff History: Germany-United States-France.* New York: H. Fertig, 1970.

Brooks, Colin. *This Tariff Question.* London: E. Arnold and Co., 1931.

Bidwell, Percy Wells. *What the Tariff Means to American Industries.* New York: Published for the Council on Foreign Relations by Harper, 1968.

Crowther, Samuel. *America Self-Contained.* New York: Doubleday & Company, 1933.

Dam, Kenneth W. *The GATT: Law and International Organization.* Chicago: University of Chicago Press, 1970.

Freeman, A. Myrick, III. *International Trade.* New York: Harper & Row, 1971.

Gaston, J. Frank, and Smith, William J. J. *Border Taxes and International Competition.* New York: National Industrial Conference Board, 1969.

Hamilton, Walton. *The Politics of Industry.* Ann Arbor, Mich.: University of Michigan Press, 1957.

Milbrath, Lester W. *The Washington Lobbyists.* Chicago: Rand McNally, 1963.

Page, Thomas Walker. *Making the Tariff in the United States.* New York: McGraw-Hill, 1924; The Brookings Institution Reprint Series.

Piquet, Howard Samuel. *Aid, Trade, and the Tariff.* New York: T. Y. Crowell, 1953.

Reischer, Otto Richard. *Trade Adjustment in Theory and Practice.* Prepared for the Subcommittee on Foreign Economic Policy of the Joint Economic Committee, Congress of the United States. Washington: U.S. Government Printing Office, 1961.

Schattschneider, Elmer Eric. *Politics, Pressures and the Tariff: A Case Study of Free Enterprise in Pressure Politics.* New York: Prentice-Hall, Inc., 1935.

United States, Department of State. *General Agreement on Tariffs and Trade.* Analysis of United States Negotiations 1960–1961 Tariff Conference, Geneva Switzerland. Washington, D.C.: 1962–1963.

———, Tariff Commission. *Colonial Tariff Policies.* Washington, D.C.: Government Printing Office, 1922.

———, Tariff Commission. *Annual Report.* Washington, D.C.: U.S. Government Printing Office, 1917– .

Wilcox, Clair. *A Charter for World Trade.* New York: Macmillan Co., 1949.

5. THE BATHROOM AND BEYOND

American Public Works Association, Institute for Solid Wastes. *Municipal Refuse Disposal.* Assistance provided by the Bureau of Solid Waste Management, U.S. Department of Health, Education, and Welfare, 3d ed. Chicago: Public Administration Service, 1970.
Benarde, Melvin A. *Our Precarious Habitat.* New York: W. W. Norton & Co., 1970.
Besselievre, Edmund B. *The Treatment of Industrial Wastes.* New York: McGraw-Hill, 1969.
Citizens' Association of New York, Council of Hygiene and Public Health. *Sanitary Conditions of the City: A Report.* New York: Arno Press, 1970.
Downing, Paul B. *The Economics of Urban Sewage.* New York: Praeger, 1969.
Ehlers, Victor Marcus, and Steel, Ernest W. *Municipal and Rural Sanitation,* 6th ed. New York: McGraw-Hill, 1965.
Grava, Sigurd. *Urban Planning Aspects of Water Pollution Control.* New York: Columbia University Press, 1969.
Gries, John, and Ford, James, eds. *Home Design, Construction and Equipment.* The President's Conference on Home Building and Home Ownership. Washington, D.C., 1932.
Griscom, John Hoskins. *The Sanitary Conditions of the Laboring Class of New York.* New York: Arno Press, 1970.
Hopkins, Edward S., and Elder, Francis S. *The Practice of Sanitation.* Baltimore: Williams & Wilkins, 1951.
Salusbury-Jones, Goronwy Tidy. *Street Life in Medieval England.* Oxford: Pen-in-Hand, 1948.
Shuster, William W. *Partial Oxidation of Solid Organic Wastes.* Washington, D.C.: U.S. Bureau of Solid Waste Management, U.S. Government Printing Office, 1970.
United States, Federal Water Pollution Control Administration. *Building for Clean Water.* A report on federal incentive grants for municipal waste treatment and future construction needs. Washington, D.C.: U.S. Government Printing Office, 1970.
Winslow, Charles E. A. *Man and Epidemics.* Princeton: Princeton University Press, 1952.

6. WATER, WATER EVERYWHERE

Brinton, Crane. *The Anatomy of Revolution,* rev. ed. New York: Vintage Books, 1965.
Campbell, Thomas H., and Sylvester, Robert O., eds. *Water Resource Management and Public Policy.* Seattle: University of Washington Press, 1968.
Fair, Gordon Maskew, with Geyer, John Charles and Okum, Daniel Alexander. *Water and Waste-Water Engineering.* New York: John Wiley, 1966.
Furon, Raymond. *The Problem of Water, A World Study,* trans. by Paul Barnes. New York: American Elsevier Publication Co., 1967.
Hartman, Loyal M., and Seastone, Dan. *Water Transfers; Economic Efficiency*

and Alternative Institutions. Baltimore: Published for Resources of the Future by the Johns Hopkins Press, 1970.

Hirschleifer, Jack, Dettawer, James, Milliman, Jerome W. *Water Supply, Economics, Technology and Policy.* Chicago: University of Chicago Press, 1960.

Jacobstein, J. Myron, and Mersky, Roy M. *Water Law Bibliography, 1847–1965.* Source book on U.S. water and irrigation studies: legal, economic, and political. Silver Spring, Md.: Jefferson Law Book Co., 1966.

Luttwak, Edward. *Coup D'Etat.* New York: Alfred A. Knopf, 1968.

Todd, David Keith. *The Water Encyclopedia; A Compendium of Useful Information on Water Resources.* Port Washington, N.Y.: Water Information Center, 1970.

United States, Federal Water Pollution Control Administration. *The Cost of Clean Water and Its Economic Import.* Washington: U.S. Government Printing Office, 1969.

Wittfogel, Karl August. *Oriental Despotism; A Comparative Study of Total Power.* New Haven: Yale University Press, 1957.

Wolman, Abel. *Water, Health and Society; Selected Papers*, ed. by Gilbert F. White. Bloomington: Indiana University Press, 1969.

7. A HEALTHY BODY

Almond, Gabriel, and Verba, Sidney. *The Civic Culture.* Princeton: Princeton University Press, 1963.

Barker, Sir Ernest. *Principles of Social and Political Theory.* Oxford: Clarendon Press, 1951.

Campbell, Rita Ricardo. *Economics and Health and Public Policy.* Washington: American Enterprise Institute for Public Policy Research, 1971.

Cray, Ed. *In Failing Health: The Medical Crisis and the AMA.* Indianapolis: Bobbs Merrill, 1971.

DeGrazia, Sebastian. *The Political Community.* Chicago: University of Chicago Press, 1948.

Editors of Fortune. *Our Ailing Medical System; It's Time to Operate.* New York: Harper & Row, 1970.

Ehrenreich, Barbara and John. *The American Health Empire: Power, Profits and Politics.* New York: Random House, Vintage Books, 1971.

Field, Mark G. *Doctor and Patient in Soviet Russia.* Cambridge, Harvard University Press, 1957.

Fritschler, A. Lee. *Smoking and Politics.* New York: Appleton-Century-Crofts, 1969.

Fry, John. *Medicine in Three Societies: A Comparison of Medical Care in the U.S., U.S.S.R. and U.K.* New York: American Elsevier Publishing Co., 1970.

Garceau, Oliver. *The Political Life of the American Medical Association.* Hamden, Conn.: Shoe String Press, Archon Books, 1961.

Ginzberg, Eli. *Urban Health Services; The Case of New York.* New York: Columbia University Press, 1971.

Gross, Martin L. *The Doctors.* New York: Random House, 1966.

Harris, Richard. *A Sacred Trust*, rev. ed. Baltimore: Penguin Books, 1969.

———. *The Real Voice.* New York and London: Macmillan, 1964.
Knowles, John H. ed. *Hospitals, Doctors and the Public Interest.* Cambridge: Harvard University Press, 1965.
Lindsay, A. D. *The Modern Democratic State.* New York: Oxford University Press, 1941.
Lipset, Seymour Martin. *Political Man: The Social Basis of Politics.* New York: Doubleday, 1960.
Newsholme, Sir Arthur. *Medicine and the State.* London: G. Allen Unwin, Ltd; Baltimore: Williams & Wilkins Co., 1932.
Stern, Bernhard Joseph. *Medical Services by Government: Local, State and Federal.* New York: The Commonwealth Fund, 1946.
United States, Commission on Organization of the Executive Branch of Government. *Federal Medical Services, A Report to Congress.* Washington, D.C.: U.S. Government Printing Office, 1955.

8. THE CLOTHES WE WEAR

Allen, James Stewart. *The Negro Question in the United States.* New York: International Publishers, 1936.
Atkins, W. S., and partners. *The Strategic Future of the Wool Textile Industry.* A Report for the Marketing Study Steering Group of the Economic Development Committee for the World Textile Industry. London: H.M.S.O., 1969.
Barnard, Alan. *The Australian Wool Market, 1840–1900.* Carlton: Melbourne University Press on behalf of the Australian National University, 1958.
Blinken, Donald M. *Wool Tariffs and American Policy.* Washington: Public Affairs Press, 1948.
Cohn, David Lewis. *The Life and Time of King Cotton.* New York: Oxford University Press, 1956.
Copland, Melvin T. *The Cotton Manufacturing Industry of the United States.* New York: A. M. Kelley, 1966.
Crawford, Morriss De Camp. *The Heritage of Cotton, the Fibre of Two Worlds and Many Ages.* New York and London: G. P. Putnam's Sons, 1924.
Elliott, E. N., ed. *Cotton Is King, and Pro-Slavery Arguments.* Augusta, Ga.: Pritchard, Abbott & Loomis, 1860.
Hardin, Charles. *The Politics of Agriculture.* Glencoe, Ill.: The Free Press, 1952.
Kester, Howard. "Revolt Among the Sharecroppers," *The American Negro, His History and Literature.* Originally published in 1936. New York: Arno Press, 1969.
Mitchell, Broadus. *The Industrial Revolution in the South.* London: H. Milford, Oxford University Press, 1930.
Olmsted, Frederick Law. *A Journey in the Back Country.* New York: B. Franklin, 1970, a reprint of 1860 edition.
Scherer, James, A. B. *Cotton as a World Power: A Study in the Economic Interpretation of History.* New York: Frederick A. Stokes Company, 1916.
U.S. Tariff Commission. *The Wool-Growing Industry.* Washington: U.S. Government Printing Office, 1921.

Wright, Chester Whitney. *Wool-Growing and the Tariff: A Study in the Economic History of the United States*. New York: Russell & Russell, 1968.

9. GIVE US THIS DAY OUR DAILY BREAD

Aykroyd, Wallace R. *Sweet Malefactor: Sugar, Slavery and Human Society*. London: Heinemann, 1967.
Baldwin, David A. *Economic Development and American Foreign Policy*. Chicago: University of Chicago Press, 1966.
Benedict, Murray Reed. *Farm Policies of the United States, 1790–1950: A Study of their Origins and Development*. New York: Twentieth Century Fund, 1953.
Campbell, Christiana McFayden. *The Farm Bureau and the New Deal: A Study of the Making of National Farm Policy, 1933–1940*. Urbana: University of Illinois Press, 1962.
Cohen, Bernard C. *The Influence of Non-Governmental Groups on Foreign Policy-Making*. Boston: World Peace, 1959.
Dalton, John E. *Sugar: A Case Study of Government Control*. New York: The Macmillan Co., 1937.
Guerra y Sanches, Ramiro. *Sugar and Society in the Caribbean: An Economic History of Cuban Agriculture*. New Haven: Yale University Press, 1964.
Hadwiger, Don Frank. *Federal Wheat Commodity Programs*. Ames: Iowa State University Press, 1970.
Lasswell, Harold D. *Politics: Who Gets What, When and How*. New York: Peter Smith, 1950.
McCune, Wesley. *The Farm Bloc*. New York: Greenwood Press, 1968.
Malenbaum, Wilfred. *The World Wheat Economy 1885–1939*. Harvard University Press, 1953.
Schmertz, Eric, and Sirefman, Josef P., eds. *Management and Regulation of the Metropolitan New York City Milk Industry*. Hempstead, N.Y.: Hofstra University, 1969.
Sheperd, Geoffrey Seddon. *Farm Policy: New Directions*. Ames: Iowa State University Press, 1964.
United States, Laws, Statutes. *Cotton and Grain Futures Acts, Commodity Exchange and Warehouse Acts, and Other Laws Relating Thereto*. Washington, D.C.: U.S. Government Printing Office.
United States Beet Sugar Association. *The Beet Sugar Story*, 3d ed. Washington: 1959.
Ward, Barbara. *The Rich Nations and the Poor Nations*. New York: W. W. Norton, 1962.

10. THE HOUSE I LIVE IN

Abrams, Charles. *The Future of Housing*. New York: Harper & Row, 1946.
———. *Forbidden Neighbors: A Study of Prejudice in Housing*. New York: Harper & Row, 1955.
Altshuler, Alan, A. *Community Control: The Black Demand for Participation in Large American Cities*. New York: Pegasus, 1970.

Bellush, Jewell, and Hausknocht, Murray, eds. *Urban Renewal: People, Politics and Planning.* Garden City, N.Y.: Anchor Books, 1967.
Boyer, Glenn H. *Housing: A Factual Analysis.* New York: The Macmillan Company, 1958.
Cardozo, Benjamin. *The Nature of the Judical Process.* New Haven: Yale University Press, 1925.
Clark, Dennis. *The Ghetto Game: Racial Conflict in the City.* New York: Sheed & Ward, 1962.
Clark, Kenneth B. *Dark Ghetto: Dilemmas of Social Power.* New York: Harper & Row, 1965.
Downs, Anthony. *Urban Problems and Prospects.* Chicago: Markham Publishing Co., 1970.
Fisher, Robert Moore. *Twenty Years of Public Housing.* New York: Harper & Row, 1959.
Freedman, Leonard. *Public Housing: The Politics of Poverty.* New York: Holt, Rinehart and Winston, 1969.
Friedman, Lawrence M. *Government and Slum Housing: A Century of Frustration.* Chicago: Rand McNally & Co., 1968.
Van den Bergh, Pierre L. *Race and Racism.* New York: John Wiley, 1967.

11. THE JOYS OF TRANSPORT

Auerbach, Carl A., and Nathanson, Nathaniel L. *The Federal Regulation of Transportation.* St. Paul: West Publishing Co., 1933.
Burby, John. *The Great American Motion Sickness: Or Why You Can't Get There from Here.* Boston: Little, Brown, 1971.
Danielson, Michael N. *Federal-Metropolitan Politics and the Commuter Crisis.* New York: Columbia University Press, 1965.
Dunbar, Seymour. *A History of Travel in America.* New York: Tudor Publishing Company, 1937.
Fellmeth, Robert C. *The Interstate Commerce Commission: The Public Interest and the ICC.* The Ralph Nader study group report on the ICC and transportation. New York: Grossman Publishers, 1970.
Ornati, Oscar A., with Whitaker, James A., and Solomon, Richard. *Transportation Needs of the Poor: A Case Study of New York City.* New York: Praeger, 1969.
Pegum, Dudley F. *Transportation: Economics and Public Policy*, rev. ed. Homewood, Ill.: R. D. Irwin, 1968.
Reische, Diana L., comp. *Problems of Mass Transportation.* New York: H. W. Wilson, Co., 1970.
Salisbury, Robert H., ed. *Interest Group Politics in America.* New York: Harper & Row, 1970.
Sharkansky, Ira. *The Politics of Taxing and Spending.* Indianapolis: The Bobbs-Merrill Company, Inc., 1969.
Smerk, George M. *Urban Transportation: The Federal Role.* Bloomington: Indiana University Press, 1966.
United States National Transportation Safety Board. *Annual Reports to Congress.* Washington, D.C.: U.S. Government Printing Office, 1967– .

12. SCHOOLDAYS, SCHOOLDAYS

Bailey, Stephen K., Frost, Richard T., Marsh, Paul E., and Wood, Robert C. *Schoolmen and Politics: A Study of State Aid to Education in the Northeast.* Syracuse: Syracuse University Press, 1962.
Bailey, Stephen K., and Mosher, Edith K. *ESEA: The Office of Education Administers a Law.* Syracuse: Syracuse University Press, 1968.
Berube, Maurice R., and Gittell, Marilyn, eds. *Confrontation at Ocean Hill-Brownsville: The New York School Strikes of 1968.* New York: Praeger, 1969.
Cahill, Robert S., and Hencley, Stephen P., eds. *The Politics of Education in the Local Community.* Danville, Ill.: The Interstate Printers and Publishers, 1964.
Campbell, Roald, et al. *The Organization and Control of American Schools.* Columbus, Ohio: Charles E. Merrill Publishing Co., 1965.
Dawson, Richard, and Prewitt, Kenneth. *Political Socialization.* Boston: Little, Brown, 1969.
Gittell, Marilyn, ed. *Educating an Urban Population.* Beverly Hills, Calif.: Sage Publications, 1970.
Gittell, Marilyn, and Hevesy, Alan, eds. *The Politics of Urban Education.* New York: Praeger, 1969.
Hutchins, Robert Maynard. *The Conflict in Education in a Democratic Society.* New York: Harper & Row, 1953.
Kirst, Michael W., ed. *The Politics of Education at the Local, State, and Federal Levels.* Berkeley, Calif.: McCutchen Publishing Co., 1970.
Martin, Roscoe C. *Government and the Suburban School.* Syracuse: Syracuse University Press, 1962.
Meranto, Philip. *School Politics in the Metropolis.* Columbus, Ohio: Charles E. Merrill Publishing Co., 1970.
Munger, Frank J., and Fenno, Richard F. *National Politics and Federal Aid to Education.* Syracuse: Syracuse University Press, 1962.
Rosenthal, Alan, ed. *Governing Education: A Reader on Political Power, and Public School Policy.* New York: Doubleday and Co., Inc., 1969.

13. BY THE SWEAT OF THY BROW

Bottomore, T. B. *Classes in Modern Society.* New York: Vintage Books, 1966.
Crosser, Paul K. *Ideologies and American Labor.* New York: Oxford University Press, 1941.
Dahrendorf, Rolf. *Class and Class Conflict in Industrial Societies.* Stanford, Calif.: Stanford University Press, 1959.
Donovan, John C. *The Politics of Poverty.* New York: Pegasus, 1967.
Evans, Robert. *Public Policy Toward Labor.* New York: Harper & Row, 1965.
Gross, Edward. *Work and Society.* New York: T. Y. Crowell, 1958.
Harrington, Michael. *The Other America.* Baltimore: Penguin Books, 1962.
Lampman, Robert J. *The Share of Top Wealth-Holders in National Wealth.* Princeton: Princeton University Press, 1962.
London, Jack. *War of the Classes.* New York: The Regent Press, Macmillan, 1912.

MacDonald, Lois, and Stein, Emanuel. *The Worker and Government*. New York: The Affiliated Schools for Workers, Inc., 1935.
Mills, C. Wright. *The Power Elite*. New York: Oxford University Press, 1956.
Muself, Lloyd D. *Government and Economy*. Chicago: Scott, Foresman, 1965.
Reagan, Michael. *The Managed Economy*. New York: Oxford University Press, 1963.
Selznick, Philip. *Law, Society and Industrial Justice*. New York: Russell Sage Foundation, 1969.
Shonfield, Andrew. *Modern Capitalism*. New York: Oxford University Press, 1965.
Somers, Gerald George, ed. *Labor, Management, and Social Policy: Essays in the John R. Commons Tradition*. Madison: University of Wisconsin Press, 1963.

14. ARRIVALS

Barash, Meyer, and Scourby, Alice. *Marriage and the Family: A Comparative Analysis of Contemporary Problems*. New York: Random House, 1970.
Canudo, Eugene R. *Law of Marriage, Divorce and Adoption*, 3d ed. Jamaica, N.Y.: Gould Publications, 1966.
Chesteen, Edgar R. *The Case for Compulsory Birth Control*. Englewood Cliffs, N.J.: Prentice-Hall, 1971.
Easton, David, and Dennis, Jack. *Children in the Political System: Origins of Legitimacy*. New York: McGraw-Hill, 1969.
Greenberg, Edward S., ed. *Political Socialization*. New York: Atheneum Press, 1970.
Kahn, Albert E. *The Game of Death: Effect of the Cold War on Our Children*. New York: Cameron & Kahn, 1953.
Lader, Lawrence. *Breeding Ourselves to Death*. New York: Ballantine Books, 1971.
Lee, Alfred McClung, and Lee, Elizabeth Briant. *Marriage and the Family*, 2d ed. New York: Barnes & Noble, 1967.
Morgan, Richard E. *The Politics of Religious Conflict*. New York: Pegasus, 1968.
Richmond, Mary Ellen, and Hall, Fred. *Marriage and the State*. New York: Russell Sage Foundation, 1929.
Shannon, William H. *The Lively Debate: Response to Human Vitae*. New York: Sheed & Ward, 1970.
Tyler, Edward T., comp. and ed. *Birth Control: A Continuing Controversy*. Springfield, Ill.: Thomas, 1967.
Udry, J. Richard. *The Social Context of Marriage*. Philadelphia: Lippincott, 1966.
United States Agency for International Development. *Population Program Assistance Aid to Developing Nations by the United States, Other Nations and International Agencies*. Washington, D.C.: U.S. Government Printing Office, 1969.
Westermarck, Edvard Alexander. *A Short History of Marriage*. New York: Humanities Press, 1968, first published in 1926.

15. DEPARTURES

Barnet, Richard J. *The Economy of Death*. New York: Atheneum, 1969.
Hayes, Carlton J. H. *Essays on Nationalism*. New York: Russell & Russell, 1966.
Hoffmann, Stanley S. *The State of War: Essays on the Theory and Practice of International Politics*. New York: Praeger, 1965.
Huntington, Samuel. *The Soldier and the State*. Cambridge: Belknap Press of Harvard University Press, 1957.
——. *The Common Defense*. New York: Columbia University Press, 1961.
Jones, Barbara. *Design for Death*. Indianapolis: Bobbs-Merrill Company, 1967.
Kaplan, Morton A. *Great Issues of International Politics*. Chicago: Aldine Publishing Co., 1970.
Kohn, Hans. *The Idea of Nationalism*. New York: The Macmillan Company, 1944.
Melman, Seymour, ed. *Disarmament; Its Politics and Economics*. Boston: The American Academy of Arts and Sciences, 1962.
Niebuhr, Reinhold. *The Structure of Nations and Empires*. New York: Scribner, 1959.
Polson, C. J., ed. *The Disposal of the Dead*. New York: Philosophical Library, 1953.
Puckle, Bertram S. *Funeral Customs, their Origin and Development*. London: T. Werner Laurie, Ltd., 1926; reissued Detroit, Mich.: Singing Tree Press, 1968.
Wagner, Johnannes, ed. *Reforming the Rites of Death*, Concilium Vol. 32. New York: Paulist Press, 1968.
Waltz, Kenneth N. *Man, the State and War: A Theoretical Analysis*. New York: Columbia University Press, 1959.

16. FROM HERE TO ETERNITY

Cahn, Edmond N. *The Sense of Injustice: An Anthropocentric View of Law*. New York: New York University Press, 1949.
Catlin, George E. G. *Systematic Politics: Elementa Politica et Sociologica*. Toronto: University of Toronto Press, 1962.
Dahl, Robert A. *Modern Political Analysis*. Englewood Cliffs, N.J.: Prentice-Hall, 1963.
Davies, James C. *Human Nature and Politics*. New York: The Free Press, 1964.
Deutsch, Karl. *The Nerves of Government*. Glencoe, Ill.: The Free Press, 1963.
Downs, Anthony. *An Economic Theory of Democracy*. New York: Harper & Row, 1957.
Duverger, Maurice. *The Idea of Politics*. Indianapolis: Bobbs-Merrill Co., 1966.
Dye, Thomas R., and Zeigler, Harmon L. *The Irony of Democracy*. Belmont, Calif.: Wadsworth Publishing Co., 1970.
Edelman, Murray J. *The Symbolic Uses of Politics*. Urbana: University of Illinois Press, 1964.
Fairlie, Henry. *The Life of Politics*. London: Methuen, 1968.
Feibleman, James K. *The Reach of Politics: A New Look at Government*. New York: Horizon Press, 1969.

Finer, Herman. *The Theory and Practice of Modern Government.* Revised by William B. Guthrie. New York: Dial Press, 1934.

Friedrich, Carl Joachim. *Man and His Government.* New York: McGraw-Hill, 1963.

Guild, Nelson P., and Palmer, Kenneth T. *Introduction to Politics: Essays and Readings.* New York: John Wiley, 1968.

Jones, Charles O. *An Introduction to the Study of Public Policy.* Belmont, Calif.: Wadsworth Publishing Co., 1970.

Jouvenel, Bertrand D. *On Power.* New York: Viking Press, 1949.

Keynes, Edward, and Ricci, David M., eds. *Political Power, Community and Democracy.* Chicago: Rand McNally, 1970.

Lindblom, Charles E. *The Policy-Making Process.* Englewood Cliffs, N.J.: Prentice-Hall, 1968.

Loewenstein, Karl. *Political Power and the Governmental Process.* Chicago: University of Chicago Press, 1957.

Long, Norton E. *The Polity.* Chicago: Rand McNally, 1962.

MacIver, Robert. *The Web of Government.* New York: The Macmillan Co., 1947.

Nieburg, H. L. *Political Violence, the Behavioral Process.* New York: St. Martins' Press, 1969.

Orwell, George. *Animal Farm.* New York: Harcourt Brace Jovanovich, 1946.

Plano, Jack C., and Greenberg, Milton. *The American Political Dictionary.* New York: Holt, Rinehart and Winston, 1967.

Pranger, Robert J. *The Eclipse of Citizenship.* New York: Holt, Rinehart and Winston, 1968.

Schattschneider, E. E. *Two Hundred Million Americans in Search of a Government.* New York: Holt, Rinehart and Winston, 1969.

Skolnick, Jerome H. *The Politics of Protest.* New York: Ballantine Books, 1969.

Spiro, Herbert J. *Government by Constitution: The Political System of Democracy.* New York: Random House, 1959.

Talmon, J. L. *The Origins of Totalitarian Democracy.* New York: Praeger, 1969.

Theobald, Robert. *Social Policies for America in the Seventies: Nine Divergent Views.* New York: Doubleday & Co., 1968.

Weldon, Thomas D. *States and Morals.* New York: Whittlesey House, 1947.

Wiseman, Herbert V. *Political Systems.* New York: Praeger, 1966.

DATE DUE

MAY 5 1978			

3-297